TRAGEDY UNDER GRACE

HANS URS VON BALTHASAR

TRAGEDY UNDER GRACE

Reinhold Schneider on the Experience of the West

TRANSLATED BY
BRIAN McNEIL, C.R.V.

A COMMUNIO BOOK
IGNATIUS PRESS   SAN FRANCISCO

Title of the German original:
Nochmals: Reinhold Schneider
© 1991 Johannes Verlag, Einsiedeln, Freiburg

The author prepared this
revised and expanded edition of
Reinhold Schneider: Sein Weg und sein Werk
before his death in 1988

Cover by Roxanne Mei Lum

© 1997 Ignatius Press, San Francisco
ISBN 0-89870-555-x
Library of Congress catalogue number 96-78008
Printed in the United States of America ∞

*Written for and dedicated to
the Secular Institutes*

CONTENTS

7

RUSSIA—CONFESSION

GERMANY—PENANCE

THE CHURCH

ROUEN—THE GLORY

ROME—THE MINISTRY

MARIENBURG—KNIGHTHOOD

CURTAIN

PREFACE TO
THE NEW EDITION

The first edition of this book was placed in the hands of Reinhold Schneider when he turned fifty in 1953, with the request not to read it if my presentation confused him and dammed up the flow of his inspiration. The preface emphasized how much his mighty work is the fruit of prayer and renunciation and the giving of testimony, in such a way that the person, harassed through and through and exhausted by intellectual and physical pain, unshaken either by boycott and slander or by the many honors paid him, wished to recede totally behind his task, and succeeded in doing so. What most fascinated me in this work was the omnipresent drama of the encounter between two missions that are equally original and yet stand in a deadly mutual conflict: the mission of the one who is entrusted with the task of administering the earthly realm and the mission of the saint as the real symbol of the kingdom of God that descends into the world. The inescapable quality of this encounter appeared to me as a guiding image, an image to be retained at all costs, for the secular institutes that had recently been permitted to exist in the Church: their fundamental aim is to combine the radicalism of the gospel with a total, active involvement in secular work, enduring in their own selves the conflict described here. At that time, it was not yet possible to recognize how deeply and variously Reinhold Schneider had thought through this problem, returning to deal with it again and again and averting one-sided solutions; one may well say that only the publication of his diaries from 1930 to 1935 (almost a thousand pages) has shed sufficient light on his ever new struggle with what he saw as the decisive and tragic conflict between life in the world and transcendence—and this in the years before his return to the Catholic faith. And what position does the writer take on this fundamental problem of Christian existence? "Faith addresses the indivisible man. This is why it is so senseless to make a distinction between the statesman as politician and the statesman as Christian, between the Christian as soldier and as the one who kneels at the communion rails. So if faith is present, it flows into the literary composition." And yet there is active here "Kierkegaard's doubt, which I cannot rob of its force: Is it genuinely possible to busy oneself with brush and paint, with pen and ink in the face of Jesus Christ: to paint Jesus Christ in the face of Jesus Christ? Where in the Gospel, in the whole of Sacred Scripture, is there one, single, even roughly adequate sentence that would provide a basis for art?" Christ, "the truth in flesh and blood, does not give teaching about himself as the truth but summons people to follow him." Ought the writer to lead people into this following of Christ through his forms and images? "But the writer has no priestly office; he does not stand in the pulpit or at the altar; it is not his task to preach. He is a child of this world and a man who is lacerated in his innermost being by the contradictions between faith and artistic activity, between the way that is the truth and his 'career'."[1]

My book may perhaps have provided the occasion—perhaps the final push—that prompted Reinhold Schneider to make the same dramatic turn in his life's history that Kierkegaard made, and the words quoted here show that they came from a deep motivation: the turning from a neutral and anonymous bearing of testimony to what Kierkegaard called "gesticulating with one's whole existence". The latter had hidden his existence behind pseudonyms, presumably already as a witness to the faith, and he states explicitly in his *Journal* that this was "because my personality does not correspond" to the personality of the one to whom witness is borne. When Reinhold Schneider emerged, one year after the publication of my book, with his autobiographical *Verhüllter Tag* (1954), this was because he, like the Dane, had no other weapons available to him now. Kierkegaard had written "Up to this point I am a writer, certainly nothing more, and it is a desperate struggle to see whether I can have the will to go beyond my boundary" (July 30, 1849). In my introduction, I had emphasized that I had omitted the entire biographical element in my presentation in order to display only the form of the work. But from this point onward, Reinhold Schneider would seek to refute the possibility of such a presentation by unceasingly arguing with his own existence, from the *Verhüllter Tag* to *Balkon* (1957) and the posthu-

---

[1] 126:59–66. (References in the footnotes of this book are to the number of the book in the Bibliography, followed by page number.)

mous *Winter in Wien* (1958).[2] The publication of his letters to various correspondents, and finally of his *Tagebücher*, only served to continue this work of yielding up his own self. If one prescinds from the "novel" (a genre that Schneider had detested hitherto) *Die silberne Ampel* of 1956, a work questionable in its delight in fables and its genealogical labyrinth, then we can see the author fighting in his last works with the sword of his own existence, obliged to pay the price (which Kierkegaard had recognized and feared) of the incongruence between the one who bears witness and that to which he bears witness; Schneider paid this price also with his "melancholy".

This meant that he handed over his work to the termite work of a, more or less, depth psychology, which was launched well and truly on its way with the appearance of his final work, *Winter in Wien*: Did the writer deny his Christian conversion here and return to his more "nihilistic" origins, or could the pitiless disclosure in this work perhaps be interpreted as the path into the "cloud" of a mystical "dark night"? Exceedingly contradictory voices clash in *Widerruf oder Vollendung* (1981). Might it be possible to unite the extreme solutions in a central point and speak of a "critical night of faith"? This analysis of Schneider's soul as a "case" has come to occupy the central ground with the result that the objective message of the great works has ceased to be heard. Their urgent hammerbeats scarcely reach contemporary ears, unless in the sense that those who are on the lookout for something more modern "see through" the themes treated by Schneider as hopelessly backward-looking and oriented to traditions that have completely disappeared, or else in the sense that his works are dismissed as questionable products of a mood of pessimism that does not help us with our own tasks. But it is only today that one recognizes the extreme courage, indeed, the audacity with which this author's chief works offered open resistance to tyranny: *Philipp II* was under suspicion; *Innozenz III* (1931) could not appear for political reasons; *Die Hohenzollern* (1933) was suppressed shortly after publication. They were "for the moment very unpopular in high places", and similarly the book about England (1936) had to be withdrawn in the same year in which it was published. There followed his exclusion from the Chamber of Writers of the Reich, the prohibition against publish-

---

[2] The short biographical notes from the earlier period (cf. 165:26–38, and F. A. Schmitt's explanations of these).

ing his books (which compelled Schneider to have them printed in
Alsace), and finally the command to go to the Western front "dead or
alive" (he was at the end of his strength), "to help in building traps
for tanks"[3] (it was only by having him admitted to a hospital that his
doctor was able to save him from this); and finally the intolerable din
of the French troops who were quartered in his house, with the result
that "much that was irreplaceable was looted, destroyed and smashed
to pieces." Reinhold Schneider survived the terror as an unwearying
helper, and he never hated: "I respect each one who has sacrificed
himself, even if he was on the wrong side."[4]

The courage with which the sufferer endured all the personal quar-
rels, the great poverty of his beginnings, the later hostility and slander
to which he was exposed, and still more his share in the suffering of
the horror of the War, ought to prevent any premature dismissal of his
work as "superseded". This is why the main part of our presentation
of this work remains essentially unchanged; a few expanded sections
attempt to ward off misunderstanding. Only then will we give separate consideration to the last five years, in which the author threw
his own existence onto the scales (1953–1958). But this can be done
only on the basis of the spirit of the entire preceding work: most of
the late statements were prepared (often almost literally) in the earlier
statements, and the biographical works cast an illuminating light back
onto what had already received its form.

What has already been hinted at here gives the proof of this claim:
the works mentioned above, as well as *Kaiser Lothars Krone* (1937)—
contemptuously rejected by the *Völkischer Beobachter*—and *Las Casas
vor Karl V*, were intended directly as a protest against the persecution
of the Jews but were not recognized as such. Numerous sonnets that
openly reject the regime, and finally the refusal to write the three-
volume history of the Reich, which would assuredly have been mis-
interpreted, show to what an extent Schneider confronted his own
period closely in the terrible events of his day. It must be emphasized
all the more strongly that the problems he perceived in the great periods of history and in the confrontations that became possible only
in these periods appeared to him to be the only appropriate response
to the questions thrown up by history. A title like *Macht und Gnade*

---

[3] 168:55, 66.

[4] 123:186.

(1940) shows this, bringing many aspects together: Schneider chose the historical high points that permitted him to display as clearly as possible the opposition and the interpenetration of the eternal laws that establish and give life to existence. We may perhaps be annoyed by the continual use of symbols like "the crown" and "the eagle", which appear to us antiquated; but the entire intellectual context of the symbol, which has its midpoint in an intellectual attitude, means that we cannot abandon it, no matter how modern we become.

INTRODUCTION

Reinhold Schneider is distinguished by the combination of the highest rank with the broadest compass: it is only in the purest spheres that he can breathe, but the integrity and holiness of the peak guarantees the well-being of the depths; the one who safeguards his high rank has also maintained the lower ranks, and the one who does not yield one foot's breadth of the height can look down on the breadth spread out at his feet. This breadth is the history of the world, with forms, movements and struggles that cannot be foreseen. But this chaos is stirred up and shaken by only a few ideas that drive it onward, ideas embodied in a few vicarious existences that are like parables: in the poets, the kings, the saints (in an ascending process),[1] but where this would bring us close to Carlyle, we are immediately flung far away from his position: the leaders are justified, not by their personality, but only by their mission and their humility in the presence of a truth that they themselves are not. The only one who can understand all this is the one who demands the highest thing of all, that which is impossible to man: namely, holiness. The only one who is permitted to enter that confusion is the one who has preserved his heart in pure renunciation and can sing his song in the midst of the turbulence as if he were quite alone by himself. Reinhold Schneider is the learned man who knows history thoroughly and describes and discriminates among the movements of the present day; but so little dust clings to him from the books he has read that he confronts our own age out of the wisdom of history but equally out of his immediate living of the faith, as a judge who exhorts, as an epic narrator, a lyrical singer, one who gives dramatic form to the idea he embodies, and a man of prayer and a teacher of prayer who leads into those most quiet zones from which all the power descends into the events of history. He is unique in our age in the fullness he displays—and even an external fullness is often enough the accompaniment of genius—especially when we reflect that this fullness is the irradiation of a passionate,

---

[1] 14:44; cf. 14:61.

inexorable choice and decision, of a one-sidedness that is foolish in the eyes of the "world": "the serious force that turns away to look on an eternal goal and, for the sake of this one matter, pays no heed to action or to world. O deeply hidden and highest passion!"[2] This is the source not only of a succession of literary works but, on a deeper level, of the will to subordinate everything uncompromisingly to this obedience, with the consequent knowledge that he is exposing himself to the stones of the Pharisees. Such an attitude would be titanic were it not the expression of the simple imitation of Christ —after the author has once rediscovered his religious starting point. Just as Christ came in order to lose everything apart from the will of the Father and thereby to win everything for the Father within this will, on the far side of death, so his servant obeys his will in the consciousness of giving up everything in order to exchange it for the one pearl. In Christian terms, the highest exclusiveness is the highest totality; it is the strictest act of exclusion that includes most, because ultimately there is nothing more outside. If one looks upward from below—from the poets and generals to the kings—then Schneider's attitude must appear to be merely one attitude among many, one out of keeping with the present time, namely, the attitude of an aristocratic legitimist, traditionalist and pacifist (a description against which he frequently protests). But since the progression continues farther upward to the saints, who "wear higher crowns", it can be seen— unless we choose to misinterpret the saints as superheroes—that it is to be read as a whole from above downward: the law of rank and of the vicarious mission holds sway only because of God; but precisely because of him, it holds sway over the lower ranks too. To take up a stance against the world while one goes to ruin would be madness, or a fruitless aesthetic perversity—even if this resulted in the foundation of a "group" or a "league"—but to go as a lamb among wolves because this is what obedience requires, and to proclaim in this way the order of true rank against one's own period in time, is the fulfillment of simple Franciscan humanity. But because this humanity is meant to lay down a law for the world, we experience in Reinhold Schneider a thought-provoking encounter between Francis and Ignatius. There is an inherent relation between the highest squandering gift of self and the highest demand that bestows a concrete form on this gift of self.

---

[2] 98:66.

It is here that Reinhold Schneider's invulnerability lies, even though his soul and his work bleed to death from a thousand wounds. Here, too, lies his irrefutable realism, even where the realists of this world accuse him of being a utopian dreamer.

Lord de Chantal's motto was "Et si omnes, ego non."[3] The spirit of the age is no compass for the conduct of the Christian. "There is a higher value in rank than in obedience to one's age."[4] Indeed, "there are ages in which those who have been grasped by that which is genuine, and who commit themselves to this, can no longer fight on behalf of men, because there is no man who upholds this properly: one can fight only on behalf of the idea."[5] This antithesis can be fruitful, "just as the value of apparently negative times consists often in the fact that they compel that which is genuine to come forth and put it to the ultimate test".[6] This is why young men are exhorted "to separate themselves with the sharpness of the sword from all that must decay, sink down and fall into corruption. No external might can compel you to enter this corruption, provided only that you become aware of what is noble."[7] But since the meaning of Christ's life was the Cross, the fact that testimony to the truth becomes the testimony of blood is no objection to this sharpness of opposition: "The artist, too, is unable to overcome an age that is totally opposed to his being and to the commission he has received; he will inevitably be shattered by contact with this age and will state precisely thus what filled him and what was the charge laid upon him."[8] "There are epochs of history in which life has only a small value, because it has all at once become impossible to live up to the highest demands"; only death can bring the solution.

Appeal is often made to Jeremiah and his face, which Yahweh hardened against his age, even in a cycle of seven sonnets ("I see all the witnesses in flight; none of them bears the destiny that I bear").[9] In the darkest time, Jeremiah "suffered the Word" and was driven by this Word into an impossible situation, when he "had to shatter the pitcher in the presence of the men of his age" and was instructed not to pray for the people.[10] Appeal is made equally often to John

---

[3] 27:16.
[4] 9:212.
[5] 9:264.
[6] 18:21.

[7] 78:18.
[8] 18:31.
[9] 69:44–50, 47.
[10] 112:57.

the Baptist, the beheaded priest of the undaunted truth, which requires him to "decrease" continuously to the point of death.[11] We
hear sometimes of Cassandra's fate, but the biblical figures speak a
stronger language. As in the case of the prophets and lawgivers, what
is involved is the razor-sharp discernment of spirits: to see guilt where
no one else sees it, to point to expiation where no one else thinks this
is possible and, therefore, also to present grace as a requirement. Reinhold Schneider did indeed protest against the attribution of prophetic
existence to himself,[12] because this label is often worn in the Old
Covenant by those who think they can set themselves up in con-
trast to true prophecy. And yet, the Church is "founded on apostles
and prophets"; these have the commission and the equipment of the
Spirit, compelled without being asked, and perhaps against their own
will, into their hard ministry. Reinhold Schneider knows that he is
one of these.

Nothing is less unambiguous in Schneider than the commission,
that is, a message that is not just coincidentally but fundamentally
and from the outset one with the existence, the form of life and the
heart's blood of the one who receives it. The existence, not the biography, belongs to the commission. "In art, a suprapersonal substance
finds its appropriate expression out of the entire force, the entire substance of the life of the artist. The idea strikes his life like a flash of
lightning: it gathers to itself all that is combustible; it is meaningless to
ask *what* it is that is burning. Nor is it so important to learn what the
artist intended or what he believed he had intended. He was an artist
only because another intended something with him: the Spirit who
took control of him."[13] In this sense, Reinhold Schneider has no message that one could separate from his heart; his *Sonette* (1939) display
the whole of him, but only in order to let the West and its mission
become visible in him. "Perhaps we ought no longer to shrink today from giving what is most personal; the greatest help lies therein.
What is most personal is our reply to God, the word that crosses
over to him from the totality of our life."[14] But this utterly personal
element remains inseparable from history in man who has received
the commission, as we can see in archetypical form in the example

---

[11] 62:88–91.
[12] 112:51.

[13] 112:9–12.
[14] 81:65.

of Newman: "We must understand the personal as the historical, and
the historical as the personal, in every phase of the conversion and
its result. The vibrations of grace that left their mark on Newman's
soul arose out of history and became history in their turn; grace met
him at the place where the religious history of England was to turn
around, where the possibility of overcoming the three hundred years'
fate became visible."[15] He himself sought only "God and the soul",
but, as one marked out and sent, he was able to perceive both of
these only as one who had been expropriated to become the person-
ification of that which was universal-historical. Thus Schneider, too,
must offer himself as "a sign, a cross on the rock-face, a testimony
in hopeless distress",[16] a beacon in the collapse:

> Hurry to the spot where the bridge is falling down!
> Become the flame that burns up your work!
> It may well be that the people calumniate and misjudge you:
> Do it all the same! The sign itself is the prize.[17]

He formulates harshly and precisely his "commission"[18] early on, the
path he takes toward this and his limitations. *Die Neuen Türme* takes
up this theme later and sets forth its articulation through poems that
address the age;[19] *Stern der Zeit*[20] develops it further, and the last lights
crown it in *Rechenschaft*.[21] Things cannot be otherwise, since the content of the message is the transcendence of history, its essence, which
it possesses through something that lies beyond itself, that is, through
something that history itself is not, something toward which it strives,
something that has its effect on history through grace from above.
Only when history obeys the Word and dies to itself does it take hold
of life. This is why such a message demands a dying existence. "The
one who challenges time for the sake of that which is eternal must accept the fact that time wants to kill him."[22] The fact that Schneider's
spiritual life, like that of Kierkegaard, begins in a deep melancholy inherited from his father and his ancestors[23] is no argument against the
spiritual character of the commission. Along with melancholy comes
the fate of illness. He has continual occasion to reflect on this; as a

---

[15] 71:113–14.
[16] 112:27.
[17] 112:99.
[18] 14:36.
[19] 14:45–47; 69:5, 50, 54.

[20] 98:78.
[21] 112:7, 27, 63, 99.
[22] 12:108.
[23] 14:5.

contradiction between spirit and body, it keeps the spiritual existence
inexorably awake (as Pascal shows).[24] It humbles in order to raise on
high; it was an extra burden for most of the saints, but it "kept them
in the state of adoration",[25] which "is the genuinely Christian state"
because it makes known "man's greatness and his misery"[26]—"it is
impossible to conceive of a Christianity ignorant of the meaning of
illness."[27] After illness has bullied the weary spirit into doing impossible things for a long time, it finally overcomes him when all his vigor
is burned out. Although melancholy and illness combine in Schneider occasionally to summon forth the wishful thinking of an "eternal
sleep" in which all images and ideas are dissolved, this continually
recurring *idée fixe* does not have the last word. Schneider's path leads
from desperation to form, and from form to figure and legislation.
He has described this path in his early *Stolz und Verantwortung*.[28] This
is not the path of Platen, C. F. Meyer or Ernst Jünger, because form is
not a protection against the encroachment of nothingness, or a mere
petrified pain, but rather grace that hardens the heart, where it turns
into clay in God's creative fingers, into a figure that bears witness.
When Schneider made himself available in the War years as the great
helper, admonisher and consoler who sent thousands of letters to the
soldiers in the field and spread countless pamphlets among the despairing people, it became clear that it was not the form as such that
was to provide salvation but rather the power of grace that revealed
itself in the form. At that period he emerged from the mantle of the
poet and historian to become the *confessor* in the patristic sense of
this word, a charismatic leader and pastor of souls who demonstrated
through his own existence the origin and proved quality of his truly
marked form. He was able to do this because he had known for a
very long time that the person is formed by a truth that lies higher
than his own self. This is why the name and the path of Newman
are in many ways the obvious point of comparison: as a very personal path that gropes out of the shadow toward the light, remaining
a paradigmatic action that is set upon a pedestal against his will, an
action that demands that each step be taken under the sign of conscience and of truth, leading inexorably and slowly to the highest de-

---

[24] 52:72–73.
[25] 16:11.
[26] 52:76, 77; 91:29.

[27] 18:120.
[28] 78:5.

cision, which then brings not only the truth but also a final loneliness, indeed, persecution. Naturally, he continues to be dependent on the unstable ground of history, in order to discern here the guidelines of his conduct in a manner more toilsome than the philosopher who issues decrees (*Newmans Entscheidung*).[29]

For *history* remains the place where Reinhold Schneider stands, the matter out of which things are formed and the primal form of existence in the world; "since the world can be experienced only in history".[30] "The prism of destiny makes visible the nature of man, by breaking him":[31] into the dispersion of time, which is always the one unique moment that demands that the decision be made now, gathering together its multiplicity into the one fundamental decision in which each individual truly becomes a person and historical. For "history is inexorable: it permits the action only once and does not excuse the failure to grasp the hour for the deed."[32] "It belongs to the essence of history that it takes its course in a succession of hours. What is possible in one hour can no longer take place in another hour. There lies an immeasurable power in the hour, in the possibilities that it mysteriously supplies and creates; this power comes into the hands of him who is one with the hour." But this hour belongs unquestioningly to the Lord of history: his time "can suddenly break into the hour; what the hour offers in contradiction to God's commandment has only the reality of a temptation; it is made of the stuff of dreams, like the world and the vision of history that Satan allowed Christ to glimpse. The power of the hour is genuine only when its possibilities are oriented to the kingdom of God and are grasped as service of the kingdom of God."[33] Here we see clearly the kernel of this interpretation of history: the central point is the event, the drama of the incarnate, teaching and dying Word of God in the world, and all genuine and perverted events are measured on the basis of this event and in view of it. The bearer of this consciousness of history is to be the Church and the believer who shares in her, together with his opposite number, the unbeliever, the "world". The Church, as her Founder intended her, makes present to the world the continuous claim of the personal Word of God, by means of which decision and history take

---

[29] 68, repeated in 71:109–40.
[30] 112:24.
[31] 10:25.

[32] 52:145.
[33] 81:14.

place ("How could Christ be victorious otherwise than in a perpetual holy 'today', in the deadly earnest of the present moment?").[34] The Church also creates for the dead, for the real past, that presence which elevates the recollection and involvement with the past to an activity that can be justified in Christian terms.[35] (*Was ist Geschichte?*, with its motto from Novalis: "The Church is the house where history dwells.")[36] The Catholic dimension in this idea is that invisible faith and visible history are not separated, because "one must not separate faith and Church."[37] No philosophy of history can be successful if it cannot stand up to being tested by the theology of history. If therefore every worldly event must be measured against the central event of the Incarnation of God—including the most hidden decisions of the conscience, which set in train the history of the world—then Christianity in its essence is also the bringing to bear of Christ's influence on history. Christian existence is mission: "Each individual fighter receives an objective, unique mission."[38] And because the appearance and existence of Christ in the world was the decisive drama, it is not at all possible for the Christian merely to take note of the perfect victory that has been achieved over the world: his only possibility is to share at once in this activity. Indeed, the recognition of the totality of Christ's victory is legitimated in the spirit of the individual only to the extent to which he is willing to share in sacrificing his life for the whole of the world. "The Christian life is never concerned only with souls but with the whole world, with the salvation of all men, with the glorification of Christ by all and the return of all men to the Father through him: it is concerned with sharing in the accomplishment of history."[39] But since Christ's struggle for the world is his immediate contact with the kingdom that is opposed to God, and ultimately means his own descent into this kingdom,

> the Christian unfailingly ends up in front of the Cross in history. The one who struggles against the darkness is overshadowed by it, and yet it may not be allowed to stain his soul. He will be assailed again and again by the temptation to use Satan's weapons to strike Satan. What if I were to sacrifice myself and do an injustice, so that no injustice would be done to others? What if I were to give away my peace, so that one

---

[34] 62:146.
[35] 14:59–61.
[36] 81:5–29.

[37] 71:117.
[38] 81:16.
[39] 81:13.

speck of ground in the kingdom of God remains sheltered in peace? But as soon as someone tends toward evil, Christ has ceased reigning in his place. Christ entered death as the pure truth.[40]

At the center of history stands the contradiction that life died on the Cross. But from the inside, this is no contradiction, because love remains true to itself in this descent. Christ's fight takes him into the wilderness, the Cross and hell, and no matter how exposed the struggle is in him, his unity is not destroyed: "When the truth enters history, it is not conquered by history, any more than the origin of the light is affected by the refractions that its rays experience."[41]

It is here that Schneider's deepest problem will lie: the contradiction between Christ and the world is an open contradiction: "Every word of the Lord contradicts that to which one is accustomed, although it is also in profound harmony with the tradition and the promise, the glowing kernel of which was no longer seen by men; the world can no longer forget the contradiction that has taken place."[42] This is a fight about life and death. But the Christian who is given his place on this battlefield is not himself truth and purity, like Christ and like his originally spotless Church. He is a "broken ray" through whom the contradiction passes with greater intensity, separating joints and marrow, increasing proportionately as he exposes his contradictoriness against God all the more to the sword of the Word of God, and is emboldened (and how can he avoid this?) to lay claim to worldly power and to deploy this for God. "Human institutions and even the saints have formed themselves in collaboration with their environment and with the demands of the present moment; they have taken on the color of the earth, although the purity received from the Lord shines through this color. All human work was bowed down, even when it was a work carried out under the influence of grace."[43] "Every single will that enters into the temporal dimension is thwarted: precisely this is the plan of grace."[44] Thwarted (*durchkreuzt*) precisely because of the Cross (*Kreuz*), Schneider will tell us—in a double sense, because the Cross is the pure form and because the impure form meets with this form. Thwarted, therefore, because everything apart from what is purest sinks down into the turbidity of guilt and because what

---

[40] 51:113–14.

[41] 52:134.

[42] 70:12.

[43] 26:29.

[44] 26:74.

is purest has itself chosen to descend into the full redemption of what is turbid.

Thus the genuine writing of history always involves the discernment of spirits. Because true history comes into being through the irruption of the transcendence of God, only sensitivity to the transcendent (which is given only by lived faith) can interpret history. "Thus we sense the outlines of a historiography that is probably impossible to put into practice: it would see all figures and events in their relationship to the kingdom of God and its coming; with pure truthfulness, it would portray the decisions that have been taken between the two banners. In this work, it would take into consideration all the earthly powers that are involved in the play of events, driving onward and apparently compelling events, but it would never desecrate the sphere of ultimate freedom." Such a historiography can never be carried out fully; it is written down in the book that will be opened up on the Last Day. But it must at least be attempted inchoatively, because it is only its idea that corresponds to the truth of real history. "How was appeal made to those who acted, the peoples and mighty men or individual generations, and how did they respond? Must we not learn to discern the spirits in the course of history, in the presence of the ultimate seriousness of history's goal? And how could we examine them if not by means of the question whether they have uttered the name of the Lord?"[45] Modern historians "have more and more lost" precisely "the simple gift of discerning the spirits", [46] the simple, clear courage to put an event into the fire of God, which is so inexorable only because it is love that purifies. Every man stands in this fire, in any case: in the "smoldering tinder of our guilt" or in the blaze of the "terrible grace"; no one comes into the kingdom of God "unless he has walked through this fire".[47]

This is why Dante is so often posited at the origin: in him is "everything included that the West must experience and say. Here is the experience of the historicity of our life, the utter seriousness of the demand that we live and act in history face to face with the Last Day, an endeavor that takes the measure of all the distances, an endeavor whose highest wisdom consists in depriving oneself of one's own

---

[45] 70:51.
[46] 70:107.

[47] 70:13.

power and letting oneself be led by grace."[48] Here the eternal ordering of the world and the unique decision are one. Christian poetic
composition "presents the temporal in its relationship to that which
is unmovable. It is characterized by a kind of chivalry. By carrying
through the judgment of the world as self-judgment, Dante has given
Christian poetic composition its definitive determination and has ful-
filled this."[49] But since all ordering and all measure are constituted
in the encounter between divine and human freedom and decision,
encounter, confrontation, dialogue, analysis and synthesis, the face-to-
face meeting of the persons who have power—all this is the concern
of the portrayal of history, just as it is the concern of poetic composition that has historic significance. As with Paul Claudel, this insight
leads Reinhold Schneider to the drama; both understand this as the
situation of encounter, although neither of them is inclined to the
theater as such. Almost all the short stories in the book *Die gerettete
Krone* contain pictures of meetings: often the simple fact of a face-
to-face encounter is enough to illustrate a focal point of history—
Philip II and John of Austria, Lord Rutland and Henry VIII, Friedrich
Wilhelm IV and Gerlach, Francis Xavier and Fereira, Las Casas and
Charles V, Celestine and Boniface VIII. Indeed, "the encounter of
two people in the same period of time is like a conversation, even if
these men should never have exchanged one single word or glance.
Such a meeting, brought about by God, is a word that history speaks
to us."[50] Two persons can often meet in the spirit of a third, who
judges them as one who is dead and helps them to accomplish their
encounter: Philip and John meet in their father; the Elector Maximilian and Johann von Werth meet in the spirit of Tilly.[51] The weight of
a man, of a time, of history as a whole is weighed from the peak of the
decisions taken; and all that is in the world and in nature (although
these remain fallen nature and guilty world in the concreteness of
history) is material and presupposition for the decision. In this sense,
the principle that *gratia supponit naturam* holds good for the historian
Schneider. Far from bringing about a harmony that would dispense
from the contradiction of the Cross, the encounter of these realities
can take place only in the Cross.

---

[48] 52:133.
[49] 112:14.

[50] 70:96.
[51] 24:37f.

Schneider thinks and shapes historically, not systematically. His work is itself the expression of the struggle of the powers; it will be understood to the extent that one enters into it and joins in carrying it out. But since the true decision is always immediately the true, representative coming into being of form in Schneider, his work is articulated by means of a clear and great symbolism of form. We need only become familiar with the outline of these forms in order to grasp at once both the development from form to form (where the later forms leave the earlier forms behind them) and the unfolding of an objective historical language of forms (where precisely the earlier forms never again lose their power). These powers are at the same time the highest expressions of historical peoples, as it were, their essential word, heard from their representatives ("for a people is like one person"),[52] figures that emerge dialectically from the posing of the questions. When they are set alongside one another like this, they light up the path of Reinhold Schneider above all, precisely because this is not in the least a private path but one that is extremely significant for the spirit of the age.

In this way, three circles arise (each consisting of three forms), each leading naturally back to the German question. The first contains the origins, whose characteristic it is to be most tenaciously retained and most passionately superseded; for the first book of a poet and thinker always remains his destiny. Schneider's path began with Camões' Portugal (1930); the Spain of Philip II (1931) speaks the antithetical word to this, and only on the basis of both of these do we find the question of *Innozenz III* (1931) about the relationships between spiritual and worldly power, then the relationships between the Prussia of Fichte (1932) and that of Frederick II (1933). The answer resounds shrilly and shows the failure of the categories that were provisionally applied. Thus a second circle opens up, spiraling above the first: England's antithetical form (1936) is laid upon Portugal's formlessness, permitting us for the first time to discern the dimension of guilt as a moving force of history. The answer to this is the secret power of Russia (1939, 1946), which is laid over the form of Philip and clarifies it in order to give it final justification. With these new, and only now truly historical, categories, Reinhold Schneider can turn for a second time to Germany (1946–1949), now in the full vigor of his historical

---

[52] 91:100.

commission. A third circle must explicitly bring out the form of the supernatural power that sets its mark on history—here the works accompany and intersect temporally the works of the first two circles. In this circle, the Church is initially displayed as the place of the saints, that is, of the absolute persons who express most fully what human nature is—the representative form is Joan of Arc—and is then described in the crossroads of her earthly existence between power and renunciation, conquest of the world and decline. The place for this is Rome: most deeply, it is the heart of the popes and the demand made that they represent Christ in history: highest drama, highest tragedy! Ultimately, the eye turns to that form of Christian existence that was the goal of Reinhold Schneider's categories from the outset, emerging with a radiant logic as the extreme point from his work, since it is indeed the perpetual living kernel that gives form to his work: the holy man of a supernatural form, but turned toward the formlessness of world and history, the religious knight at the border fortress of Marienburg, "Europe or Christendom" looking toward the East, clearing the earth in the humility of his Christian mission so that it can bear culture. And this is no longer utopia and contradiction, as in the first of the circles through which we passed, but the summons of the hour to some individuals who dare to confront it without a safety net.

This book was written for the sake of this summons. But it must finally occupy itself with Schneider's concluding period, in which the final veils were drawn aside from what was still half-hidden. This final act (as I have said already when making the comparison with Kierkegaard) indicates both that the final store of proofs is being put forward and that a shadow is thrown across the testimony that has been given hitherto. Is it possible to resolve this antinomy into an unambiguous final form? This question can be answered only at the close.

ORIGINS

PORTUGAL—THE DREAM

The Coast

The experience of the collapse of culture, of the transience of life, an unsurpassable measure of melancholy and the hopeless flight from the sinking ship: this is the beginning. No nihilism can be more profound than that of the twenty-three-year-old for whom all faith had disintegrated, every firm outline had become fluid, every sheltering wall had been shattered, so that he emerged from the crumbling house of history into an existence with nothingness as its most certain mark. Kierkegaard's melancholy was subjective when compared to this new melancholy that arose from the evidential character of the meaninglessness of events. Nietzsche's despair could find relief in his own willing and creative activity; Heidegger's horror could change in an instant to a state of resolution. Here, however, a heart was exposed even more vulnerably to the icy winds; and no path was in sight. The anxiety does not take on the concentrated form of a clay that can be modeled, as in the hands of Rilke. Life itself is impossible, no matter how it may establish itself; even more impossible is the work this life generates. "The fact that I cannot live abroad, or in my home country",[1] the fact that a hidden and a public existence are equally impossible, makes the poet "the enemy of that which is similar and the enemy of duality",[2] one who doubts both form and freedom. Existence now is only the impossibility of the one or of the other, of every part and counterpart.

Reinhold Schneider will set up his realm "on the far side of a despair" experienced far more profoundly than that of any existentialist. He does not flee in cowardice from ruin but rises up precipitously from the abyss. Thus no harshness will ever again be able to terrify

---

[1] 14:7.
[2] 14:6.

him, since he himself comes a priori from that which is harshest of
all. The flight that stands at the beginning is something elementary,
something that lays the foundations of his existence: from the collapsing midpoint, Germany, to a periphery; but his instinct impels him
away from the direction that would have taken him to the origins
(Greece or Asia) to take the opposite direction, to the place where
the West (*Abendland*) becomes ever more evening (*Abend*), until his
flight halts at the uttermost coast, where the West subsides into the
ocean. Here, on the edge, its name and its essence are discovered
in their truth. "The problematic concept of Europe becomes a total
utopia here."[3] The sphere that opens up is utterly alien. "On the
margin of the continent",[4] the life that will later be interpreted as
Herz am Erdensaume (Heart on the margin of the earth)[5] comes into
its own. "The step taken over the boundary leads into the innermost
realm."[6] "A Rocky Massif on the Portuguese coast": the eternal ebb
and flow washes it away into nothingness, and he bends down into
this flood in a "ray of lost light": "the sky and the water await me
—nothing else."[7] *Estremadura*: "Wretched houses scattered helplessly
abroad in the vicinity of shattered stones", the wilderness grows in
ever more rarefied air, time is pushed to its boundaries: "Is this the
first day? Is this the day of the judgment of the world? The beginning becomes the end, and the weary life's dream builds its house of
stone."[8] This land is not only "foreign" but the very embodiment of
all that is foreign: "alien to the earth in its uttermost depth",[9] just
as it also remains the land of the great oscillation: "a land of earth-
quakes from the beginning".[10] Others had fled: Hölderlin and Byron
to Greece, Platen to the south coast looking toward Africa, to the
"border of the continent and the uttermost boundary of the kingdom", all three with the intention of raising the classical form out of
the waves there;[11] Hugo Ball had dared to take the leap on the sea
cliffs of Athos from the utopia and the asceticism of unbelief into the
holiness of the fundamental renunciation of the heart, something that
permitted the form of faith to arise anew; all of these found help in

---

[3] 3:7.
[4] 3:8; 3:118.
[5] 82.
[6] 6:51.
[7] 14:10.

[8] 14:12.
[9] 3:20; 3:139.
[10] 5:11.
[11] 18:45.

the form that already existed and was offered by the historical basis of the Mediterranean. Schneider's nakedness is much more exposed. He takes up his position at the point where the continent descends into the ocean, and he absorbs into all his pores the oozing away of the West. Portugal: the land of the colors refracted in the sea mist (as it is invoked again majestically in a final vision),[12] a beginning that is never brought to completion, ruin and dissolution, a fragment that is the antithesis to the Spanish form at its back,[13] deliquescence, melody and atmosphere.[14] The unfinished monuments still stand to an epoch carousing in the dream of historical greatness, "in an unexampled hypertrophy of feeling";[15] the soul still oscillates between the unfounded sadness that destroys and denies everything and the enthusiastic affirmation, indeed, the cult of precisely this feeling. *Saudade*, the word for the innermost contradiction between this yearning that consumes itself and yet wants itself to live in this very act of consuming[16]—only Graf Keyserling succeeded in giving an equally intense and paradoxical description of this existential feeling in his *South American Meditations*—and this contradictory life that is the glorification of all the powers that are hostile to life, this contradictory act of existence as passivity and passion, of a passion that destroys itself and enjoys itself in death—this is experienced and felt as the "reversal of all Western values".[17] The image of a perverted orientation of life occurs again and again: "since my branches tend toward the depth, and my roots ramble in the air!";[18] but this reversal can prompt the question: Is not precisely this the peak of the intellectual life, indeed, the essence of the spirit and, thereby, the very essence of the West—an essence that must penetrate to the point of this contradiction: "That the heart loves to fight against itself, that it is better to yearn than to receive . . . all of this seems to be something other than Western"—and yet: "The soul of the coastal population, which had received the charge of speaking the final, uttermost word, is in truth a genuine Western soul, a Christian soul in the most beautiful sense of the word":[19] a soul that crosses over into eternity at the point where it burns up in the glow of yearning.

---

[12] 18:137f.
[13] 3:10–11, 40; 3:58f.
[14] 3:8; 3:7.
[15] 2:85.

[16] 2:86, 91; 3:7.
[17] 3:146.
[18] 14:23; 2:107.
[19] 18:137f.

This contradiction had become more and more acutely the stigma of the Western spirit: Faust lived in the shadow of the one who denies from the beginning; Hegel sees truth as the phoenix rising from the ashes of Yes and No; Schopenhauer sees pain as the essence of the world and compassion as virtue; Nietzsche understands spirit to be the life that carves itself into life, its most secret cruelty; for Kierkegaard, intellectual existence means melancholy; for Klages, the spirit is the foe of life; for Scheler, the spirit is the heroic midpoint between the power from below and the powerlessness from above; for Freud and Thomas Mann, the spirit is a sickness of life; for Heidegger, spirit is the place where Being is afraid of its own self; for Sartre, the spirit is the intolerable possibility among all the possibilities of essence. But we do not yet see the linking of the tragic dimension of existence with a noble pride that bears this tragic dimension and arises from it as a precious form: this is the genuinely Iberian linking that Schneider first discovered in *Miguel de Unamuno*, the thinker of the tragic contradiction between spirit and life. It was Unamuno who gave Schneider the most decisive stimuli—without giving him more than the confirmation of what he already knew and sought within himself—and it is Unamuno who must be seen (together with Schopenhauer, who was likewise received on a deep level) behind the Iberian beginnings of Schneider. One ought to have Unamuno's "descriptions of landscapes" (*Por tierras de Portugal y de España*, 1911) echoing in one's mind when one reads those of Schneider; one ought to recall his *Del sentimiento trájico de la vida* (1913) and *L'Agonie du christianisme* (1925) when one attempts to understand the way the German feels about the world. For Unamuno, spirit is the tragic sense of life, for "life is a tragedy, and tragedy is a continuous struggle without victory, without the hope of a victory: a contradiction."[20] It is above all a contradiction between life and reason; "reason is an enemy of life",[21] covering up the abysses, seeking harmony and happiness. No, it is pain that reveals the genuine reality. For although consciousness is a "sickness of life",[22] "nevertheless this madness is at the same time the source of vitality and the recovery of health. Out of the abyss of

---

[20] M. de Unamuno, *Philosophische Werke: "Das tragische Lebensgefühl" und "Die Agonie des Christentums"* (Vienna and Leipzig, Phaidonverlag), 19.

[21] Unamuno, *Lebensgefühl*, 116.

[22] Ibid., 24.

the sense of our mortality, we rise up to the light of a new heaven."[23]
It is the knowledge of one's death that distinguishes man from the
beast: it is death that makes the consciousness alive.[24] Thus Schopenhauer is taken on board, and a bridge is erected toward Heidegger. "In
happiness, one forgets oneself and one's own existence, one merges
with that which is alien to oneself, one become alien to oneself. One
gathers oneself only where one is 'I' in pain."[25] The consciousness
of God is the embodiment of the pain of all contradictions.[26] "Pain
is the substratum of life, the root of the subjective. It links to all that
exists; it is the divine blood in all its vessels",[27] the contradiction that
is suffered, but at the same time the contradiction that is fought out
to the close: spirit is *agōn*,[28] the linking through the struggle of that
which is fleeing from its own self. The conquering thought remains
always a ravishing of oneself.[29] But the matrix of the spirit, antecedent
to all life and thought, is the power of the imagination,[30] from which
(along with the contradiction) the saving images, dreams and ideas
arise. True religion is "despair" or, precisely, a "tragic sense of life",
and its expression can be either the image of God or the burning of
this image: "Out of despair one affirms, out of despair one denies, and
out of despair one refrains from every act of affirmation and denial."[31]
The highest consolation of existence is "the holy, sweet, saving uncertainty"[32] that makes faith possible on the far side of crazy reason.
Thus (although his intellectual stance is consciously anti-English)[33]
Unamuno's arm embraces with equal cordiality the cruel Marlowe
(who burrowed much more deeply in his *Faust* than did Goethe in
his)[34] and Ignatius of Loyola (a Basque like himself) and Philip II,
and above all the utopian chivalry of Don Quixote,[35] which generates only the highest form and ideality of the tragic sense of life. A
daring arch swings across from Schopenhauer to Christ, indeed, to
God the Father, who shares in the suffering of the Son of Man on
the Cross.[36] The agonistic life attains its peak in the agony of the

---

[23] Ibid., 54.
[24] Ibid., 52.
[25] Ibid., 179.
[26] Ibid., 191.
[27] Ibid., 255.
[28] Ibid., 144.
[29] Ibid., 41.

[30] Ibid., 36.
[31] Ibid., 156.
[32] Ibid., 152.
[33] Ibid., 394.
[34] Ibid., 372.
[35] Ibid., 382.
[36] Ibid., 254.

Cross.[37] Although Unamuno almost everywhere experiences Catholic dogma as a compromise,[38] he finds the Protestant decline of life into the letter of the law to be even more intolerable.[39] He feels that the Catholic sphere has at least retained the tension between form and impossibility, between nobility and downfall.

Reinhold Schneider was never tempted to blend such epigonic philosophic ideas of a weary European spirit in the melting pot of a glowing passion. The line of melody of his lament is much purer than Unamuno's: it is humble and without philosophic pretentions. But how many motifs sound related—all the more so because the Spaniard had drawn his main ideas from Pascal, Kierkegaard and German philosophy! The category of contradiction remains in the background for the German, but it surfaces at decisive points.

> You must do the uttermost that is possible for you; but this "uttermost" is also the end: you cannot avoid arriving at the point where you must contradict your own being and essence, where you can no longer exist; it is precisely the power that drove you to action that now drives you beyond the action, and there exists nowhere a deeper suffering than on the highest peaks of human existence toward which great souls strive with an innermost yearning. While the world is still celebrating your name, you have already experienced the end.[40]

This is what he says about Corneille. And now Camões: "Because death shatters the sphere in which fulfillment is impossible, it bears in itself the promise of eternal fulfillment. Death is the strongest impulse: when life is driven to its uttermost boundary, life flames up most passionately of all."[41] The primal contradiction becomes visible in Portugal as mourning and a lamentation over existence: as a life that leads to death, but since death is indwelling in life, as a life out of death and through death. Destiny does not come upon us from the outside: "The curve of the path of life is only a projection of the inner constitution of the soul or, to use the words of Novalis, 'Destiny and temperament are the names of *one* concept.' "[42] "Ivy and tree trunk are made sisters by their enmity."[43] "Because the soul wants to live, it also wants to lament. And it almost seems as if Portugal experienced

---

[37] Unamuno, *Agonie*, 11; *Lebensgefühl*, 78.
[38] Unamuno, *Lebensgefühl*, 98.
[39] Unamuno, *Agonie*, 45.
[40] 13:36.
[41] 2:109.
[42] 3:141.
[43] 3:147; 18:137–38.

the tremendous epic of its conquests only so that it could bleed to death because of them, in order to experience impoverishment, decline and the long turning away from history, in order to transform the impossibility of what is earthly into a song and a dream."[44] The one who lives and acts is aware of the innermost transience of life and action—"nothing was ever so certain in Lisbon in the course of all the centuries as catastrophe"[45]—"the same principle of life that impels its unfolding contains in itself the necessity of decline",[46] as we see so pitilessly in the image of the sunflower:

> O excess of life that has attempted to find a form!
> You bend the stalk down before it brings fruit to maturity,
> you take the sap before the capsule closes.
>
> So ultimately the sun glows in vain,
> because it reaches too deeply down into your roots
> and your marrow flows too fully toward the sun.[47]

Thus nothingness and futility must flow into life and action from the very origin; "the ultimate demand" made of the one who acts "aims at his unification with the tragic law of history: at the decision to take the eternal nothingness into our own action".[48] This is why there exists in the most serious sense a will to suffer,[49] even "out of the whole glowing passion of the heart";[50] the one who loves "demands" that the beloved "destroy" him.[51] What Schneider says here about Camões comes close to the lovers' passion in Claudel's *Satin Slipper*. It is life, not death, that is tragic; one who wished to overcome death would cut life to the quick.[52] This can be reduced to the most formal terms by saying that it is time, the "eternal decline", that deals out death and life in being and in action:

> Time slays time; at the end there circulates
> that which ever kills us and snatches us from death.[53]

And it is precisely for this reason that the organ of time, the power of the imagination, is the deepest element in the soul, disclosing the dreamlike quality of existence, indeed, disclosing in the "dream" the

---

[44] 18:135.
[45] 3:72; 5:120.
[46] 7:21.
[47] 14:37.
[48] 7:304; cf. 18:9.

[49] 2:91f.
[50] 2:29.
[51] 2:91; cf., e.g., 3:50–51.
[52] 6:240.
[53] 14:35.

most wide-awake and clear dimension of the spirit. Thus the three
Portuguese short stories end in a metaphysics of the dream. Despite all
the genuineness of transcendence, indeed, all the truth of faith, "still
we do not know of any deeper wisdom than the Spanish science of
the dream, which is at the same time a German experience. And since
they all dreamed, they also lived; indeed, it is certain that the one who
dreams most passionately lives most deeply."[54] The Portuguese realm
of the dream oscillates between earth and heaven;[55] to enter "reality"
and to enter "the dream" are one and the same thing: "When earthliness is intensified to the highest degree, it becomes transcendent."[56]
"Men never awake: all they do is turn around in a half-sleep so that
they can begin a new dream and seek the possibility of a new deed;
there is no deeper dream than that of the one who acts." Thus the
dream is everything:[57] it is the "truth" of our existence that weighs
as much as our existence, and nothing more; thus it is also the "men-
dacity" of our existence; it is above all the ego: "seven shadows".[58]
"A German experience", says Schneider; and so he finds Jean Paul
in Portugal again and again,[59] and he even finds the Russian element
there: "the lethal breath of passion under the humble devotion, the
passion that triumphs in self-abasement".[60] It is important that such
extremes meet. The final pair of concepts that can give expression
to this dream-soul is the related pair of tragedy and idyll, each arising out of the other, challenging it and in turn overcoming it. The
idyll is not only a pause, a floating recreation from the weight of
the existence that makes excessive demands: it is this existence itself
raised to the second power; it is seriousness at play, the serenity of
mourning that is all too sad.[61] In Evora, we have the fountain, the
Roman temple, the gracious pavilion: "So much serenity, so much
grace was not permitted to Europe." "Would it really be possible for
me to believe in a continuity, an equilibrium here?"[62] The nobility
of the perfected form rises here like an unconscious, voluntary fruit
from the mourning that allows it to ripen slowly.

---

[54] 5:149.

[55] 2:22.

[56] 107:144.

[57] 9:424.

[58] 3:43; 14:9.

[59] 2:21; 3:80; 3:142.

[60] 2:92.

[61] 2:111; 3:31; 3:98f., 101, 125;
107:281; 8:94; 13:23.

[62] 3:128–31.

The Idea

It would not be worth mentioning Portugal between mourning and dream were it not for the fact that the poet who justifies everything arose from its decline as full accomplishment with his idea. "On the clouds of our heavy earthly dream, which often lift only to spin their web even deeper around us, shimmer the lights of eternity; and it is only the artist who elevates these clouds to become a structured form."[1] Camões provides the example of the power of this transformation. The poet lives the entire contradiction in himself, for the only poem he can compose is his own self: out of the death of his own soul is born the eternal life of the idea; and in relation to his work, his life is the index of the world and its history: out of the lethal contradiction of historical reality arises the idea portrayed in the poem, transfiguring and justifying this reality.

Das Leiden des Camoes, Reinhold Schneider's first work, is constructed in four stages: the first describes the "hero" of the *Lusiads*, Vasco da Gama, and his milieu, the period of Portugal's conquests, with pitiless realism: plunder, murder, inhuman cruelty, the total inability to make plausible in the act of colonization the Christian idea that allegedly impels it, indeed, the inability to achieve even the most elementary balance of powers. The mother country bleeds to death and is impoverished in the intoxication of the unlimited distant realms and their riches. The second stage shows the poet, his Portuguese blood, the incurable state of his soul—"a man enters a world in which he cannot exist." His "abysmal and endless lamentation is uttered a whole life long in all lands and on all seas and intensifies finally to become the terrible curse that the old man invokes on the day of his birth, shattering both the world and his own life"[2]—the tragedy of his love, which consumes itself and desires its own ruin (Penthesilea is not far away), his involvement in Portugal's adventure, on far seas, in numberless journeys where the horizon is ripped open on all sides, in all spheres and cultures: all this provides the basic material for the construction of the *Lusiads*. Out of the doubly bleeding contradiction of history and of the existence of the poet who is held captive therein arises, thirdly, the kingdom: aware of what he is doing,

---

[1] 10:28.   [2] 2:70, 71.

aware of the "deep contradiction between matter and form, the basic problem of the *Lusiads*",[3] Camões changes his hero into an apostle of the faith, the pirate voyage into a Christian mission of the elect Portuguese people, the failure and shipwreck of the entire undertaking into a grandiose victory. "He cannot accept things as they are, for they inflict a mortal blow on him. So he must change their nature, so that they become what he needs them to be." This is the "consistent idealism". Thus the poet elevates himself above his people, which do indeed know the dream "but not the idea".[4] Within the world, he offers his people what God does for his creature in the act of justification: a creative verdict that contains the truth in its genuine nature, providing a dwelling place and a dream of existence for the existence that is breaking down and falling into decay. Camões' shipwreck, out of which he rescues himself naked, holding the manuscript of the *Lusiads* high above the waves with one arm, is certainly symbolic of what remains to be shown in the fourth section, "the extinguishing earth": how the idea, which is taking on ever clearer outlines, becomes the "ethical criterion"[5] of what is real, the judgment in the double sense of the saving adjustment and the condemnation of all that is inappropriate. In order for the idea to be pure, that which is real must disappear: it is the highest justice that the royal dreamer Sebastian should die in 1578 in his meaningless African campaign, but also that "Camões dreamed his last dream with this king",[6] falling down with him as a man, where only his spirit survives. "Is not a princely price paid for the decline of a nation when a poet writes the inscription on its tomb?"[7] But justification takes the form of a judgment in the Christian sphere too: only the one who is humbled in faith enters the glory of the new state of being a child of God.

The poets stand in a dialectic relationship to history. They "come either too early or too late, either to prepare what is to come or to elevate into lasting continuity what is transitory and perhaps has already passed away";[8] but precisely in this sense, they must be judges. "For the poet is closest to the spirit that composes the poem of history, the greatest poem of guilt and judgment; but whereas the law of the judgment of the world indicates itself only at long intervals,

---

[3] 2:133.
[4] 2:136, 137.
[5] 2:148.

[6] 2:226.
[7] 2:241.
[8] 13:18.

like the hours sounded by the clock in the night, the poet proclaims
it through the accomplished destiny in the firm, strict boundaries of
his work."[9] The idea becomes the conscience of the world, because,
like the concluding section of the *Lusiads*, it progressively absorbs
into itself the entire structure of the world, rising up to become the
vision of the world that is imparted to Vasco when he returns home;
over all the seas and their depths, all the cultures, all the powers of
the cosmos that have a genuine presence as the classical gods and yet,
according to Paul, have already withdrawn before the omnipotence
of Christ, over all the kingdoms with their kings, over the entire
contradictory and lethal struggle between the life of the passions on
earth and the "tragic anemia of the ideal".[10] But by absorbing this
totality into itself, Schneider's composition takes the decisive step beyond Unamuno. What is involved in quixotry is not only that the
hero "is ridiculed and conquered, for to be conquered is the same as
to conquer; he is the master of the world in virtue of the fact that
he has made himself an object of laughter to the world."[11] Rather,
the point is that the whole of Portugal, from Manuel the Happy to
Sebastian, from Vasco to Camões, itself behaves quixotically in reality and that therefore the idea not only rings out like a mockery
of reality but belongs to this reality as a power that judges and that
accordingly has historic force. Schneider's appeal to the lord of La
Mancha is already superseded as it is being made:[12] no matter how
much he may portray the relationship between the real and the ideal
as a relationship of struggle and hostility, the fact that he experiences
reality as something that is already decaying and broken open means
that the idea possesses a priori an indwelling function of ethical judgment.[13] The poet's responsibility is stated in very strong terms; fame
is not something ultimately striven for and, in any case, is bestowed
only in decline and renunciation;[14] the poet "forms the tragedy of
his own life, of his fame, which is perfected and survives, as the victorious shout and the mourning of his soul".[15] Kant, too, to whom
Schneider will turn for information, is thereby in principle already
superseded, and all the doors are opened for a further development

---

[9] 18:100.

[10] 2:197.

[11] Unamuno, *Lebensgefühl*, 406.

[12] 2:136.

[13] 2:116.

[14] 2:94; 107; 108; 110.

[15] 13:36.

that is as yet uncertain: a development to become the one who acts ethically within history, the one who stands above history as its responsible shaper. And one can understand why he loves to place his own mission again and again in the shadow of Camões[16] and makes a poet's work depend on his possession of the "exalted freedom over image and dream":[17] it is only this freedom that allows one to see the idea.

For the moment, of course, everything remains expressed in razor-sharp antitheses. Adamastor, Camões' figure of destiny, the tragic giant of the Southern Cape "on which the ships are wrecked",[18] remains the real hero: "The delight in completion is inextricably joined to the delight in shattering one's own form":[19] "Dare to praise the sailor and the rock on which he is dashed to pieces!"[20] It is characteristic that the real king is not as yet any image but only a quixotic figure, that instead of this, Pombal enjoys a certain shuddering admiration,[21] that as yet the saints are wholly absent, or that their position within real history is mentioned only with irony,[22] and when the real unfolding of power is cursed, the curse remains on ground level and determines everything.[23] The fundamental category of real history remains the (Buddhist-Schopenhauerish) "thirst",[24] the greedy, tragic passion for power and possession, a primal cruelty of life against itself (most wonderfully in the chapter of the Portuguese diary entitled *Die Langusten*, which is equal in rank to the best of Nietzsche). "No enmity is greater than the gluttonous hostility of life to itself",[25] but the milder melancholy of Schneider allows tones from the world of *Tristan* and the *Götterdämmerung* and their tragic vision to be heard too: "So all that remains is a sleep without images, a limitless forgetting, the highest joy—the only joy",[26] an *idée fixe* that recurs again and again until the very end. There is surely little that is more German than this contradiction between life and form, which Schneider took with him to Iberia, in order apparently to discover it there: "the tragedy of the Germans, who have never united power and spirit, nation and

---

[16] 35:47.
[17] 98:79.
[18] 2:105f.
[19] 2:108.
[20] 82:13.
[21] 3:61f.; 5:123f.

[22] 2:138.
[23] 2:156–58.
[24] 2:130.
[25] 3:124.
[26] 7:238; 83:66; cf. 79:13; 112:63.

culture, history and formed ethos",[27] remains the eye-glass through which the escaping poet sees the world of the Latin countries; a dialectic between the power of instinct and the powerlessness of spirit, which pins down the precise point at which all the modern protests gather against the antimediaeval image of the world, a dialectic that remains most profoundly unchristian (and this also means: unhumanist): the Protestant protest against the Catholic "ordering of being", the possibility of uniting heaven and earth (and idea and existence) that is portrayed and established in the Incarnation of God.

The Image

In the tragic world, the image remains the only meaning: "How much consolation there is in the image; yes, all our consolations come from images."[1] The image is not a concept abstracted from reality, for it is not possible to deduce anything eternal from what is contradictory and declining; nor is it without any relationship to reality (in the sense of the symbolism of "art for art's sake"), since it comes from the power of the imagination, the fundamental power of the soul, which suffers because of its existence in time and history. In the case of Corneille, we are told: "The basis of tragedy is an emotion, the fate portrayed is an image of life."[2] If the drama of the poet is the reproduction of an original existential emotion, namely, the tragic existential emotion, then it is also destiny and history as a whole; this means that the image is not alien to reality. But whereas the drama as event and clash of the powers that destroy one another reveals the tragic, dying sides of existence, the image is the transfigured, saved, surviving side of the same existence. Thus the image of the poet is indeed the highest and clearest image but not at all the only image: history itself is able (and indeed ought) to produce images in which it transcends in the very act of declining; and its highest meaning will be to give birth to real forms as images, models, representations of the eternal meaning. Alongside the poet, two others will take their places: the ruler and the saint. And whereas "the truth changes without standing still",[3] it will suffice to note that the great, lawgiving figure is exempt from

---

[27] 7:184-85.

[1] 107:310.

[2] 13:39.

[3] 7:304.

this change; as such, and through its own self, this figure "bestows value on the world", although it is precisely man, who in this way becomes an image, who is the site of tragedy par excellence: he becomes this through his harshest antithesis to his own life, to which he dies, and through the most radical transcendence to the world of the supernatural.

> Sometimes history forms images that stand above the ages with the power of allegories; they have a deep meaning; indeed, they are as impossible to interpret exhaustively as is the word of one endowed with grace, almost like a revealed word. . . . If we penetrate more deeply into history, we shall find that it is very rich in such images, which use the means of earthly reality to express the reality that lies beyond this world and which make visible the substance of an epoch in its relation to eternity and often anticipate this; perhaps it would be possible to summarize the history of peoples, and the salvation history hidden in this, in such images, out of which the directing spirit itself seems to speak. Naturally, the accomplishment of this task would require not only the strongest personal force on the part of the one drawing the portrait but also a dedication to the supernatural, to that which exists and works—and such a dedication is exceptionally rare.[4]

Nor does the image float unrelatedly in itself; rather, it is the true revelation of the essence of the world, namely, that this apparently aesthetic meaning is rooted in a religious meaning that was later understood to be Christian:

> All images point back to the archetype that is veiled in light, just as things subsist in the Son as the reflection of the glory and the copy of the Father, in the Son through whom the Father created the world and who sustains the universe through his word (Heb 1:3). The entire being of the world has the quality of an image, a reflection of the Divine Being. The soul can satisfy itself only by means of that which is an image, not by means of an event that has not yet been raised to an image.[5]

"History, too, must be an image if it is not to destroy, and it is perhaps the task of those who have the responsibility to maintain and to prepare the path—the kings and the poets—to create, to respect and to preserve such images . . . (to) hold the protective, elevating image in front of the reality."[6] "In mediaeval Russia, a holy image was

---

[4] 18:262.
[5] 18:289.

[6] 9:379, 380.

brought to a sick prince, so that he might get better through looking
at this picture. Even today, peoples and their mighty men could become healthy by means of images of genuine ordering, provided they
have maintained the ability to look at such images."[7] But the price
paid for the supratemporal validity of the image is the life that belongs
to time: life must die to itself in order to become an image; indeed,
the image itself is most eloquent precisely where it is in the process
of arising out of death, as the perpetuation of the life that sacrifices
itself, as tragedy that has taken on form.

These last quotations have taken us almost ten years farther on in
time; the Portuguese horizon does not allow so much. Here, the image is still almost only a form of mourning: its praising and perpetuation. And Reinhold Schneider will never detach himself completely
from this origin. The life that ends in death supplies the greatest image and is at the same time the most extreme historical situation and
the symbolic situation. Thus kings are portrayed above all in their
dying; the description swells toward the end and reaches the broad
delta when it enters death. The death of Philip II will be unforget-
table, the "painless hour" at the end of tremendous sufferings,[8] the
hour that is the stigma of his living life in the king's existence. Un-
forgettable too are the death of Charles V and the celebration of this
death, slowly considered in advance,[9] the death of Frederick William I
of Prussia, the description of which comes close to that of Brahe's
death in *Malte Laurids*,[10] the end of Frederick the Great, which is
only the conclusion of a lifelong decline,[11] of Frederick William IV,
in which "the last king had departed",[12] then the death of those who
had been brought to accomplishment, like that of Tilly during the
battle[13] that he accompanies in spirit, in prayer, but also the death
of the mighty ones in the claws of the demon: of William the Conqueror, who ends in the night that had been exacted by force and in
poverty,[14] the endless dying of Louis XI, the rebel for whose soul the
saint struggles,[15] the death in the terror of the deprivation of power,
in the case of Boniface VIII,[16] death in stony silence in the case of

---

[7] 92:33−34; cf. 51:103.

[8] 107:354−64; 71:101f.; 14:63; 98:72.

[9] 107:177f., 184−86.

[10] 7:154−67.

[11] 7:280−93.

[12] 94:120−38.

[13] 24:41f.

[14] 9:153; 110:88.

[15] 67.

[16] 108:271.

Elizabeth of England ("the queen sat, stripped of her splendor, in the twilight on the earth, looking down at the ground, her finger in her mouth, waiting"),[17] the death of Henry VIII, which had already been survived in his repentance,[18] the grandiose parable of the beheading of Charles I,[19] the death of the Sun King in repentance and extinction,[20] Czar Alexander I, who penetrates even deeper into humility and vicarious representation.[21] "What belongs more unambiguously to the future than the last sound of a dying man? The high peaks of death permit one to take in the widest panorama; for Philip, as for his father, death is the decisive action."[22] Alongside this there is the tragedy of getting older and especially of the abdications,[23] and then, as the image that runs through all the works, the long list of crypts with their self-perpetuating mysteries:[24] Speyer, the grottoes of St. Peter's, Königslutter (with Lothair in the middle, his wife Richenza to the right, and Henry the Proud to the left),[25] the Capuchin crypt into which Maria Theresa has herself lowered on a rope every year on the anniversary of the death of her husband (and once the rope breaks),[26] the church of St. Michael into which the old Elector Maximilian descends to pray, the crypt in the drama *Der Kronprinz*,[27] and the crypt of Paul I.[28] This has not the slightest connection with Romanticism—rather, it is classicism: a strict form that comes out of death. But the images always compel the reluctant eye to look inexorably on the ultimate harshnesses of historical reality, not in order to try their taste in a perverse manner, but almost with a pastoral tenderness, in order to obtain precise information and to draw the correct consequences from this. All meekness now yields place to a patient perseverance in the horror that seems to have been registered with a slow-motion camera: the fire of London (as the crowning of the history of England),[29] the destruction of Lisbon in *Erdbeben*,[30] the slow and precise description of all the cruelties of the Inquisition

---

[17] 9:394.
[18] 9:328f.
[19] 9:451f.
[20] 13:96f.
[21] 65; 110.
[22] 107:202.
[23] 107:55; 24:16.

[24] 8:33f.; 81:34; 14:15.
[25] 11:11–12; 18:169.
[26] 18:260.
[27] 24:23; 101:39.
[28] 110:124.
[29] 9:488–96.
[30] 5:103f.

and the conquistadores in *Las Casas*.[31] Few battle narratives can equal
that of Hochkirch,[32] and few scenes can be more tormenting than the
temptation of Celestine V in *Der Große Verzicht* and the fall of the
demonic Boniface in the same play, or the mental torments of the
women suspected of being witches in the short story about Spee.[33]
And yet, the images of muted, intimate joy arise again and again out
of the terrors, the wonderful idyll of the fishermen in *Inselreich*,[34] the
prophetic evocation of the holy early period of Ireland,[35] the long,
satiated sequence of images in *Macht und Gnade*.[36] Here it would be
necessary to show in greater detail how Schneider's experience of history begins in landscapes,[37] so that the sensuous image discloses not
only the past but, as it were, the metaphysics of the place, the city,
the country (one can think here of that church in Coimbra filled to
half its height with sand from flooding and of the meditation that at
once pierces into the ultimate dimensions yet always remains attached
to the symbolism of the image).[38] *Auf Wegen deutscher Geschichte* offers
many examples of this power to see the historical picture in a landscape, the meaning of the world in a historical image.[39] Often a few
scraps of biography suffice—the fundamental outline falls into place
in an instant.[40]

All the image are completely open, unlike the symbolism that understands them as something ultimate; they are as open as the wound
of existence from which they flow. The concept (as its very name indicates) is something that closes; the image is something that opens,
because it points to what is depicted in the image. In the sonnet
"Form und Freiheit",[41] the *indifferentia* between image and nonimage
is achieved, and all the poems in *Herz am Erdensaume* show with pre-
cision (in a manner very close to Eichendorff) how the images clus-

---

[31] 2:44f., 123f.; 12:39f.

[32] 7:219ff.

[33] 34:195–226.

[34] 9:369f.

[35] 9:13f.

[36] 18.

[37] Cf., e.g., 3:5 for Portugal, for Potsdam in *Die Hohenzollern*: 7:125–31.

[38] 3:46f.

[39] 8.

[40] Cf. the portrait of Corneille's life: 13 and 91:93, or of El Greco's life: 91:117f.

[41] 14:6.

ter and then dissolve again: their transitional character, their twilight existence, that which is finally summarized under the name of "the falling glory" or "the rustling of the falling mantle of glory".[42] The image is itself distilled from the "extinguishing", decaying earth, but this too can become invisible:

> Dear roses, the voice of my soul is dying—
> let my whole soul look on you!
> In your radiance, as you breathe your last, you weave me gently
> into the great mystery of the rising night.[43]

Thus the perfected form can appear as a tomb, and true beauty can lie in the act of dying and crossing over ("an evening light sheds its glow around all beauty"),[44] the fear caused by the fact that one must die can conceal within itself a most secret joy, and the falling silent of the voice can be the most precise statement of this joy. "That which is beautiful is surrounded in a special way by the terror of death, by a yearning for eternity that is contradicted by all experience."[45] It is here that the first cycle of experience is rounded off, the cycle that has arisen from the land at earth's margin, the land of the dreamers and of the poet satiated with suffering. We do not forget that Reinhold Schneider fled here instead of to Greece, with the inheritance of German dialectics as the thorn in his heart. Here it was possible to combine classical humanism with an eschatological-utopian radicalism and thereby to lay the foundations of an interpretation of existence in extreme terms as historical struggle. This country looks across to Africa, where Tertullian glowed with fervor and Augustine looked on the world as the struggle of the city of God with the demonic might. Until the very last, there will be no place in the Western vision of Reinhold Schneider for the Greece of the Aristotelian "midpoint", the Stoic "nature" and the philosophy of Thomas Aquinas, which is constructed on the basis of these. When he encounters Aquinas (something that happens seldom), it is almost always only in order to indicate his limitations: Thomas remains attached to the creation and its orderings, while the most concrete historical ordering, as the Apocalypse reveals it, this ordering full of tensions and catastrophes, "shatters the world of St. Thomas";[46] here, an eschatological thinking

---

[42] 82:32.
[43] 82:27.
[44] 69:53.

[45] 83:67.
[46] 112:75.

that is at the same time a radically christological thinking is set against thinking on the basis of the creation.[47] The only way in which Greece is represented from the beginning onward is through its tragedy, about which Schneider has something essential to say: *Der Mensch und sein Leid in der griechischen Tragödie*[48] begins with the *fortissimo* of all terrors and nights, bypassing all cheap solutions to the riddle of the world to praise as the highest achievement of the Greek genius its leaving the religious question reverently open (instead of an almost inevitable revolt against the gods). This is Schneider's *gratia supponit naturam*: "We venerate the song of the tragedians. It contains truth about suffering, not about God: yet God has revealed himself by means of this truth",[49] by means of the world of Antigone, Iphigenia and Oedipus, "where valid orderings contradict each other", indeed, where "gods rule against one another".[50] But already here there is a boundary to tragedy: the reverence, the acquiescence, the image that is set at rest, so that God's revelation does not become incarnate in the contradiction *tout court*, but in a fear of God, even if this is blind (and Paul, too, speaks of this). Nevertheless, this image that has been set at rest, as it shimmers over the decline of Portugal, is not Plato's *eidos*, still less Aristotle's essential form. It is the "immortal", detaching itself from that which is tragically dissolving, but only because this latter breaks down. One should never forget the position of the words in the title: *Das Leiden des Camoes, oder Untergang und Vollendung der portugiesischen Macht*. From the coast of failure, Reinhold Schneider will have to clear the path back into the European midpoint, and he will never forget that this boundary was a midpoint for him.

---

[47] 112:76.

[48] 86.

[49] 86:31.

[50] 86:14, 15.

SPAIN—THE FORM

The King

There lies a leap between *Camoes* and *Philip II*: the primordial experience of the Escorial and of its lord. In Portugal, the kings, the kingdom, Belém and Mafra belonged to the dream world; only the poet transcended them in the structured form of the idea. But in Spain the idea intervened in reality once and for all to give it form. Where the poet stood, the king now stands; where the poem stood, the palace stands—more than this, the state built on the model of the palace stands. Now the subtitle has to be: *Religion und Macht*. It is only now that all the threads run together, what had liquefied crystallizes; the exact figure detaches itself in the precise distance between the primal Spanish *nada*, in which Reinhold Schneider finds his entire provenance, and that form of life toward which his life is traveling, although he does not yet have any idea how it can come to look. It is the figure of a king, of *this* king, but in him the image of every king. He is like a matrix of human existence; inimitably exalted (as the genuine idea must be) over all copies, yet these copies in turn are to be interpreted in their confused endeavors only by means of this purest figure.

Nothing of the presuppositions is abandoned: life is a standing in impossibility, an excessive demand, a rape. But precisely as anvil, life becomes the hammer; as something broken on the wheel, it becomes the wheel; as something crushed to death, it becomes the form. In *faith*, living out of the power of that which lies beyond this world, the life that denies itself brings the idea into this world. Schneider has said everything in five pages about the tragic existence on the basis of faith in the world here (*Das Ethos Spaniens*).[1] "The dreadful determination and certainty" with which "a destiny of the greatest

---

[1] 18:227–31.

dimensions" is passionately taken up, "the courage to go to the uttermost", is Spanish: to dominate the world out of a transcendent idea,
to make an irrevocable decision once in life, "the courage to fight
to the finish the conflict of life between this world and the world to
come with the active commitment of one's whole existence".[2]

Philip must be misunderstood by all who do not live out of faith
as he does.[3] His existence is the end of psychology, because the force
out of which he lives and constructs lies beyond his soul. Psychology,
the wretched and pernicious surrogate of faith, has been left behind in
principle in the world of the king and of faith, in the world of Reinhold Schneider; he quotes with approval the words of Novalis: "The
so-called psychology, too, belongs to the masks that have occupied the
position in the sanctuary where genuine images of the gods ought to
stand."[4] One who does not wish to die to himself and to the claims
and abilities of his own soul will never grasp the greatness of an existence as office and representation. Fichte's words about the ruler are
the prefix to Philip's life: "In this manner, the idea takes hold of him
and penetrates him thoroughly, absolutely and without reserve, and
there is nothing left of his person and of the course of his life except
what continues to burn as a perpetual sacrifice to the idea. And thus
he is the most immediate appearance of God in the world."[5] He is
installed in his office through the unheard-of renunciation his father
makes; "Philip's most burning desire is to become like him. His nature
aims at what belongs to the past, at what is passing away; now that
his father is slowly taking his leave, withdrawing himself voluntarily
from the earth in Juste and yet bearing on his pallid face the shadow
of the necessity of passing away, he must inevitably entice his son
to imitate him."[6] What the son takes on himself is "wholly office",
a "divine task", "only burden and service".[7] "No value counts less
for him than happiness." The great kings "all made decisions under
the idea that elevates and destroys the personality".[8] "Great ideas are
incompatible with a certain mercy. The commandment sounds forth
into life inexorably; its constraint will form life. The bequest, too,
grows only under compulsion. Thanks to the violation that has been

---

[2] 18:227, 228, 229.

[3] 71:44f.

[4] 90:123.

[5] 107:141.

[6] 107:167.

[7] 107:175.

[8] 107:312.

endured, life will one day bear witness that it existed and will in turn awaken life."[9] (Still more abruptly about Frederick II: "He does not belong to himself; and the same is true of the family that is the living representation of power and loses its unity and prosperity because of this power; all its members are secretly enraged with one another: the terrible commission of power consumes all that is human.")[10] One cannot distinguish the thought here sharply enough from every kind of legitimist theory that is tied to blood; what is involved is a spiritual, metaphysical decision by the person.

> The mystery of this appearance does not lie in the blood but rather in the demand made; this is the genuine nobility of kings. Where the greatest demands are made, the greatest fruit will be borne, and there is only one presupposition for this: that this demand is completely understood and is grasped as a new life. The decision depends on the thought's not being adopted and carried farther but being born anew in the individual, so that it begins to grow in him, and every power of the man in whom it lives is subordinated to it. This thought will destroy: it will impel to completion by destroying. A king is never bourgeois; his task is to live out in the eyes of his subjects that which is most rare and uncommon: the consuming service of the idea. There is at least *one* moment in the life of a king when there is surely no possibility for any counsel or voice or consideration from the world to gain access to him—this is the moment in which the question is whether the office entrusted to him by God is to have more weight than the existence of his trusted intimates—or even than his own. How would it be possible for a genuine king to take advice in this moment? The decision is made between him and his God —yet it was already made when he ascended the throne.[11]

And thus the law of being becomes visible in the king: "It is an unchangeable relationship to life that kings must supply: the relationship of the tragic man who no longer attaches any significance to being itself, because of the necessity to be and to act in one particular manner."[12] Once again, in the case of Corneille's king:

> The one who stood highest in life had also paid life the highest price, indeed, perhaps he belonged no longer to life at all, as those he ruled, those who looked up to him, understood life. The lawgivers and orderers of this world have all died a secret death, since the renunciation of all

---

[9] 107:193.
[10] 7:274.

[11] 7:10–11.
[12] 7:303.

that is personal is a death: it may be that the real theme of Corneille the
tragedian was this death of the mighty man and hero, which does not
coincide with physical death but is, on the contrary, the first condition
for the historical task that must now be mastered. Thus existence appears in a dreadful self-contradiction: laws are imposed on life, laws that
contradict life, and yet those who carry out these laws are surrounded
by the rays of a light that bestows on life its purest value. . . . All is
sacrifice, even life itself.[13]

"The kings have not acquired for themselves this relationship to
suprapersonal life; they have only preserved it; in reality it is congenital to them as the particular genus of their soul that determines
all their feeling and thinking, even the ebullitions of their blood; they
are copies of a form that was created long ago, epiphanies of an idea."[14]
"As the essentially tragic person, the king symbolizes the tragic fate
of the world."[15] He, and only he—but all men through him. Here
lies the starting point of an "aristocratic metaphysics": the real nature
of the world appears at *one* point, but because this point (through its
dying) is a vicarious point, that which is real can reveal itself everywhere. The "historical metaphysics" of existential philosophy (Being as time and history) is transcended in the only direction that is
creative of values and of the world, which unintentionally justifies
the highest culture and past and overcomes nihilism, without again
neutralizing the rent that has been made in existence. The concept
of representation, simultaneously historical and philosophical, forms
the nodal point of this ordering of the world, and it is this that will
find its highest justification in the theological sphere: this is the place
where the vicarious existence (as model or as copy) will later prove
appropriate as the vessel for the archetypical revelation of the God-
man.

The king is expropriated into the universal dimension. "Kings experience the fates of their peoples as their own life; even in the most
personal dimension, they are not only a person; and if the mystery
of kingship consists precisely in the fact that the one who bears the
crown lives not only the present time but equally the depths of the
past and of the future, so that he is in a comprehensive sense the ex-

---

[13] 13:26–28.
[14] 13:75f.
[15] 13:72.

pression of the historical being of the people whose crown he bears",
then the king lives in representative existence.[16] "The history of his
people also lays an obligation upon him. It is only by accepting the
validity of these powers that determine destiny that one will understand the life of a king, which becomes a totality, not in itself, but
only in union with the past."[17] More says to Henry VIII: "Yes, you
are a king, and that is why your personal life and your decision, your
destiny and the destiny of the country coalesce, and none of your
subjects can distinguish between what you have done for your own
sake and what you have done for the sake of the country."[18] "Even
when they err, kings experience more than their own destiny; as long
as they are still bearers of history, and the people want them to be
such, the most personal dimension of their life contains a decision
that determines what is universal."[19] The prince is a *universale concre-
tum*; this is why we must suppose another concept of society here
than is customary. The customary concept holds that one can make
the demand of the many that they should not live for themselves but
should forget themselves and be available for others. But such an attitude is always presupposed in the being of the prince, and the opposite demand is made of him: he is to be himself to such a degree
that all are included in him. Unamuno had understood this, but he
had expressed it "democratically" once again: "There is nothing more
universal than what is individual. Each individual man has the same
weight as the whole of humanity; one cannot sacrifice the one to all,
but only sacrifice all—to the extent that they *are* 'all'—to each individual."[20] What is thought of here in Hegelian terms as a universal
proposition will be applied historically and in a unique way in Reinhold Schneider. His aristocratism has a most profoundly social nature:
the officebearer has died to his own individuality—the crown itself
compels this death—and is from now on only vicarious existence.
The theme in *Kaiser Lothars Krone* is the power of this transformation through office: through the crown, the rebel becomes a genuine

---

[16] 18:46–47.
[17] 18:93.
[18] 34:45.
[19] 9:235.
[20] *Philosophische Werke: "Das tragische Lebensgefühl" und "Die Agonie des Christentums"* (Vienna and Leipzig, Phaidonverlag), 58; cf. 113.

prince; one could virtually speak of an *opus operatum*. The same is true of Grillparzer's Rudolf I: "The transformation of the one crowned is not brought about by the changed political position alone; it is a miracle that is generated by his consecration, and the crown works in history with a power of its own."[21] "The crown is an act of faith, and man and world are referred to this act. . . . Here it ought to be the testimony to a man, the inalienable element of himself, more than his life."[22] "Offices have a force that continues to work even when the bearers do not correspond to their offices."[23]

It is only now, in the Escorial, that the link between palace and monastery can be understood: the prince himself is one who has died, and his inner life is related to that of the monks, although their office makes a distinction between them: "The king and the monk stand each in his own place; neither of them is allowed to exchange his office for that of the other. The king ought to have had the experience of the monk and to rule with this experience."[24] Thus "Philip is king and monk, ruler from the East Indies to Hawaii and slave of eternity."[25] "This is the only form of life of the Catholic monarch, the form now discovered at last: as his kingdom is a fief received from God, so he himself dwells in God's house together with men who are subject to God, not to him."[26]

This is the union of humility and pride that is appropriate to princes and blossoms to its ultimate unity in Philip: these two are not antagonists, or elements to be brought into a difficult harmony (as in bourgeois ethics), but originally belong together: as a feeling for the rank that as such is a fief and a service: a form bestowed as gift, not according to one's own merit. Indeed, it is the "pride of humility",[27] just as "highest pride and deepest humility" are the distinguishing mark of the saint of Assisi himself.[28] Once again: all this is not psychology but ontology. We are shown from this highest point the form of which the finite being is capable. Not a drunken reeling between a presumption of omnipotence and the experience of the crash into powerlessness, but the absoluteness of command and obedience, of the

---

[21] 55:29.

[22] 101:51.

[23] 9:379.

[24] 9:66.

[25] 107:291.

[26] 107:294f.; cf. 18:229.

[27] 71:49; 107:204.

[28] 26:70.

authority that comes from humility, a form that is never hidden but
sets its mark completely on everything. All the twitches and cramps
of religious subjectivity from Luther to Kierkegaard remain ultimately
bourgeois and in the deepest sense unserviceable for an objective mission in which one is put to use. Philip's humility has forgotten itself;
it serves the cause, and thus it constructs it.

Deeply moved, Reinhold Schneider looks up to this height, fascinated by the loneliness in which the office shuts up those who
are sacrificed.[29] Love, the relationship to women, remains essentially
tragic, because here, too, the personal is sacrificed to the official; or,
where this does not happen voluntarily, it is inexorably demanded by
the office.[30] Philip's life suffices as exemplification; one scarcely needs
the explicitness in Corneille's themes. Schneider is also fascinated by
the silence that surrounds the ultimate decisions, its image that room
in the Escorial where the king writes ("man counterfeits, the voice
counterfeits . . . but when the pen slides over the paper in a room
where no human presence confuses the stillness, where the silence
stands motionless between the sides in a glass, setting one sign after
another in deep black on the pure white page, then the word purifies"),[31] and then the contemplation and the weariness (on Titian's
and Valázquez' pictures of kings): "They depict the one chosen to
establish order at the summit of his power, without passing over in
silence his suffering, his weariness, his weakness; indeed, it is precisely the shadows that fall on the ruler's soul that give his picture
the genuinely kingly stamp",[32] and finally there lies "the shadow of
transience" over the king's long work and toil.[33] The image of the
king's window, lit up in the night, recurs very often: while the rest
of the country sleeps, the ruler is awake, plagued by care, working,
struggling with God.[34] And while the king is one sacrificed before the
eyes of everyone, the queen is often one sacrificed at a much deeper
level but in secret. The destiny of women on the throne is shown in

---

[29] 24:6.

[30] 107:212, 216, 308; 7:173f., 275f.; 13:31; 110:44, 75.

[31] 107:207.

[32] 18:271.

[33] 71:105.

[34] 101:18.

the "Death of the Queen" Margaret of Scotland[35] but also in the wife of the Bavarian Elector and in Philip's wives: "worn out early on by the burden of duties, the heaviness of the form, the perpetual sacrifice, that are the destiny of kings".[36] And yet, the enormous burden of the world, claiming the active involvement of all the soul's power and overwhelming it with this demand, does not make the chosen ones broken cripples but, on the contrary, makes them the most beautiful images, the most perfect personalities. Instrumentality, as understood here, is the opposite of the anonymity of modern man. "Philip II became a personality under the influence of the suprapersonal; it is the essence of the personality to stand before the absolute and be under obligation to it."[37] The purest image is born where "the form and the image, which are demanded *ab extra*", fuse with the "soul", so that the perfect personality of the ruler emerges,[38] indeed, where the soul in death is victorious in the form, as we see in the death mask of Frederick II: "He served power and stood his ground. He confronted power with his innermost force, the person who neither can nor may become an instrument; with the force of the person, he bore the power he had seized impetuously; the person will last longer than the power."[39]

It is not Frederick but Philip, however, who provides Reinhold Schneider with his criterion, since faith is required in one who is to be the perfect ruler—only faith guarantees that the burden of the world will not crush the soul. It belongs to the idea of the king—no matter how much the historical copies of the idea may fail—that his soul is open to God; "The genuine kings are compelled to look up to God; they are, as it were, involved in a perpetual conversation with him."[40] We are told of Philip: "The king, the human administrator, the *hombre Rey*, lives in an unbroken dialogue with God. But only God, no one apart from God, gives commands to the king."[41] This is the ruler of Plato's *Republic*, as he was later transfigured in Poseidonius and Philo and in the Neoplatonic, Christian and Arabic-Jewish mysticism and politics to become the mediator between heaven and earth. But when Reinhold Schneider associates kingship and holiness

---

[35] 103:63f.; 24:35.
[36] 71:85.
[37] 71:46.
[38] 25:4.

[39] 25:12.
[40] 77:15.
[41] 107:205.

so closely, this is for substantive reasons, not because of history: for the expropriation of every fiber of the private existence into an unreserved service of ruling, the form of the king's life, is per se, as a form (and prescinding here from any question of content) the objective form of holiness; of itself, it demands that the bearer correspond to it through personal-subjective holiness. The "consecration that stands higher than all human wisdom" and lies in the crown demands that the bearer "have a consecration that penetrates to his very heart and be kingly even in his thoughts": "A dreadful truth, that means death to us!" says the "Crown Prince" in the play of the same name.[42] And thus there is "something holy" that floats around Shakespeare's kings, "something that becomes visible precisely in the dying king who has been stripped of his power".[43] And it is never more clear what a king really is than when he is genuinely holy.

> Almost every people has been granted to see its crown once on the head of a saint, and to see the most pious man in the most powerful man, whether in good times or in bad. Thus the Emperor Henry II ruled in Germany, Edward the Confessor in England, St. Louis in France, St. Stephen in Hungary, Olav in Norway; St. Elizabeth wore the Portuguese crown at the side of her husband, and Margaret the crown of Scotland. All these could bear witness that the crown does not destroy the soul of the one who wears it reverently. For it was the strength of Christ that bore the power in them, so that a reflection of their similarity to the king and judge of the world may have become visible on their faces.[44]

This statement also tones down those traits drawn from tragedy with which Schneider executes his first portraits of kings; what he had seen then as a fatal contradiction between soul and form is now caught up, beyond every philosophy, into the Christian mystery of the Cross. But Schneider is as yet only en route to this position; what is called "faith" here is still one of the symbols of the transcendence that is inherent to existence. But already we can say that when Reinhold Schneider affirms the Catholic dimension in Philip, this is not out of any love for an aesthetic form of life or even a cult of form such as we find in Maurras—he has been affected by the overwhelming truth of the form of the expression and, in search of its source, has stumbled on

---

[42] 101:50.
[43] 77:13f.
[44] 25:7f.

humility. Teresa of Avila called him the holy king: "eso nuestro Santo
Rey Don Felipe".[45] Philip's mystery was to set the profane in order
on the basis of the sacred, letting the reflected splendor of prayer fall
on all secular business and understanding the service of the state and
of justice as responsibility in the presence of the God who is close at
hand and accompanies all that the king does. Schneider illustrates the
same principle by means of St. Louis, whose acquisition of the crown
of thorns in 1239 remains a great symbol: he always has this crown
in view when he has to carry out the duties attached to his own. He
is concerned about equity and jurisprudence; when he comes from
Mass, he sits in judgment under the tree of Vincennes "out of the
grace of the illumination of his office, just as the German emperors
left the cathedral in Speyer and sat in judgment, not as lawgivers, but
on the basis of the responsibility of their priestly-historical power and
of the wisdom that was linked to this".[46] We have already seen the
relation between monastic life and kingly life; now "priest and king,
the chosen distributor of heavenly grace and the one installed in office to administer the fragile earthly power", are associated with one
another as "related", "since they encounter one another under the
mystery of the crown of thorns, the sign of kingly priesthood hidden
in history".[47] Louis' kingship is brought "into the proximity of the
sacraments":[48] this statement is not meant in a Romantic, legitimist
sense but derives from the essence of earthly power when this is illuminated by the light of faith. Naturally, the light of the Catholic
faith cannot be separated from the form of the Catholic Church, so
that Schneider will soon have to ask what the relationship of the consecrated kingly power is to the equally consecrated authority of the
Church; logically enough, his next work, *Innozenz III*, will portray
the tragic collision between these two.

But for the moment, prescinding from all the historical conflicts,
let us note that Reinhold Schneider is never concerned either with
an abstract philosophical doctrine of the state (of the *bonum commune*
and the various constitutional possibilities of realizing this) or with
the description of pure historical forms and situations, no matter how
"ideal" these may be: he is always concerned with concrete human

---

[45] 107:273, 365; 71:106.

[46] 62:105.

[47] 62:109.

[48] 62:108.

existence as this *ought* to present itself in the historical sphere in its ideality. As man truly is, he can never wholly detach his "temporal" and "universal" good from the relatedness to his eternal salvation; he is the man of guilt and the man of redemption, and every doctrine of history and of the state that abstractly bypasses this fundamental definition in its thinking will fail to do justice to the essence and the concrete situation of man. No matter how well constituted and autonomous the temporal well-being of the people may be, the one who administers it cannot dispense himself from looking to that which is eternal; and this look is objective only when it makes him available to God in *indifferentia* and prayer, and with the expectation that the form of the highest responsibility, the crown of thorns, will impress itself upon his own responsibility—or (to make the same point in different terms) that secular power must be administered under the law of the voluntary powerlessness of the Redeemer: "The thorn of this terrible contradiction cannot be detached from the crown."[49] Naturally, a ruler who wished to do justice to this highest law and understood the administering of earthly power, not in a personal sense, but in the sense of service, would have some hope of being able to carry out this resolve only if the people he ruled had the same view and (at least in the best of its members) endeavored to look on the image he wished to set up: that is, if the form of the king could become everyone's form. In this *mutuality* of the people's will and the king's will, which is for Reinhold Schneider the crowning of his idea of the king, every external legitimism is left behind. The genuine king is possible only when a country thinks in kingly terms, and this thinking leads it to demand the corresponding image of its ruler. Then the visible crown would be so strong that it would make the secret, invisible crown shine in all hearts.

Thus it is indeed true that the king justifies all life in the country: "It is only he who makes possible the existence of those who live in enclosed houses. There must be at least one who is strong enough to will even that which is of no use; he must have overcome in himself the collapse that has not yet happened if the quieter world of the others is not to collapse."[50] But the vicarious dimension becomes the model: "They are to serve as he himself serves."[51] The king must

---

[49] 62:104.

[50] 7:11.

[51] 7:101.

be an image, and "his nature must be rich enough to provide the people with the material for such a kingly image";[52] according to a remark of Frederick William IV, "the unshakable consciousness of the distinction between what is above and what is below", which creates and maintains this image, presupposes not only in the people but also in him "the living, sharp, logical recognition of the unutterable distinction between the Creator and the creature",[53] with humility and distance as the highest commandment. "For it is the dignity of man", indeed, even the dignity of the king, "that he can bow down and that he is raised up as one who is bowed down."[54] The king also justifies the nobility as a class, for "without kingship there is no nobility; and even if the nobility continually follows its own nature, which vacillates between pride and devotion, and (rightly or wrongly) opposes the kingship, nevertheless it would annihilate its own self the moment it harmed the marrow of the kingship."[55] The king is a genuine idea, and his elevation over everyone permits him to set on everyone the stamp of his own self, permitting even the most bourgeois existence to share in the kingliness of his existence. The acknowledgment of the representative form of life of the king by all and for all leads to the requirement that all live under this image, which remains alive only as long as all recognize the demand it makes of them. "The crown is a very heavy burden", says Nikolai in *Zar Alexander*, "I can bear it only if you help me and obey me."[56] We are told of *Kaiser Lothars Krone*: "It would never have been able to send its rays into the world from the head of the dead king unless it had shed its light in the hearts of all who had served him: their force and faith had borne him as the head of the people who were called to the kingdom."[57] Finally, as a conclusion, Schneider says about Shakespeare's kings: "A light goes forth from the ruler and just administrator of power, the 'one who is at the origin of customs', and this wishes to encounter the light of the ruled; light depends on light, and the whole world depends on this confluence of light, which has its real origin in the eternal light. . . . Conscience and insight and an unbroken heart are the crown of every individual: the forces of such crowns unite a thou-

---

[52] 18:69.

[53] 18:20.

[54] 51:100.

[55] 9:179.

[56] 110:172f.

[57] 11:195.

sandfold and are exalted in the graced crown of the king."[58] "For the crown lives from the hearts that revere it, and it is extinguished along with these hearts; it is a symbol, just as much as it is an expression, and this is why it is absolutely never based on power."[59] Thus Reinhold Schneider can make his own Uhland's words (which are astonishing on his lips): "No head will shine above Germany that is not anointed with a full drop of democratic oil."[60] But what Schneider means is a "religious democracy, the universality of genuine faith and truthful humility, which can no longer be presupposed today. The lack of this makes a genuine kingdom impossible. For the crown could rule only where it was raised up in the soul of each single individual among the people."[61] Pre-Christian kings were a possibility because those times were an advent, according to God's plan: "A path led from the classical period to Christianity, in the sense of an unfolding of ac-quired values; but there is no path leading from Christianity toward its opposite", and so it is no longer possible today to conceive of a real king unless he were a Christian king, because it "is quite simply impossible to envisage a world, still less a culture, that would not be anti-Christian but would leave Christianity behind and construct itself in virtue of new values of its own, coming together to form a totality."[62] This is why we find among the most tragic figures of his-tory those kings who are born in a kingless time and lack the material on which are to set their stamp. This destiny is portrayed in Freder-ick William IV,[63] and it is the theme of the drama *Der Kronprinz*.[64] Who can even truly understand a king like Philip today? ("So one must say that historiography has been very unchivalrous in dealing with this ruler, the representative king of a chivalrous people; all too often there has been a refusal to see him in his own world and reality —instead, he has been subordinated to ideas that this man passion-ately endeavored to fight with all the pride of his being.")[65] But how could it be possible for the scholarship of a profoundly unchivalrous age to contemplate knighthood and kingship otherwise than from the outside? How could such scholarship avoid speaking from the out-

---

[58] 77:46f.
[59] 11:36.
[60] 113:173 (47).
[61] 18:24.

[62] 18:85.
[63] 94:120–38; 18:18–24.
[64] 101:86.
[65] 71:45.

side, without faith, about the faith that this knighthood and kingship presupposed?

Philip remains Schneider's midpoint and touchstone. He inherits Camões' Portugal. He is the adversary of the rigid Elizabeth, who embodies the opposite island kingdom. Indeed, he stands behind the kings of Prussia; Reinhold Schneider turns from the Escorial to Potsdam. Philip is the criterion for Corneille's French kingly tragedy. He is the vanishing point of the encounter between Las Casas and Charles V. "He stands absolutely in the center of the Spanish world."[66]

The Castle

In the Castilian landscape of *nada*, out of which Teresa of Avila's invisible castle of the soul arose, too, like a mirage, there arose at the same time the visible "castle of the truth", the king's palace, which was simultaneously a church, a monastery and a funeral monument, in which the spirit of faith was to become stone and art and the law of all spiritual form was to provide proof of itself before the eyes of all the world. It is the prerogative of kings to build, and the spirit of representation demands in terms of its own concept that it become an image. Naturally, the building put up here was a sign of the salvaging of what was already under threat, the perpetuation of what was already collapsing in time, a building almost more for the dead and their relics than for the future. Charlemagne, Henry II and Louis of France could try to depict the kingdom of God in measure and weight, looking to what was to come: out of the time that is passing away, Philip builds a Noah's ark leading over to eternity. His building stands on the boundary where the representation portrays itself for the last time and achieves completion as it perishes. At this boundary, what has been achieved must be a consolation, a straight line pointing into a future that is no longer sufficient. But what faith builds is exalted over the laws of earthly history; its passing away gives it as much as its completion: Philip builds in the same spirit as Teresa when she establishes her *moradas* and her foundations and as Ignatius when he outlines the crystalline plan of his Exercises. This

---

[66] 71:50.

is the Spanish dimension, namely, that the highest transparency, even where it means death in earthly terms, generates from itself the form and image, deep and sharp in a manner befitting eternity. "Not in the evening or in the morning mist: the high plateaux of Castile and its mountain ranges reveal themselves at midday, in the brightest light. In an excess of clearness, it becomes possible to see that which lies above the world. The stronger the form, the more impossible it is to reject the symbol."[1] Whereas the North casts the images down in the name of faith and of transcendence, dissolving the firm framework of the world, the South constructs out of faith and in the name of transparency. The question mark that the North sets after the concept of "Christian art" troubles the South so little that the only art it knows is Christian art. Faith provides the task that "includes also the purest possibilities of art".[2] Faith is the basis of art; when art becomes possible for the artist, grace becomes doubly visible in the world, in the king and in the saint; and both images, since they belong together, are reflected in each other. Both impose on the world an ordering from above; it is not forbidden for the king to have his origin as high as that of the saint—he is allowed to turn his palace into a monastery and a place of perpetual prayer—and the saint is not forbidden to root his own working as deeply in the world as the king does. Ignatius and Teresa want to renew the face of the earth out of the spirit of mysticism. The king is not "more turned toward the world" than the saint, nor is the saint more "turned away from the world" than the king. These words have no meaning where they stand. They have no Catholic meaning at all. "Where the truth has not entered the thinking of men from above, where man has not bowed down—instead of inventing or even creating something that never existed before—then no form has succeeded, no statement has been conclusively made, no path has been shown."[3] But to bow down to the truth from above means to die to oneself and enter the form of God, which alone is the original form of man (and thus of his art). In the short story "Der Sklave des Velasquez", the encounter between King Philip and the artist becomes a genuine reciprocal influence of both offices, which represent the eternal in the real and the ideal spheres, and can do so only if they let their life become a work of God, as the saints

---

[1] 107:243.
[2] 18:236.
[3] 52:26.

understand this.[4] In the unity he embodies, Philip's building is the
harmony of all three: holiness, politics and art. And art and politics
in their idea serve holiness, just as holiness takes on flesh in both of
them. "A perfect house is the pure imprint of a life, the condensa-
tion of an existence into its strictest and at the same time appropriate
form."[5] But Philip embodies the same clear, mathematical law in his
state and in his government: they are the counterpart to the Escorial.[6]
And both are the law of his life, which makes itself available humbly
to God's forming hand.

> Nothing in this stone is cold; the tide is coming in and rising; the mea-
> sure serves only to gather things together; an untamable might lies in the
> numbers. Every block is a number that is exploding with energy, pulling
> others along in its wake, because it goes ahead, and making demands,
> because it gives support. The intensity of the discipline that is imposed
> betrays the intensity of the power within. Did life precede the form, or
> did the form precede life? The question does not end; the heartbeat does
> not turn to ice any more in the stone. Feeling is form.[7]

> > The gray cupola and the gray room,
> > in which the king listens to God's voice,
> > abide unchanging like land and mountain.

> > When the builder has turned to stone, he scarcely quivers,
> > when the flight of his victorious eagles passes away,
> > and he serves and dies and remains in his work.[8]

The palace, which is at the same time a monastery,[9] is ultimately the
highest memorial of a reverent tradition: it becomes the mausoleum
of the Habsburgs; the crypt lies under the church, and the statues of
the imperial family kneel to left and right in the choir; it also becomes
a reliquary in which the sanctuaries imperilled in the North are won
back and find refuge. The king knows that he does not negate life by
looking thus into death: the dead kings and saints are living, and they
join in the work of shaping the future in the communion of saints.
What the son did was only the completion of his father's work and
renunciation, bringing his father's living heart home into the eternal
form. The slow procession of the dead to the palace has a grandeur

---

[4] 94:80–93.
[5] 107:298.
[6] 71:90f.

[7] 107:303.
[8] 14:32.
[9] 107:309–21.

surpassing human grandeur; its rays form on all the streets; it rests at night in the churches; then there is the solemn reception in front of the building, while a storm rips away the brocade from the coffins— "the crowns, the weapons and the flashing signs of lordship, the broad initials in gold whirl out into the wilderness like the dead leaves of last year."[10]

"The precondition for the epiphany of the eternal is that something is broken to pieces",[11] for the Christian existence is tragic. But its breaking to pieces is always itself the birth of its eternal form, the framework of which forms the presupposition of the true tragedy both in life and in art. In *Drama und Königtum*, Reinhold Schneider develops the apparently very harsh but logical idea that tragic art presupposes the image of the world that finds expression in representation.

> A tragedy can occur only when immovable, iron laws hold good; where there is no form, there is no necessity. The person of the king himself, its value and merit, can be called into question in the drama but never the kingship or the crown, that is (in the most general sense), never the form of the state. Thus all of Shakespeare's kingly dramas end with the reestablishment, the renewed foundation of the crown, which enjoys an inviolable respect, no matter what fate it may have suffered. The highest measure of structuring power, or inner order, is demanded of the tragic poet, and this means that he cannot be a revolutionary. Tragedy describes a cycle that goes from the disturbed ordering, via confusion, back to the ordering; it sees in rebellion an ineradicable element of the world but not an absolute value. There is no revolutionary tragedy: the very concept is a self-contradiction.

Nor does the "ethical law in man's breast or in the stars" suffice "to govern an action", for this law is not sufficiently incarnate to judge man; faith and the form of the state remain "uncertain, mutable, dependent on the individual aspect".[12] To speak of tragedy is necessarily to posit a transcendental value, "not for the sake of consolation: what is involved is the law of existence and of the form that expresses existence"; indeed, death cannot be understood otherwise than as "the fatal breakthrough into the eternal ordering. But

---

[10] 107:315.
[11] 107:189.

[12] 18:27–29, 27f.

it depends on mortality. The life beyond death and the eternal law in antithesis to earthly life: these are what bears tragedy."[13] But this law judges only when it shimmers visibly through the framework of the human ordering (which always breaks down). This takes place— as Schneider will later recognize—in the Incarnation of God and in the ordering of the world that bears the Incarnation's stamp: in the epiphany of God's power in the creation as grace and in the transcendence of secular power in the direction of grace. "In the immense movement of history, there is only one place of rest: at the point where power and grace are united."[14] The "clarifying parable" is Shakespeare's *Measure for Measure*: the drama of guilt takes place under the eyes of the masked Duke of Vienna, the mild prince, who at the end, as a symbol of the judge of the world, comes forward with power and creates justice, but his justice is a function of grace: "I find an apt remission in myself."[15] This is why the Baroque is the apogee of the drama: the period between Shakespeare and Calderon, when the old image of the world, in which the earthly is still understood as a symbol of the grace of the Incarnation, has freed itself from the mediaeval immobility of Thomas and Dante, enticed into a dynamic event where the world itself has become a drama without thereby losing its strong form—just as in Ignatius of Loyola's Exercises, for example, the Christian life becomes a process and a decision, taken within the process of Christ and his decision, but borne by the unshakable "principle and foundation", which gives strong expression in itself to the whole dynamics—or as the spirit of the Escorial finds its final sublimation in Calderon's drama: the ordering of the world as an ever new, immense event, gathering together all the dramatic meanings and fables to produce a universal meaning, the resolution of all the tragic tensions under the sign of the forgiving grace, the proximity of the theater and the Eucharist (the primal drama in the world): only in its shadow is it possible to play, to bind and loose aright.[16]

This brings us to the theme of Reinhold Schneider's later theory

---

[13] 52:64–67.

[14] 37:53.

[15] 77:39–41. The quote is from *Measure for Measure* 5.1.497.

[16] On Calderon: "Ein Drama Calderons", 18:194–202. "Calderon" in: "Philipp II", 4:317–28, and in: "Iberisches Erbe", 107:365–74. "Die Wahrheit vom Menschen in Calderons geistlichem Theater", 52:47–55. "Calderons geistliche Dramen", 81:77, 78. "Das Spiel

of art. All true art is religious and is born of a will to obedience. It is a service of the idea, and it is great precisely through this humble service. There is so little tension between aesthetics and ethics that aesthetics presupposes the perfect ethics of the artist and of the epoch for which he creates and continuously demands this in the producing of the work. "Genius as such is neither good nor bad, it is a commission and gives a task; its value depends only on the service it renders to the immovable truth. The genius can be evaluated only by being related to values that do not have their root in man and are not dependent on him." Genius is no legitimation, nor even a mission, but only the presupposition of a mission: a capacity for greater service. But the Lord of the missions stands in freedom above the capacity that derives from him and that must listen to him if it is to receive the correct idea. The true artist would have to be a saint.

Faith

The mystery of the Spanish power is the faith. Its power becomes most visible where the secular power begins to dwindle, where earthly certainty sees decline and doom as inevitable. It is here that its line intersects the sinking human curve and draws up out of it what must be salvaged. This faith is the end of psychology and of world history, revaluing all downfalls because these can be the decisive dawns of the invisible salvation, and the faith in this can once again embody itself visibly in life, work and influence. *Gratia non tollit naturam*; on the level of nature, the downfalls remain what they are: a humiliation and a disgrace unto death. But they are woven about with the mystery of germination, indeed, of public triumph; in God's eyes they are not what they appear to be on earth.

Thus Reinhold Schneider's *Philipp II* is pervaded inexorably by the consciousness of the end. The Portuguese melancholy lies over everything; it is the hour of the great withdrawal, the salvaging of the last goods before the storms come from the North, the *eternizar* of what is almost lost in earthly terms. The Escorial is citadel, redoubt, mau-

---

vom Menschen, Belsazar, frei gestaltet nach Calderon", 105, with an introduction about Calderon's theater.

soleum; the Netherlands fall away; the Armada is sunk and gives the hostile kingdom the definitive advantage; Philip has a solemn Mass of thanksgiving celebrated in all the churches when he hears the news of this. Soon all that is left is suffering, the endless torture of the final illness that makes the king definitively a saint. The earthly land is parceled out bit by bit, and faith withdraws into the innermost chamber: "A narrow stone passage leads from the king's room behind the choir to a cell that is scooped out like a cave in a rock. There Cellini's marble Christ bows his head on the Cross. No one sees the king on his path into this room, where the Spanish granite encloses the Roman marble. This chamber is the innermost cell of his state and remains the inaccessible foundation of silence from which all activity flows."[1] "We do not master the dark field when we lose ourselves in it. We must go back into the innermost sphere of our faith, into the final sanctuary that contains God's power."[2] Philip's surrender, indeed, his flight into the citadel, leaving behind an immeasurable quantity of booty to the foe, saved only one thing: the faith and its form. And "only the formed faith creates form in turn and maintains it";[3] thus despite all its booty, the North, which abandoned the form of the faith, has won nothing, and despite all its losses, the South has lost nothing. The faith that "is and works only as a form"[4] "is the power that penetrates everything, unites and rises: as such, it has brought about the history of the West and given the West its form and its substance; it has awakened the soul and given it the gift of a claim that it will not renounce, even if man should long since have forgotten what he himself is and what his soul desires." Faith has set its mark on history to such an extent that man has no longer any other choice than that of being a servant or an enemy of the faith, and one cannot fail to see "that everyone who hates is a servant of what he hates. The foes bear a testimony that is no less weighty than that of the adherents"; "faith triumphs even on the funeral pyre of mockery."[5] For faith is accustomed to losses: faith is so essential a death to one's own will and feeling that no internal losses weaken it —they serve almost only to confirm the truth of faith. "The faith is already mortally wounded by that incomprehensible and invincible

---

[1] 107:306f.
[2] 62:140.
[3] 18:112f.

[4] 18:88.
[5] 18:83f.

heresy; but like one of the old knights whose armor is shattered by a shot, it is ready to lose castle or land, provided only that it can live. The idea in which all life is gathered together must subsist without any admixture."[6] "After everything promised by the dream had been won, the king became a monk, so that he might die as a saint. Thus, and not otherwise, the kingdom of the crusaders had to end: the faith that had helped them to achieve victory demanded the restitution of the symbols of power, so that it alone might rule."[7]

Philip's faith was still able to give visible form to his work, but it was a leave-taking.[8] His politics was the outward form of his faith; his whole state was faith that had become form.[9] When he was on the defensive, he approved in principle of the Inquisition, the judgment on faith; like his father, he was severe against the heretics[10] and likewise against the pagan Moors.[11] That which is achieved today can suddenly become an impossibility tomorrow, the naked emergence of faith from the form of power lent to it can sweep away the last claim made by earthly pomp (as the brocade was swept away from the coffins) and immerse the soul in the night of pure faith. The same West that had been formed by the force of the faith is now driven like a ship in distress on the sea, and those on board, shut into the "bottom cabin" in a hopeless situation, can no longer do anything —all that they can do is "to believe" and "to be something". Now the "withdrawal" is completed: where "in the face of the probability of the destruction of *all* values, faith has struggled through to the affirmation that can permit us to survive today."[12] It may be that the word faith uses in prayer will be the cry of the one abandoned on the Cross: "Of course, *my* God is still Father even for the one who is abandoned; it is faith and the unshakable knowledge of God that cry these words. This is the God of believing despair, of despairing faith, the God who *is*, for how could we call to him and ask him questions if he did not exist?"[13] Today faith is assayed, to determine its pure essence, viz. the courage to get out of the (sinking) ship of the world and all its unsteady certainties (including one's own inner uncertainties) in order to go to meet the Lord across the

[6] 107:269.
[7] 107:366.
[8] 107:189.
[9] 107:194.

[10] 107:190f., 322–34.
[11] 107:195ff.
[12] 112:59–61.
[13] 88c:30, 33.

waves.[14] Faith is courage,[15] unbelief is "lack of courage, the great sickness of our time".[16] Faith is "the courage to accept the truth that, if our heart accuses us, God is still greater than our heart (1 Jn 3:20)".[17] "This courage contains all that is lasting in this age, everything in this age that belongs to the future."[18] This is not the courage that wants to salvage the debris of the ship with superhuman force.

> The point is not that the ship should be salvaged; we can entrust it to the Lord. It would be foolish to reply on the day of judgment that we had had to look after the ship and were not able to leave it. The point is the conversation that Peter once had with Christ, the believing question the apostle put and the simple, mighty word: "Come!" We are not to seek the shore but the Lord. The meaning of our age and of life lies in obedience to the command to walk on the waves.[19]

But obedience to the word of Christ means entering into the form of the Word itself, taking on the stamp of an "overwhelming life in which one's own life perishes". Faith is imitation and deed, or else it is nothing: from our side, it is a blind trust in love—on the side of the one who accepts us, it is an act of seeing that forms us into his own form. For the one who is sinking, it is "a deed that makes excessive demands of our forces", "a deed that goes beyond our own selves"[20] —for we ourselves are the waves across which we step; we ourselves are the tomb in which the stinking corpse lies. But in the gift of the Lord's power, this is a simple service we perform for him, carried out all the more simply and uncomplicatedly because man knows he cannot do this out of his own resources. Faith becomes the office with which one is invested, and the officebearer performs in virtue of this office something that he would not be able to do as a person.

And suddenly this service—which makes the highest demands of man and, indeed, poses excessive demands, so that it is carried out on the far side of what is highest in him, after what is highest in him has perished—becomes his true, his only mystery. In faith, God entrusts his power to man, so that man may be able to do through this what he cannot do of himself. But this power "cannot be possessed—only

---

[14] 78:24.

[15] 70:15.

[16] 71:125

[17] 80:10.

[18] 70:8.

[19] 70:15–22.

[20] 83:43, 42.

administered''.[21] "The crown is received while kneeling: the sign of the highest dignity can be borne only when it is understood as the sign of the deepest humility.''[22] Peter wanted to run away when faith filled his nets—to run away from God's overwhelming might as a failure, a sinful man. "But Peter is not to be afraid of the one whose might has suddenly caused the net, so long thrown out in vain, to fill up; nor is he to be afraid of the office of fisher of men that awaits him." The fish are prepared for the one who believes, "the office of Peter and the redemption of the creation are profoundly interconnected. As soon as he enters on his office, all beings and things become dependent on his net." While the act of his faith is out of all proportion to the subsequent catch of fish, even this "great catch" remains merely a symbol, indeed, almost an arbitrary symbol of the harvest of faith that the Lord really intends; the entire visible kingdom of God on earth, the kingdom of the popes and the kingdom of the Catholic king, remains a metaphor for the real ingathering of the world, which will take place in the power of Christ, but not without reference to the faith and the office of the Petrine Church. "What Peter has gathered is saved; but with an incomparable power, the divine fisher will throw the net over all the stars that swim away from our gaze in the universe filled with night and will pull them in toward himself as he drew all the souls to himself out of the darkness of perdition and sin. When the net has been drawn in with its burden of the creation, there will once again be astonishment about the man who is Rock, and about his companions.''[23]

If the being of the world is an appearance only, in Portuguese terms, then faith, in Spanish terms, is the penetration from appearance to being, "from the apparent power of men to the power of the Lord, from the apparent glory of the earth to the glory of the kingdom of God''.[24] But the intermediary concept between appearance and being is that of allegory: the reflection of being in the appearance, the form that the kingdom assumes in the temporal sphere. It has validity yet exists only because of the force of faith; one must always look through this form to see its foundation, and this foundation always has the potential to dissolve it, for the sake of the faith that must be accomplished

[21] 91:17.
[22] 91:30.
[23] 91:59–62.
[24] 26:15.

more purely. A faith that saw would no longer be any faith.[25] And a faith whose law was not the night of the cross would not be the following of Christ. The world is "the broken reed" that God did not reject: those who suffer and those who believe "see the secret crack that runs through all life and being in time; the hidden writing of the Cross runs through the whole bright carpet of the world."[26] It is only face to face with this crack, and on the basis of the knowledge of it, that faith can administer the office and construct the form. The building derives from the same transcendent power as the Te Deum that was sung in the face of the debris of the fleet: the king who administers is none other than the saint who stands above it. It is time to point out again that faith demands holiness and that the one who truly believes must be holy[27] and must precisely for this reason allow himself to be laden down with all God's commissions for this world and its administration. A king, on the one hand, monk and priest, on the other: Philip has minted the form of contemporary and eternal faith.

Once again, we have anticipated here many statements that were not yet ripe at the time of Schneider's Spanish book—as that time, the Catholic faith was merely a metaphor for transcendence—and yet it has been made clear at the same time that there is no rupture in continuity between the early and the late Schneider but only an unfolding. But one must not overlook the distance between the two.

Reinhold Schneider knows that all earthly images are conditioned; he draws the boundaries sharply, coloring darkly the shadows of his hero. The antithesis of the Reformation is not overcome by the thesis of the Escorial: "For the first time, a second truth stands alongside the one truth; the age of relativity begins under the sign of stony intolerance."[28] And "whereas in Spain earthly life was, as it were, subordinate to the life to come, a compensatory balance takes place in Orange, where the life to come is something that gives support to earthly life."[29] But one does not overcome this new truth by hiring people to murder it. Philip is on the defensive, and the great offensives of history never lack some truth. Everything remains open at the end of the Spanish book, even the interpretation of the book

---

[25] 58:13.
[26] 83:51, 52.
[27] 89:9.

[28] 107:325.
[29] 107:339.

itself. To what background and absolute value does its author refer
it? Ought one to interpret it with reference to *Camoes* (and hence
to nihilistic origins), so that the life that is accomplished in death is
understood as a universal philosophical category that has found one
expression (though certainly a significant expression) in the Christian
sphere? Is Philip an epiphany of the tragic will of the world, which
is baptized in his case in the name of faith? Or are we to see the
Christian faith truly as the absolute, and ought we to hear the strains
of melancholy, drawn from tragedy, as something unreal, something
that merely dies away, while the basic melody is the Cross, which
is never melancholy? The author's later works will allow the second
interpretation, but one must examine the first interpretation to the
bitter end before it is definitively rejected.

This is why we must recall one more work, which followed shortly
after *Philipp*. Although it was completed in 1931, the political situation prevented its publication. It saw the light only in 1960, as *Innozenz III*, long after the completion of the great drama *Innozenz und
Franziskus*, and in a harsh antinomy to this. Three German emperors
are in conflict with the Roman See, occupied by the "great pope"
—the Hohenstaufen Philip of Swabia, Otto the Guelph, and Frederick II—and each of these in turn is excommunicated. Schneider
gives only a brief summary of the history, in order to leave all the
space for his fundamental tragic problem: both the pope and the emperor stand on the same ground: the power of the Roman Caesar.
For both, this power is sacralized in a Christian sense: the empire is
subject to the emperor, but he receives the crown from the pope.
Innocent has Rome in his possession and makes use of the spiritual
power (of excommunication) in order to make the emperor obey his
will. Thus both become "epigones of the Roman emperors".[30] Each
stands, with a claim of his own, in the highest place. Schneider portrays the later Innocent, who composed a text "On the Contempt of
the World", as the antithesis of Philip, the man of renunciation and
ascetic disdain, whose negative attitude is a form that anticipates later
power over what is disdained. Now it is "as if Caesar were to crown
Augustus, so that he might rule along with him".[31] Unlike the case of
Philip, where power and holiness embraced, now the tragically insol-

---

[30] 138:53.   [31] 138:87.

uble dilemmas fly apart from one another; these are emphasized both by the emergence of Francis, the true saint, as a third person alongside the two rivals and by the underlining of the position of power that the Fisherman's vicar holds through the cruel war against the Albingensians. Holiness becomes purely objective, both in the crown and in the ecclesiastical office. No matter how a pope and an emperor may act, "They must be enemies; all that brings them closer to one another is the impossibility of accomplishment—something that they may never admit."[32] But the main theme is not the tragedy of the emperor—Otto's death is described very movingly—but the double contradiction in the man who has charge of the Church. "The church contradicted herself twice: when she summoned the emperor of the North and handed the world over to him, without renouncing the symbols of might; when she took back for herself a piece of earth from the kingdom of the emperor, so that she could rule freely over it; she made herself free and bound herself once again; she made her servant free and set the seal of a vassal on him."[33]

For Schneider, this antinomy is the public proof of the indissoluble contradiction that lies even in the Christian use of earthly power. He absolutizes the mediaeval situation in this way because the sacralization of the crown is something he cannot renounce. Nevertheless, the disappearance of the great emperors and the lordly popes does not mean the end of the conflict for Schneider: for him, this conflict has a constitutive nature because of the religious transcendence of humanity: "The conflict proceeds from men to peoples, from princes to thinkers; it becomes more burning, more universal."[34] But, if we measure it against Francis, the highest model remains that described above; to understand this, one must open Schneider's diary and read the comparison it contains between the Escorial and Rome, between the expression of the power that makes the renunciation and the will to have power over the whole world, for example, in the tremendous pomp of St. Peter's: "Buildings the size of St. Peter's are always tombs; they are the petrification of what is passing away";[35] Rome has no style of its own but only that of the Caesars; "the organization, the only thing that appears to make the universality possible, is

---

[32] 138:100.
[33] 138:106.

[34] 138:110.
[35] 164:328.

Roman."[36] The contradiction of the gospel for the poor and home-
less has been brought to perfection: "There is no path that leads any
farther."[37] Schneider feels "an ever-growing opposition to the whole,
incurable Christian contradiction, which compromised metaphysics
in the most fateful manner".[38] "The tragedy of Innocent is that as a
Christian leader he cannot free himself from this Roman leader."[39]
And already Schneider begins to reflect in Rome on Fichte's doctrine
of the will. This may be surprising, but the steps outlined in the diary make it comprehensible. Hitherto Schneider was interested in the
form that is established out of nothingness and is placed in front of this
nothingness as a protection. But what will begets its miracle? "The
world as will and mental image" was Schopenhauer's thesis, but his
concept of the mental image was not the same as Schneider's concept
of form. This is the reason for his long and passionate involvement
with Nietzsche, who interpreted the will in a positive sense as the
will of life for power. But Schneider's criticism becomes ever more
resolute: Nietzsche's will remains immanent to the world, and form in
the elevated sense arises only in the tragic process into the religious-
transcendental realm. He will never retreat one step from this insight,
although as yet this religious dimension remains something he cannot grasp. Even the word "God" is at best a cipher. And since the
Catholic will in Rome appeared to him to be a will that refused to let
go of paganism, his attention turned initially to the Prussian North:
form, now unambiguously political form, as the product of a primary
Germanic yearning for the transcendent. With clarity of vision he
sees in advance in his diary the boundaries he will meet; but he finds
that the task bestowed on him is the attempt at a portrait of this.

Rome's dominance frightened him off. He felt well only in front
of the mosaics of the small old churches, which he describes in detail:
"The faith of the year 600 is no longer related to the faith of the year
1600."[40] Yet the mosaics had spoken to his heart, and so we find in
the pages of his diary from 1933 onward signs of his indignation at
the face of power that Rome presents, and we hear notes that resound
from his far-off Catholic youth: it is not through the ecclesiastical office but through the Cross that Schneider will find the way back to his

---

[36] 164:329.
[37] 164:334.
[38] 164:396.

[39] 164:333.
[40] 164:373.

faith. The events of the period made their own contribution to this, so that in 1938 he goes "into the church every day, to Mass every Sunday", although he does not yet dare to approach the sacraments; then he knocks at a monastery door and asks a brother "if he would help me to make my confession", and then finally he dares to kneel at the communion rail on New Year's Day.[41] We find invectives in the diary against Rome and for Luther[42] but just as many invectives against the Reformation's lack of style;[43] the insight grows that prayer is as effective as action, that the true substance of our existence is the experience of God, that, in order to produce a genuine work, we must have died to the earth before we die.[44] Finally, we read that transcendence does not succeed without the Catholic form and that faith without dogma must shrivel up.[45] But then comes once more the victory of "the doubt" that a religious form can have absolute validity, especially "in view of the contradiction between the modern historical and cosmic consciousness and the Christian doctrine of salvation", a contradiction "so great that not even the most believing man would be able to overcome it".[46] So for the time being his attitude to Christianity wavers—not least when confronted with the contradiction discovered in Innocent. It is only while working on the *Inselreich* that this will become his firmly chosen standpoint. Schneider writes in a letter twenty years later: "Twenty years ago, I tried to write about Innocent III: I did not succeed."[47] Now it is Fichte, as the exponent of the Prussian will to take responsibility, who comes on the scene first in the sequence of time.

---

[41] 123:149ff.
[42] 164:725.
[43] 164:529, 782, 816, 820.
[44] 164:708, 711, 718.
[45] 164:829.
[46] 164:728.
[47] 145:29.

PRUSSIA—POWER

The Misery

Should he return into the heart of Europe with the vision of Iberia? And what ought he to do with this vision? Ought he to return to the country behind which lay the empire, like an excessive weight from the past, and in front of which lay uncertainty and nothing? For faith had broken in two here, right through the heart, and the beautiful form of the South could no longer succeed. Must the images he had acquired now fail? Or will they not prove to be true precisely by standing up to the test here? The task was to construct the audacious arch spanning the gulf between Spain and Prussia, between the fortress on the mountain of Castile and the citadel on the sand of Brandenburg. Had not Fichte supplied the right motto for *Philipp*? Was it not in secret the same will to service, the same lordly, heedless harshness to oneself, that compelled the emergence of the form in Iberia and compelled here the emergence of the more severe, more meager, but still more moving, still more praiseworthy structure: the visibility of the naked soul in the garment of power?

The question about power and its tragic presupposition, a question posed out of misery and virtually out of compassion, created Philip and Innocent but also the next two characters whom the author rejected almost as soon as he had produced them, although it would not be possible to form a proper image of him without them: *Die Hohenzollern, Tragik und Königtum*, built on Frederick William (the father) and Frederick II (the son), and *Fichte, der Weg zur Nation* as a sketch of the metaphysical background belonging to this. *Tragik und Königtum* shows that the question posed remains the same, that Frederick is set as a nocturnal brother alongside the Spaniard who is lit up by the lightning flashes of holiness; and, more deeply, that both worldviews are seen in contact with each other, just as Oswald Spengler, too, drew the line of continuity from Spain to Prussia, the continuity

of the attitude, of the aristocratic form, and of the power that is measured out and held in check. Even the new accusation is something
that belongs to the past, something that has already passed away; it is
Grillparzer who supplies the motto: "The king has departed. I abandon him. It is only the kingship / I want to preserve for the world,
which needs it." The same question will arise in greater intensity at
the end of this book: What is kingship without the king? What is the
demand made by form in the age of formlessness?

If it was El Cid, "the absolute man of action", who stood at the
beginning of *Philipp*, still utterly familiar with the earth, acting in
the most flexible mobility and negotiating between Christians and
Moors,[1] the beginning of *Die Hohenzollern* is the vision of the border
fortress of Marienburg and the Knights of the Teutonic Order, who
are the first to wear the color of the future power: "The black cross
stood out against the white of their mantle."[2] The only way to tame
the endless sand and the steppe was through a strict law, that of the
Cross, which dominates their form of life; and this form of life in
its turn wants to dominate the formless landscape. "It is life beyond
death that is determinative; and the forms of the earth grow up toward this." "The mystery of the work of the Order consists in the
alternation between asceticism and the desire for war."[3] But the contradiction grows in proportion to the growth of power in the name
of the Cross, because "the very same principle of life that impels to
unfolding contains also the necessity of dying."[4] But where the inner
spirit was extinguished, the external collapse before a higher spirit
is already justified, and "thus the gravest injustice appears to be perfectly accomplished justice, when the spirit that set its mark on the
law has died, and the law forgets its goal and rules only for itself."[5]
The form of the Order provides the dominant image of Prussia, and
the fatal doom that has just been described remains the tragic law of
Prussia's history. And if the spirit died in the rending caused by the
Reformation, what can the building be that this spirit nevertheless
brings into existence?

---

[1] 107:145.
[2] 7:15.
[3] 7:19, 21.

[4] 7:21.
[5] 7:24.

The portrait of the great elector is drawn under the title *Die Macht*, and this image is at once set in the framework of an iron necessity, an almost crude realism, which dominates it totally: politics is the struggle for power, that finite earthly reality that can be neither increased nor reduced, "this most unambiguous and brutal of all laws" that "necessarily makes foes of everyone" and "allows no fidelity" other than "a fidelity that demands sacrifices and is able to bestow nobility on this struggle: fidelity to one's origin, to the piece of earth that is to grow into the sphere of power through its representatives".[6] We are shown a soul humbled by the laws of power ("How was he to overcome himself, in order to make a league with his enemies, to break faithfulness, to revoke the revocation?"), conquering and then losing again, penetrating deep into the East ("the snowy wilderness is shadowed over by the foreboding of futility"), then retracing his steps, a "pleading, exchanging, negotiating", "the goal remains the same: to come out and break through into power; but the path becomes a detour; it ends in futility."[7] The summary of this restless life: "Victory is always futile, whether it brings gain or not; only the symbol is immortal. This is its bequest, more valuable than the army and the fleet, more valuable than Stettin: the consuming passion of its service."[8] Ultimately, power and its tragic law are only a riding school of the soul, which steels itself and grinds itself down therein and shows in bleeding to death that it was greater than power.

The meaning of the picture in the middle of the triptych, Frederick William, is the same, as the new motto from Grillparzer shows: "It is the man who is the highest, no matter how great his limitations; / in the king himself, it is in the final analysis the man who is the best": the power of the one who forms a whole people, of the harsh and kindly Prometheus who himself is close to the soil and forms men in his own image ("they are to serve as he himself serves").[9] Frederick, in his turn, colonizes eastward, creating the dangerous instrument of the Prussian army and hastening on the work of the ever-incomplete city on its stakes in the marsh, until the torso of his work is rounded off in his grandiose death, which is, as it were, chiseled out of stone. A Christian "who stands firmly on the earth, serving this earthly life

---

[6] 7:35.
[7] 7:36, 54, 58.
[8] 7:68.
[9] 7:101.

with the best of his powers and precisely thereby acquiring for himself a right to eternity".[10]

A third latecomer is the real object of this exercise. He begins in the idyll of Rheinsberg and in a philosophy consisting of nothing but light and skepticism, as if this would allow him to escape from his coming fate, as if he could parry the fatal tragedy of power with his "Anti-Machiavelli", sketching "the image of a prince who does not rule for his own sake or in order to cool the consuming fever of power. No, the hour inevitably comes upon him when he will give his whole life to his subjects, in order to make them happy (as he hopes), but at the same time without despising himself in the least."[11] Machiavelli on the one side, the virtuous ruler on the other—where does reality lie? "Morality is imputed to politics, and this is not correct; one takes refuge in the opposite position and holds that the greatness of a state is achieved only by its crimes or its sin; but one must leave the level of good and evil if one wishes to enter the field of historical decisions. It is not a question of sin or of its opposite—it is a question of necessity alone."[12] Reinhold Schneider ties the knot in a few sentences: The tragic leader

> will not escape from guilt or from the "judgment", if one chooses to consider it a judgment that the leader who accomplishes history loses his own life and the possibilities of what one can call "happiness" among those he leads; the people, too, will take its own path to the zone of eternal ice that encloses all historical experience and that has never yet been crossed; every earthly commission contains, as the innermost point of the force that impels it, the annihilation that is only the promise of the transition into another sphere: the ultimate decision of the unconditional that alone permits the existence of what is conditioned. Thus one will find atonement everywhere, if one looks for it, just as certainly as one will find guilt: but it is only the experience of the historical necessity that justifies us.[13]

This is the overture to Frederick's invasion of Silesia, the cities of the empress, an "unhappy woman". "His ancestors are the best justification of what he is doing. But it was only the work of his father that gave the determinative summons. Prussia, which had grown large out

---

[10] 7:91.
[11] 7:188.
[12] 7:191.
[13] 7:192.

of the idea of defense, could no longer exist in peace." The perfect army demanded to be put to the test, but it is only the Habsburg weakness ("God's will is in the end too")[14] and ultimately the profoundly divided faith ("the contradiction of what exists is the greatness of Hohenzollern; the maintenance of it is the destiny of Habsburg")[15] that justify the incurring of guilt in the eyes of history. For although he naturally becomes guilty through what he does, "the choice was only between one guilt and another guilt: between guilt in the eyes of the written law and guilt in the eyes of history."[16] All that remains now is to describe the tragedy of this unutterably exposed heart that has surrendered itself to the claim of power without the strength a Christian faith would have given, without the possibility of a friendship; it is the tragedy of one who is sacrificed and who himself sacrifices his friends, his wife and his brother to the law of his loneliness, one who must literally endure in the "sphere of annihilation",[17] so that he can become a myth for his people there.[18] He carries on his breast the oval box with the pills that could free him from suffering ("I have already wanted to take my own life, / But then—O greatest suffering!—duty issued its order",[19] he says in a poem he wrote); he lives on the far side of desperation, in a nothingness in which only misery and its relief exist: perseverance in his service. Nothing, literally nothing survives here other than the quality of the soul that endures in the deadly contradiction. "Only the *adagio* of his flute, its tones dying away without an echo, disclosed the innermost reality of his soul."[20]

"In this transformation of the Christian ideal from the ascetic greatness of the Knights of the Order to the cheerful earthliness of Frederick William"—and, let us add: to the heroic nihilism of Frederick the Great—"lies a substance rich enough for centuries."[21] This observation was published in the very dangerous year 1933, perilously close to the truth that was current then. Once again, one must ask this observation how the evaluation is made and what criterion is being used. Is the origin in the Christian faith the norm? Or is it rather the

---

[14] 7:204.
[15] 7:210.
[16] 7:200.
[17] 7:268.

[18] 7:284.
[19] 7:169, 233; cf. 79:18f.
[20] 7:245.
[21] 7:91.

end, because it is only here that the soul presents itself in its whole
extension, because it is no longer ennobled by the law of an Order but
is strengthened for its solitary last song by the terrible law of nothingness? Perhaps the historian believes that he should read history as
a phenomenology of greatness where greatness of soul would be the
absolute value, relativizing philosophy and religion, and that the occasion for a new testing is the contradiction of the systems, which generates tragic history. Philip was to be interpreted on the basis of the
Catholic sphere, Frederick on that of the Protestant sphere; Germany
was never wholly converted,[22] and there is an ultimate dimension to
the shifting waves of the struggle between Rome and Anti-Rome.[23]
Thus all that remained in the end was Frederick's deeply moving
death mask, modeled by extreme suffering, which found no one to
sing about it (as Philip found Calderon), because Weimar passes Potsdam by, and "the division between the two cities remained unrecon-
ciled."[24]

The Deed

Schneider's *Fichte* was to expose the ultimate concern even more
clearly.[1] The idealistic categories in which Reinhold Schneider understood Iberia emerge in a naked and extreme form, all the more so
because the historian sees them as portrayed in the life of Fichte the
man, this time in his restless existence, contradicting itself and setting
out on new beginnings again and again. He begins with some lines
by Fichte:

> Let him not imagine that anything is his own: possession
> is a limitation on him, and death is repose;
> the essence of freedom is an eternal struggle.
> Let him never worry about what has fallen down behind him.
> Let the thought change, destroying and creating.
> Let what is purest be selected for the grave the flames provide,
> where God's spark may meet him and make him young.

---

[22] 8:15f.

[23] 8:13f.

[24] 7:300.

[1] On the conception of *Fichte*, see the indications in the *Tagebuch* (164) 446f., 451–67,
476f., 482–84, 491, 505, 535, 539–40.

What concerns us here is not Fichte himself but the image that Reinhold Schneider bears of him, the experience he wishes to express
through Fichte. Fichte is only one of many images, but a particularly
impressive image, of the tragedy of the representative existence on
which is laid the burden of a commission. "Philosophy is an attitude;
in the highest case, it is a deed; and the history of the truth is the
history of the personalities who represented the truth."[2] "Thus the
personality continues to exist, even when none of the constructions
that it erects for itself lasts any more; the one single law of the appearing of the personality is more than the laws that it makes known;
this is the only law that applies when creative power takes on form."[3]
The essence and kernel of *history* is this taking of form by the soul
that binds itself into the world and precisely so frees itself from every compulsion in what it does. This category achieves a fundamental dominance. It was not genuinely present in Iberia: there was only
the immense intensity of the life that suffered in the dream and died
in the form. It was possible to see the elements of the construction
of the world, as it were, in an abstract nakedness. In the German
sphere, the dynamic, the primal process, the intensity of Being as history awakens. The soul (as Schneider says), the "I" (as Fichte says), is
deed, the portrayal of itself in the image and the law of a world, and
no law and command is harder on the one who performs the deed
than this necessary reversal of his own work, which everything in the
"I" serves even to the point of dying. But the soul is no worldly
image, and, therefore, in order to be and to become, it must shatter
and forget every earthly image in an indefatigable transcendence, in
an essential infidelity—out of fidelity to itself. A consuming readiness
to serve becomes one with a proud and nonchalant self-assertion; this
is the sphere of Faust.[4] Schneider takes hold of Fichte at the point
where he desires real action: initially, under the sign of Rousseau,
it is revolution against tyrants—the misunderstanding of a freedom
as happiness—then comes a sharp reversal when the German nation
takes up a position against the tyrant Napoleon, but in each case in
an incurable dialectic "between paradise and the unattainable goal,
between progress and a contented standing still, between the tragedy

---

[2] 6:15.   [4] 6:90.
[3] 6:16.

of the deed and an idyll in earthly and then in religious hues".[5] The
reflection of this incurable state is the conflict about atheism: the absolute, self-portraying "I", which dies and becomes free in its work,
became a cause of annoyance, but its thinker "is unable to listen; silence never dawns over him, he is unable to experience the infinite
as an overwhelming that comes from outside himself because he only
feels it in himself as a burning summons to the deed."[6] Yielding to
the pressure of opinion and yet remaining true to itself, the final deed
of the "I" changes into a suffering; "that which is boundless rises up
in him; up to now it served, but now it must destroy itself in order to
exist." The deed becomes passive, "and thus a will that is almost full
of hatred turns against the 'I': it must be totally consumed by God."
But even this is still dialectic, "the pain still echoes in the flood of
the new proclamation; the fracture has not healed completely: the 'I'
wavers between annihilation and deification."[7] Such an intermediary
situation, "the tension between pride and humility, is the life of this
religion". "The bow of the forms stands eternally above Being: a part
of the essence itself, imperishable, like that which it reflects. The tension will never be reconciled; for it is love itself, the blessed act by
which the one takes possession of himself; it is life. The one hovers
before the individual, attainable by love but separated from him because of love. Thus there is no extinction, such as the East dreams of;
there is endeavor and embrace, a passive deed." What Fichte dares to
cover with the name of love is a "blessed life" in the same way as the
life of the one who is chosen and sent, the individual, the one who
makes it known, the one who lives the most tremendous tension and
laceration.

> Happiness is the most heroic word. The one chosen, in which the di-
> vinity makes the gift of a new idea that changes the world, belongs to
> this life of the idea in him; unnoticed, he loses his goods, love falls
> silent, praise disappears; no one sighs over this renunciation, no one
> ever mentions the name of the victim. For only happiness suppresses the
> bright warmth of things, the consoling closeness of people's lives; God
> consumes all that is created; in deed and in waiting, in proclamation
> and in falling silent, this life in the deep bliss of the divine presence is
> enough.[8]

---

[5] Ibid.   [7] 6:162f.
[6] 6:148.   [8] 6:164.

This bliss does not await any life beyond death, for the eternal moment of the encounter between God and "I", essence and image, "is a reality of the earth". Appeal is made soon to the image of Philip II, who is perhaps the only one who completely carried out this "sacrificial service",[9] and we are reminded that Fichte also had to translate Camões[10] and that he himself gave the expression "solemnly, in mighty sonnets" to the deathly bliss.

If the "I", or the soul, is the primal history—that which portrays itself in the world, that in which and through which God portrays himself in the world—then this history is also directly world history: "The tremendous drama of the world is God's taking on form in the material of destinies and kingdoms."[11] Thus new civil constitutions and also Church orders are sketched again and again, until at last the restlessly quivering needle comes to rest at the idea of the nation: here infinity has been compelled to take on form, in a form (in the case of the German nation) that is characterized by its knowledge of its own inherent infinity and by its continuous self-transcendence. It is here that Fichte finally finds his form: in the *Addresses to the German Nation*: language, never more sovereign and powerful than its swelling flow here, "alone is already the answer, language itself is content".[12] The Spaniard builds; the German talks. His form is the art that belongs to time and that always pushes farther on, so that what stands beside it cannot see it fully, the art that is always different, the art of the eternal process of becoming. A struggle rages between the Latin world of space and the Germanic world of time, the kingdom that exists and the kingdom that is in the process of becoming; and the ending of this struggle would be the end of Europe. "And even if Europe were to bleed to death because of this struggle, still it would be what it must be, and what it is, until the last hour of its bleeding to death. For this struggle created every achievement: no German word would have been spoken if Rome had not been the enemy." But the German achievement is the eternal invasion of becoming into Being: "a deification of becoming in thought, in word, in sound, in deed, carried through to the last sacrifice. Thus the kingdom becomes a mockery: For what is the point of holding out? Thus those who want to en-

---

[9] 6:167.
[10] 6:168.
[11] 6:170.
[12] 6:193.

trench the kingdom in a Roman wall are betrayed—these wear the highest nobility of tragedy in history, Otto, Frederick and Henry, the Roman emperors of the German nation, whose name combines the incompatible to produce a deadly contradiction. But where everything the earth ever gave in the form of promises—crown, kingdom and power and the inheritance of one's sons, the good of one's ancestors—is sacrificed, life itself glows in the highest reality of its misery, and it is a futile folly to seek to induce it to convert."[13] "But no one on the other side of the border will ever understand the divine language of becoming."[14] "State and kingdom are nothing; the foundation and transformation of the state and the kingdom are everything; those who impel this onward and exaggerate it, whose work is shattered in a Gothic spire, belong most deeply to our own tribe."[15]

It is only logical that Fichte ultimately discovers Machiavelli and that he yields "with passion to this thinker, whose demands stand in the sharpest antithesis to the ideals of German classicism and German philosophy".[16] For contradiction is the heart of becoming and of German thinking: ultimately, this is the conclusion between a reality of power and its absolutization into a utopia: both of these are bound together in dialectic identity. For the real power is the soul that portrays itself, creating and destroying, over all worldly form, and so it is impossible for another value to be valid in the sphere of reality than power as the allegory of the soul. "This is the only real politics, based on the tragic law of life, which arises and swells and can never come to rest: the politics of power, the politics of Machiavelli. Even the great king of Prussia refuted the Florentine only before he ascended the throne; when he was a ruler, he followed him."[17] The new confession may appear to be a discontinuity, seen from the standpoint of the early Fichte of the Enlightenment and the Revolution; but seen on the basis of his original pathos, it is only a fulfillment: "Only now, under the sign of the downfall, does the herald find his most sincere and necessary relationship to the world."[18] The idea of power occurs "against the will of the thinker, in antithesis to his dearest hopes, and yet in harmony with the life that created these hopes for itself".[19]

---

[13] 6:197.
[14] 6:203.
[15] 6:244.
[16] 6:216.

[17] 6:217.
[18] Ibid.
[19] 6:218.

Once again, Reinhold Schneider is not Fichte; for him, the thinker is only the exponent of a life that is to be portrayed in history, this time the German life. But life in history is the very Being of the world, and this is why every historical portrait has its metaphysics in itself. Schneider sees and shows the limitations of Fichte, agreeing with his contemporaries' criticism of him, above all that of Schiller and Goethe. Limitations of substance reveal themselves in all too noticeable personal limitations. But the tragedy of the historical form only confirms Schneider's own metaphysics, in which the idealistic "I" and its "thought" are transposed onto the level of life, of the "soul" in its historical existence, thereby appearing as an existential dialectic: spirit as life that itself intersects life. We hear the axiom of the "philosophy of life": "Life *is* not, it *becomes*; it cannot dwell in any form of the earth, but it will pour itself into all these forms in order to break through them, and there is no life in the kingdoms and the goods of the earth but only in the innate idea that cannot be perfectly realized."[20] And we see the consequence of this: "The immortal aspect of the idea has a destructive nature. Life lives on the basis of impossibility. It is the innermost dimension of every strong deed, every broad hope, every great love, and while it rushes onward without resting, the scenes and struggles unfold, the works and the days are rounded off: the deeds alongside the deed; the words fall away, but the Word does not fall away."[21] The abiding element of Fichte's intellectual construction is history as *absolutum*:

> History: the indeterminable life of ideas, flowing on toward infinity, inundates the creating work of the one who gives form. It does not permit one to dictate any direction to it; for history itself, and history alone, is the commanding power. Those who thought they were resisting history served it without their own knowledge; those who dammed history only accumulated its victorious power; those who drove history onward were run over by it. History froths onward in eternal transformation, nonchalantly using and throwing away its servants and its foes alike.[22]

It is not the "I" (as Fichte thought) that generates history from itself, not even in its ultimate passivity vis-à-vis God; the tragedy makes an even deeper incision: "Destiny has a double countenance: it appears

---

[20] 6:212.
[21] 6:224, 223.

[22] 6:235.

to bear the mark of the will of the individual, and it appears, when lit up by further experience, to be the pure effect of an alien force that displays itself in the overcoming of the resistance of the individual. The hour of its appearing rules over the work; the essence falls a victim to the era."[23] But this primordial tragedy, translated into existential terms, is only once again the primal ambiguity of all idealistic religion: it is consumed by the god that it itself has created.

The Rift

The criteria that have been applied here to German history have brought Germany right up to the abyss. Reinhold Schneider, who will soon demand the great confession of sin on the part of the German spirit, will first have to decide against these criteria and admit their total insufficiency, indeed, their pernicious character. He has ventured on something impossible: the attempt to look from *one* standpoint on the Catholicism of Philip and Camões, the Protestant pantheism of Fichte and the atheism of Frederick the Great, and to understand them positively. This standpoint was that of heroic tragedy, as this begins in German Idealism, reaches its midpoint in Nietzsche and has its end and its catastrophe in Hitler and in existentialism, in a rift that goes through to the cataract brought to light by the inherent consequences of the intellectual contradiction, the dialectic. This dialectic, lived through logically, has led to the abolition of every genuine historical situation, since every temporal continuity and regularity is made impossible, and more deeply still, because human existence is traced back to a mere agglomeration of mental intensity, a purely formal force devoid of substance. "When I portrayed Christianity hitherto, I did not do so as a Christian; it was and is for me the form of reverence."[1] Nevertheless, Rome remains one of the presuppositions: "There is no German state of the German nation, that is, no German state without a Roman-Romance ligature."[2] (But the Roman, too, bore its indissoluble contradiction within itself.) When Schneider comes to speak of *Mein Kampf* and its author, we read: "Truly, a foolish primitive quality in the thought! The technique of manipu-

---

[23] 6:236.

[1] 164:174.

[2] 164:826.

lation of the masses is set out with unique openness. No statesman, just a demagogue. The secret of the effect he has: the fanaticism that keeps on renewing itself."[3] The unambiguous result of this: "As far as I can see today, what lies ahead of me is clearly the confrontation with Christ himself." And he likes to look across to Shakespeare's England, for what is involved is the choice between the reconciler and the greatest tragedian of the West. "One must dare to look at both simultaneously, with the most profound reverence and with the will to ultimate justice."[4]

If we look at things from the standpoint of *Fichte* and grant that the idealistic-dialectic conceptuality was only a *garment* for Schneider (which could if necessary be exchanged for another garment that fitted better), used to clothe and present an event of historical greatness: What experience would this then be? It is the admiring vision, full of compassion, of the great soul that sacrifices itself to give its testimony in the sphere of history, constructing its order and disclosing its eternal meaning. The sacrifice proves that a rift yawns between the "upper" sphere of the soul and the "lower" sphere of external history; no matter how intimately we may conceive of the attachment of the soul to external history, it must transcend this in order to portray itself in it, it must want to be eternal (and therefore die to all that is temporal) in order to leave behind in time a valid monument to its presence. The soul derives from the absolute: this is its nobility. Nothing that is relative, not even the relative and worldly aspect in the soul itself, which is subject to psychology, can grasp it and satisfy it. Since it derives from the absolute, it is power pure and simple; and it proves to be such in history through its ability to transmit to world history a gleam of the eternal and the holy (what Reinhold Schneider calls "the crown") in the highest sacrifices it can make: in a life based on the pure commission, in representation. But seen from the viewpoint of history, the soul is powerlessness, because it is not of this world and is a priori the one who is mastered in the power politics of the lower sphere, the one who is abused (in Hölderlin's sense) and sacrificed. Thus the soul will reveal its power "from the life to come" only in an earthly dying that is not in the least an es-

---

[3] 164:755f.   [4] 164:612.

cape: it is a perseverance that means ennoblement in the midst of
what is contemptible. But since the soul does not find itself flung out
into an alien element only at some subsequent stage (in a Platonic
fall out of the idea) but always finds itself already present therein, all
the historical existential struggle and tragic drama that can unfold is
originally gathered together in an existential feeling that includes with
equal immediacy both the marvelous glory of Being and the shuddering at the necessity of existing in one particular manner. "The basis
of tragedy is a feeling, the destiny portrayed is an image of life."[5]
Although this primal experience of the "secret rift that runs through
all life and Being in time"[6] is a genuinely tragic experience, it ought
to be possible to formulate it on the basis of the forms of thought
of Protestant German philosophy and its offshoots. It was not necessary to give it the form it took in *Innozenz*, in *Hohenzollern* and
in *Fichte*, that of a heroic-tragic metaphysics in which it was exposed
to all the absurdities of the contradiction. For who knows—perhaps
it was already a primordial Christian experience that could find its
appropriate language only in a Christian *theology of history under the
sign of the Cross*. Reinhold Schneider's endeavors take him more and
more consciously in the direction of such a theology of history.

This path is possible because it is a "path back" from a secularized
form (for what is German Idealism if not a secularized theology?)
to the original form that set its stamp on the West. This path is so
correct because it is possible to acquire an original theology of history on it and because no one has yet taken it. But it is difficult and
full of dangers, for the provenance of Idealism is the Reformation,
and its provenance in turn is the nominalism that rose up against
Thomas and essential philosophy. When the soul was interpreted in
Reinhold Schneider under the sign of the "will", and its sphere of
working under the sign of power in the world, this was essentially
Protestant.[7] One will have to follow the conceptual changes very attentively, without using any other scale of values than that Reinhold
Schneider himself chose. The path cannot fail to be dramatic.

When one examines it thoroughly, the modern philosophy of the

---

[5] 13:39.

[6] 83:51.

[7] On this, see the important observations by Richard Hauser, *Autorität und Macht* (Heidelberg: Lambert Schneider, 1949), esp. 295–54 and 383–421.

rift is anti-Christian, or at least anti-Catholic. Scheler reduced it in his late period (*Die Stellung des Menschen im Kosmos*) to the exceedingly sharp formula: The (blind) instinct is power, the (seeing) soul (or its divine dimension) is powerlessness. Power is per se devoid of value; value is per se devoid of power; man stands in a tragic titanic position between what is above and what is below, sharing in both and compelling both to find their unity in himself. The whole philosophy of life but also its foe, the philosophy of value, both live on the hidden presupposition of this rift: the idea cannot and must not realize itself (in the latter case); the intellect cannot and must not apprehend life (in the former). Against this thesis stands the old Western philosophy of spirit as the true life and of the theoretical and practical power of the reason; even more resolutely, the theological insight of the genuine Incarnation of God stands against this. The great renunciation of the organic unity between spirit and body, between God and man, which modern thought and life make is therefore anti-Christian and may not be equated with the great renunciation made by the Son of God on the Cross. There is no dialectic that can mediate between Christ and the Antichrist. Even when Christ's sacrifice becomes the ultimate law of the world and its history, it is God's free deed and never the expression of a metaphysical situation of Being. But the mystery of the hiddenness of salvation exists under the forms of ruin, and if the mystery of ruin presents itself as the powerlessness of the spirit and of value, how can man distinguish between these? Schneider's entire work seeks to serve the discernment of spirits, and this is why we must practice the same discernment on his own work itself. Up to now, we have looked at origins and access roads, not yet at the finally valid work itself, which begins with *Inselreich*. One must not tie the author down to paths he has explicitly characterized as superseded and abandoned. We take two insights from these origins, which will constantly accompany us, freed of all metaphysical encumbrance: the Iberian insight that the whole greatness of man lies in obedience and in self-forgetful service, and the Prussian insight that the source of all history is an invisible decision in the inner sphere of the soul. Both emerge in Marienburg, the spiritual origin of the empire. But it is also from here that the supposed contradiction in the Roman-institutional aspect must let itself be resolved.

HISTORY

ENGLAND—THE GUILT

The Island

The first voyages out to the boundaries brought ambiguous booty home; there is greater experience behind the new voyage to the other coast on the North (which is even more abandoned), the coast of holy Ireland and of England with its solitary power; this is no longer an escapade of youth but the conquest of a mature man. "This book has chosen its standpoint."[1] This is the decided Christian standpoint, applied to history. "History will be considered here *only* from the high point of faith. The decisive question for men and peoples is whether they have succeeded in filling themselves with the eternal, or (to put it more humbly) whether they have allowed the eternal to be operative within them."[2] Metaphysics is resolutely surmounted by faith, and the purely ontic contemplation of the world (statically in Spain, dynamically in Prussia, but both times in the equation of Being with event) is resolutely replaced by history. This is the new element: the vertical line, which looked on the situation of the world in the timeless cross section of a representative figure, is given a new position in the horizontal extension of time: the essence of history is now to reveal itself in the longitudinal section of the destiny of a people. The tremendous claim is made here—not out of curiosity or hybris—to read the theological substance of this process out of it, to take up anew the commission given to Augustine with regard to the Roman empire and the *civitas Dei* and, without any model or preparatory work in the modern period, to present a theology of history that is not only formal but full of content.

The first attempt of this kind, the only one completed, is *Das Inselreich* (The island kingdom). The intention of the author would have

---

[1] 9:10.
[2] 9:14.

been much wider: he planned a three-volume presentation of the history of the German emperors and the empire. The adverse situation of the time allowed him to present only fragments and studies made in view of this work ("Auf Wegen deutscher Geschichte", 1934, and numerous episodes shaped as short stories). Since he understood that his work would have laid itself open to every kind of abuse in the turbulent years of Hitler's state, he turned to the negative realm of meaning, so that the intended image could appear in its reflection. Only *Kaiser Lothars Krone* was completed as part of the counterevidence, the history of the German empire. And yet, is the Christian permitted to decline to undertake the discernment of spirits and thereby a concrete theology of history? Is he to leave to the pragmatists the stupendous revelation of the concrete sovereignty of God in the world, in a great renunciation of interpretation, a refusal to share in the work of giving shape? Hegel dared to turn the pages of the book of judgment, though without having faith. This time it is a believer who dares to decipher a few pages in this book. Only Léon Bloy attempted something similar: to portray the history of the world from the viewpoint of tragic symbolic figures with historical names, but his choice of figures is violent, and they do not reach the luminous serenity of Reinhold Schneider's.

If the leitmotiv of this history is guilt, one should never forget that there is no pragmatic intention (still less a political intention) lying concealed under Schneider's bewitchingly beautiful narrative of tangible historical processes—as if England were more guilty, on earthly criteria, than any other people. His intention is theological: to exemplify here the guilt of all history, although the concrete event is not reduced to an example of a "universal truth" but stands as a visible symbol of the never totally invisible kingdom of God and of his justice. When Schneider turns to England, he makes the transition from a pan-tragic universal guilt, which coincides with existence and in which the concept of guilt dissolves itself, to a demonstrable ethical-religious guilt, to particular wrong decisions taken in history, in which of course there is revealed the deeper mystery that the representative persons who (initially alone) incur guilt do this in the name of history: in social terms, they burden down the people and those who come after them with their mistaken decision, just as they themselves can be burdened down in advance by the already existing weight of the people's guilt. Here for the first time we have a clear view of the concept of guilt that belongs to the theology of history: this is an inalienably two-sided, representative-personal and collective-social concept, and its emergence demands as a later, necessary echo the correlative concept (also belonging to the theology of history) of expiation, which the Christian cannot see otherwise than in connection with the sacramental confession of guilt, which here discloses, perhaps for the first time, its social-collective meaning alongside its personal meaning. If confession fundamentally presupposes that concrete guilt can be established and a concrete judgment in which the true Judge is present (no matter how hidden he may be), then the theologian of history may draw the consequence for himself that the guilt of the peoples cannot be totally hidden from the eyes of faith, nor can it be (in the Protestant sense) an anonymous universal guilt that is simply another name for existence on earth as a whole.

No matter how one may wish to evaluate the details of Reinhold Schneider's assessment of the history of England, even if one were to find it substantially mistaken or misleading at some points, or even *in toto*, this does not mean that his intention is refuted as something impossible. One can perhaps discover presuppositions of a non-theological nature that have had some influence on his assessment; one can attack the architectonic structure of the book as being itself such a presupposition: the idea of the *island kingdom* as the part of the empire that insulates itself and separates itself ever further from the mediaeval empire until worldly reason and worldly power truly bear off the victory there against the spiritual foundations, viz. faith and the crown. Indeed, in the face of the development of the other European peoples, the geographical allegory can only be grasped as an allegory, not as the theological matter itself.

Nevertheless, he demonstrates in his history that "guilt remained the greatest and most genuine motif of English literature";[3] the three structural moments of English history are characterized by indelible personal-social guilt: the conquest by the Bastard, the separation from Rome carried out by Henry VIII and completed by Elizabeth, and the murdering of the crown under Cromwell. The three parts of the book are built around these three midpoints. We find also the mission and the backdrop in the West and the history of the world: as overture to the first part, the relationship to the Rome of Caesar and

---

[3] 9:213.

to the Rome of Gregory the Great, as a foil to the middle part, the opening up of the sea and the lifting of the anchors, and as scenery in the last part, the farthest coasts: Australia, the Indies, America, where the "answer from Saratoga" is given and the spirit of emancipation, the true spirit of the island, reaps what it has sown: the betrayal of unity.

Caesar was the first there; although the withdrawal of the Romans left nothing tangible behind, the spirit of the mighty man floats over the island like a shadow full of mysteries. But it is a holy Rome that united England and made it a kingdom; Reinhold Schneider can never find enough words of praise for the peaceful planting of the cross by the monks who were sent out by a holy, nonviolent pope; this is the wonderful early period of the islands, dominated by holy monks; despite all the storms of barbarians, that hierarchy which is expressed in the legislation of Alfred, "the perfect Christian king", remains intact: earthly law coming from the source of the sacred law of God, as lived faith, is able to grasp this.[4] This synthesis belongs to the early period, because the poles in their essence pull tragically apart from one another, "faith unites with power; there is something in its depths that opposes all power, and there is in power a coercion that has no respect for any faith; yet neither of the two forces is able to exist in the West without the other."[5] But already William the Conqueror is beginning his raid on the island; cunning forces the law onto its side; power subjects to itself the Rome of diplomacy, the episcopate, the monks, the faith. Now we are told, in an echo of *Hohenzollern*, which clearly goes farther: "Not even the necessity of the earth creates any right in the eyes of God."[6] (This makes it necessary to discern what is meant by the statement: "Guilt can be necessary, but even necessary guilt will be judged.")[7] None of the favor shown by "fate", "heaven" or "the Church" at the Conquest itself and in the following period can mend the rent torn in the sacred fabric. Guilt, like a malignant ulcer, begets further guilt, and the fire that smolders for a long time

---

[4] On Gregory's colonization (apart from 9:39f.): "Kreuz und Geschichte", 18:32–38, and "Papst Gregor der Gross", 40 (reprinted in "Gedanken des Friedens" 51:119–34). On England as "holy island" (apart from 9:13–82), cf. the sonnet "Irland" (14:19) and "Der Traum des Eroberers", 110.

[5] 9:28.

[6] 9:155.

[7] 9:100.

is kindled into new life again after many centuries.[8] In *Der Traum des Eroberers*, Reinhold Schneider sought once again to pin down on the stage, in mythical dimensions of allegorical power, the decisive leap from justice into power: the image of the brutal and cunning man in the hour of his death and judgment, to whom the angel relates the story of his life ("Heaven and hell are mingled here in a way that chills my blood"),[9] and who dies in the arms of the angel without seeing anything but the night. The Normans build the cathedrals, but these enclose the relics, the holy inheritance (for what can art be other than the praising of holiness?), yet the vaults do not rise up so boldly as on the Continent.[10] In the Magna Charta, despite all the political meaningfulness and correctness of the decision, we begin to see the deeper wound that will lead one day under Cromwell to the murder of a king. "The ruler was no longer free." Although a great deal was said in the Magna Charta about justice, "only one thing was lacking: the feeling for the consecration of the crown that shares in shaping state and life. The king had sinned against the spirit of his office; was this an argument against the office? Did the failure of the officebearer establish a right against the idea?"[11] Edward I remains handicapped by the nobles and by parliament, "England was no longer a good land for a king";[12] "the equality of men before God was to be turned into an earthly equality".[13] The evocation of Langland's Piers Plowman, out of whom "time", which was aware of its guilt, "spoke and stammered",[14] is one of the most moving elements in the symbolic portrayal of this people. "The pure faith was no longer a historical power."[15] The refusal to distinguish between the idea and the one who bears it impels to the central decision, the turning away from Rome, which is now seen as the only source for graced healing of the island power.[16] The island tears itself apart from the mainland and

---

[8] "When Henry Tudor boarded the ship again, on August 1 in the year 1485, he sailed with not much greater right on his side than the Duke of Normandy had once had, when he sailed to his conquest" (9:236).

[9] 110:39.

[10] 9:162.

[11] 9:181f.

[12] 9:206, 198.

[13] 9:211.

[14] 9:212.

[15] 9:216.

[16] 9:230–85; 9:552.

becomes a ship, a power that is isolated as the "hostile kingdom".[17]
With Henry VIII, who appeals to his "conscience", this withdraws for
the first time from the external visible portrayal in life, as an internal
dimension that cannot be verified from the outside, abandoning the
external sphere to pure power. Schneider now recognizes the rift between these two as something that is arch-Protestant.[18] In this milieu,
the fate of Catherine, whose idea is closely related to that of Philip II,
becomes a pure testimony of suffering,[19] like that of Chancellor More,
the living conscience of the king.[20] More deeply moving than either
fate is that of the "Pilgrims of Grace", which Reinhold Schneider surrounds with the highest pathos of tragedy—these thousands who aim
at the good and are no longer able to act because of the misdeed of
one single man.[21] Robert Aske is the man "in whom the conscience
of England strove against itself and wavered about whether it should
exhort to faithfulness to the country and its lord or to faithfulness to
God. For things that never should have been separated had been separated."[22] "Out of this double faithfulness, which must be *one* faithfulness, something divided had come into existence. Only death in the
faith could set them free."[23] What follows after this is a postlude: the
unfruitful virginity of Elizabeth ("England's heart must remain cold.
England's politics was the loveplay of a woman who was resolved not
to give herself to anyone"),[24] Shakespeare, under obligation to the
powers of the old world but broken open by what was new ("a provisional roof rests on the mighty columns, on single groins of vaults
that span wide arches"),[25] Marlowe, the poet of Tamburlaine, Faust
and Barabbas, accused of atheism, in whom naked power breaks forth,
along with hell; Shakespeare writes the epilogue to the old England
that is disappearing, Marlowe writes the prologue for the new England that is coming into being. John Knox brings the "new form"[26]
from Calvin's Geneva, and in both conceptions of power, that of the

---

[17] 9:555.
[18] 9:253f.; 9:280f.; 18:46f.
[19] 9:259ff.
[20] Cf. "Der Traum des Heiligen", 34:37–56.
[21] 9:297–315; 18:74–82.
[22] 9:308.
[23] 18:81.
[24] 9:383; 9:388–93.
[25] 9:401.
[26] 18:53–60; 9:403–21.

Stuarts and that of Cromwell, the former is condemned a priori: the one who has the power has right on his side; the office and the mission have died, to be replaced by the person. In Cromwell's decision ("Happy the man who is free enough to obey necessity!"),[27] Reinhold Schneider has explicitly burned up what he had adored in Frederick the Great; once again, the highest tragic pathos surrounds the expiatory death of Charles I, while the "parliament of saints" performs the unholy grotesquerie of power's self-transfiguration. The end is formed by the paths of the conquerors that lose themselves in the far distance; by the gaze of the blind and bitter Milton into the abyss ("Satan, the eternal rebel who fights against the light, is wholly form. He is the most naked one, reality, power");[28] and the burning of the old London, on the ashes of which a stony heart of power is to arise. The Tower survives, "the gloomiest symbol of guilt and of power, and of their unity",[29] the "gray monstrous fortress that concealed throne and chapel, court of justice and executioner's block, room of state, council chamber and dungeon":[30] the decisive counterimage to the monastic palace of Castile.

All that we have been able to show here is a cold outline of this work, which swells with poetic power; if one asks what is the idea that bears it, the answer must be: It is only the faith that can be the ultimate guideline for the reason in the sphere of the sinful and redeemed world; but the true faith is faith in the incarnate God and in his Church, and (since Mary-Ecclesia is the mediatrix of all graces) there lies upon the worldly power not the faintest gleam of the grace it needs in order to exist, except for the grace that is mediated through the Church. The mediaeval form for the expression of this necessary relationship, the investiture of the prince by the highest spiritual lord, was only a time-conditioned symbol of this inalienable truth. The visible Church is not indeed identical with the kingdom of God, and we have the hope that even what has been split off in the course of time will be saved for the unity of the kingdom by the eternal grace. But it holds true on earth and in heaven that there is no salvation outside the Church, and that, because the Church is visible, there is something like a visible mediation corresponding to her invisible me-

---

[27] 9:451.
[28] 9:486.
[29] 18:8.
[30] 9:245.

diation of salvation and that the gleam of grace on the worldly power
must not merely be present but can also be seen and observed.

As if to solidify these ideas, numerous great and small figures of Western history appear in a constellation around *Inselreich*. These are apparently chosen arbitrarily, but, taken as a whole, they provide a sufficient illustration of the methodology that is attempted. The only
representative of the German empire is *Kaiser Lothar*, to whom Reinhold Schneider's most tranquil book is devoted; this is also the first
book in which the tragic element does not have the upper hand,
but we are permitted to see the movement of an ascent, indeed, of an
earthly transfiguration. Before becoming emperor, Lothair is the born
agitator, the faithless man ("indeed, it seems as if the role of emperor
may not be left vacant for one moment, if history is to remain what
it is: a testing that always permits two decisions but demands one
single decision").[31] When he becomes king, he must discover what
he himself has done; he must rule among the total insurrection of
the princes; he must establish order and unity in a centrifugal chaos,
until he almost reaches the abyss of total dissolution ("Was this the
fate of the empire, eternally to enter into conflict with itself and to
irradiate out into the world, not the entire power, but only what it
had left after this kind of conflict?");[32] and he must allow the law of
the crown, which is imposed on him as a cross, to penetrate down
into the marrow of his existence. The office perfects in him what the
person failed to be; he puts himself at the service of the office and
becomes the true guardian of order, contrary to his own merit, out
of the grace of the office. On the second Italian expedition, when
he went with the pope to battle against Bari and a golden crown descended from heaven in the sight of the people in the cathedral of
St. Nicholas during the sacred liturgy, in order to confirm the reconciliation of Church and empire, only a few perhaps

> felt with painful clarity that such a vision revealed itself only above the
> ruins of earthly endeavor, in order to make its hidden meaning visible
> one single time and to transfigure its failure in the light of an invisible
> goal; for who could think these ruins of any value, unless he were able
> to discern in them the arch of the bow they were meant to serve? And

---

[31] 11:32.
[32] 11:126.

perhaps only a few sensed that this hour could come to pass only because one of the viceroys of Christendom belonged to the earth only as a guest; a gleam of the heavenly crown that had appeared in the air played around the snowy head of the emperor.[33]

Lothair's visit to Monte Cassino recalls Philip II; the emperor and empress "washed the feet of the poor, dried them with their hair and kissed them, then the hosts themselves served their guests with food. Here, in the house of St. Benedict, the pious ruler could delight in the similarity of the imperial garment to the priestly garment; he set himself in the place of the abbot, out of that need for sanctification which no worldly business ever satisfies." The emperor does indeed die on the return journey, and the dam bursts at once; but an image of the eternal order has been set up in the metaphorical realm of the earth. And just as the images of Teresa and Ignatius shine in the center of *Philipp*, so there shines in the heart of *Lothar* the image of St. Otto, bishop of Bamberg and missionary in Pomerania: without violence, just as Augustine had converted the Angles and Columba had tamed them, the highest power of grace goes forth from the German saint, the true power of which the harsh power of the emperor remains only a reflection.

In the following year (1938) appeared the *Szenen aus der Konquistadorenzeit: Las Casas vor Karl V*, a passionate episode shaped like a short story, in which the shift from *Hohenzollern* to the later view displays itself for the first time in all clarity as something accomplished. (Those in power did not recognize that Schneider intended the book as a protest against the Nazi persecution of the Jews.) The cruelties of the secular power in the conquistadores, which had already been described in *Camoes* with a shudder (and only apparently in an objective manner), return intensified, but this time it is not the transfiguring poet who is the counterpart but the Dominican who cleanses himself of the same crime and now overflows in Christian rage, the father of the humiliated children of nature, and his disputation with the lawyer Sepulveda in the emperor's presence. But the author is concerned, not with humaneness, but with something much more precipitous: the discernment of what is Christian. The conflict is "about whether, as Sepulveda taught to the applause of the colonists, a large number

---

[33] 11:179f.

of the higher officials and even of the clergy, the conversion of the Indians must be preceded by their subjugation, or whether, as Las Casas and his Order were convinced, the work of conversion, with only the instruments of faith and in a certain sense independently of consideration for the state, was the real task of the Spaniards in the New Indies."[34] The position of the lawyer is no doubt overdrawn— one should note the year of publication—since he supports his "state law" with a racial law, whereby "a more highly developed people— and we Spaniards are the only such people—'possesses' for the good of the world a right over peoples who stand on a lower rank, as Aristotle and Plato already taught."[35] War as such is righteous and holy for the dominant caste.[36] But behind this there is the moderate view that it is not possible to help the faith otherwise than through an ordered state[37] and that "nature" precedes "grace", so that the unavoidable war also precedes baptism. Las Casas counters cuttingly: "If we baptize, we have no right to punish idolatry; if we do not baptize, then we have no right to travel to the Indies. This is why I consider the war against the Indians to be forbidden and slavery to be un-Christian."[38] One of the great themes is touched upon: Europe's mission in the age of the discovery of the world, the commission to spread the one Christian kingdom over the whole earth and the failure of the West vis-à-vis this mission. We shall return to this theme later. The question arises now: Was it possible to succeed in this task? Is it possible to arrive at a clear solution in this dispute between "grace before power" and "power before grace", between nature and the supernatural (with natural law as its basis), on the one hand, and the supernatural with its commandment before nature, on the other?[39] Does the thorn of contention between these two lie so deep and unavoidable that one must speak here of a "contradiction": "contradiction between the Christian commission and the power that had sprung up overnight and yet must continue to appeal all the time

---

[34] 12:70.

[35] 12:139.

[36] 18:10.

[37] 12:126.

[38] Ibid.

[39] 12:128f.: "Let the first law be, to create order on the earth; let the requirement of the Christian life hold good only when this order is established. . . . For it must be clear that the endangering of a Christian state would threaten Christendom itself with the gravest harm."

to this power",[40] "contradiction between the commandment of God and the life of men, both" demanding the totality "in their terrible reality" and yet standing in opposition to each other.[41] The first sentence refers only to a fact that has been observed: Spain was unfaithful to its mission. But the second sentence seems to have a deeper entry point: it uncovers a law that is irrefutable: the contradiction lies in the very constitution of the world. Las Casas is victorious in Spain, at least for the moment; the emperor issues the "new laws" (1542); the idea triumphs (in Philip) against brutal power, although the latter, in keeping with its nature, soon swims back to the surface. Sepulveda's solution triumphs in principle in England.

Thus the unity of these three works becomes clear but also the profound question that they force open. *Las Casas* could give the impression that what is involved in history is a decision of precedence and priority: grace (the law of Christ) before power (the law of fallen nature), or vice versa. And the "contradiction" would mean that the Christian was false to his true mission and made grace a function of earthly power, "setting the state created by men in the first place and God's commandment in the second".[42] And it would perhaps be possible to establish the harmony between grace and power by giving the precedence in principle to grace in most situations, if it came to a genuine contradiction that demanded an exclusive choice. Even then, the way one would have to choose would be laid down in advance, since one must obey God rather than men, and since there stands on the side of nature only the "*state created by men*", while God's commandment stands on the other side. But can one truly harmonize things in this way? Does not God's commandment stand on the side of the earthly state too? Did not Alfred the Great and Lothair (to say nothing of Philip II) recognize the immediate mission received from God in the work of the state? Was it not the fatal great renunciation, the apostasy from the real Christian task, when the state was relativized as merely the work of men and refuge was sought in the absolute sphere of "grace"? But does not the contradiction once again become perfect if God's commandment stands on both sides and the law of the earthly state in this fallen world demands power—

[40] 18:188.
[41] 12:108.
[42] 12:114.

and this is the power that concrete human beings have and can apply
—the same power that the Sermon on the Mount obliges us to turn
the other cheek to? Is this contradiction rooted in the heart of the
Christian existence? And it is not then God himself who ultimately
contradicts himself? Does not the specter of the *necessary* guilt return,
and is not William the Bastard ultimately correct to venture the audacious leap onto the island and to put a sudden end to the utopian
kingdom of a "holy power", an administration of the earthly harsh
reality from the domains of heavenly asceticism and prophecy? Is it
not better to come to grips with things and to take upon oneself the
necessary guilt than to flee into an unworldly holiness? Lothair, too,
became guilty, like all those who came to grips with things, but at
least he could reflect a gleam of the eternal into the realms of power,
and what else can the "kingdom" be than this gleam?

Here we are at the heart of the terrible problematic that moves
Reinhold Schneider and that makes a mockery of every attempt to
neutralize it (as in the *abstract* thinking in terms of the natural law).
The Cross is set up and lies heavy on the world and humanity. It is
the watermark of the creation. But it is still important that the Cross
be interpreted correctly. The system of the world that Schneider used
in his first period to interpret tragedy had been inadequate. Now it
was a matter of following the transformation of this first system of
the world into something new, a Christian theology of history. Two
complexes of questions can be discerned: that of the relationship between nature (power) and the supernatural (grace), with the special
problem of the right and claim of power (we shall discuss this under
the heading of England), and that of the unavoidable Cross in history
(which we shall discuss under the subsequent headings).

The Parting of the Ways

The spirit (or, as Reinhold Schneider insists, the soul) is not itself history, but it *has* history; it is more than history, it creates and endures
history. Where the spirit is, history comes into being. "Everything
depends on the soul",[1] on its presentation, preservation, redemption;
and this is its history. The kernel of the spirit belongs to the eternal:

---

[1] 13:81.

it is there that its history is. The kernel of the spirit belongs to the eternal: it is there that it is at home; it longs to return there; it must be in contact with the eternal in order to undergo the destinies of the world. "The soul dwells beyond the border of the state."[2] A continually recurring image is the height above the field of historical action, the height of interiority above that which is external, the height of contemplation above action, of prayer above deed, of Being in eternity above working in the temporal sphere, the height of distance and of transcendence as the presupposition of all genuine closeness and immanence. "Beyond history there lives only the believing soul; so one ought not to look in the work for what is lasting."[3] More strongly still, indeed, almost mythically: "The spirit does not come into being in history but is sent down into it from a foreign sphere; it cannot work without entering into history, and yet it will never get over its original foreignness."[4] The man of the classical period, from Plato to Origen and Augustine, would have said "fallen down" instead of "sent down", thereby establishing an undialectic precedence of contemplation over action. Reinhold Schneider experiences the same foreignness, but as a modern man, that is, with the primary consciousness of mission. But no matter how much the world may lay claim to the one who is sent, he comes from somewhere else, and he knows his own nobility. The mountains are necessary in order to breathe here below. "The law was once given on a mountain; the Lord spoke to his disciples from a mountain; he was transfigured on another mountain; he met his accomplishment on a mountain. It is here that history was and is overcome. The one who overcomes no longer denies; he has an overview and a recognition; he has left the realm of the powers and subordinated himself to the law of a pure, ever-flowing truth."[5] History needs these heights on which the light dwells and from which it flows down into the valleys, even when the one who lives up there only seldom appears in history as a man of action but is "much more frequently a witness and bearer of an irresistible shaping force". It is ultimately through this force that "alone brings about transformation", the soul's orientation to eternity, that history is what it is; it is most deeply marked by the invisible, from the most silent

---

[2] 9:151.

[3] 13:42.

[4] 13:7.

[5] 18:214.

decisions made before God, from the hiddenness of contemplation and prayer; thus this force is not the same thing as power and action. One can call this most hidden element historical, because it moves history on the deepest level, but one can just as well call it unhistorical, because it is essentially superior to the worldly zone. "Every life, even the most hidden and the highest, is a historical life; but this does not exhaust its content, because it includes a soul that was sent into history and will once again be free from history by proving its worth in history."[6] The necessary reference of the spirit to history but also the highest effectiveness of contemplation and of its fruits in the field of action distinguish modern spiritual-intellectual life from that of the classical period and even from the teaching of Scholasticism. "The spirit is not absolutely free; it comes from above, but it enters history and works in it, collaborating with historical life. In the struggle with the reality of its sin, it accomplishes the task of giving form that was entrusted to it."[7] In this sense, the soul is radically historical; the deepest reason for the corruption of modern culture is the failure to recognize the historical power of all that is born of the spirit, from the most secret thoughts to the most explicit idea.[8] "Outside history there is no service and no life."[9] In all these words one discovers a change of direction that has been taken quietly. Whereas in the early works the will (in Schopenhauer, Nietzsche, Fichte) made the act of transcendence in an upward direction, and this transcendence counted as "the religious dimension", from now on the ultimate and decisive transcendence is based in the grace that enters the soul from above, not suspending the will but giving it an orientation.

As the idea that the orientation of every soul to God is a most profound power in history wins through, the more important becomes the individual, alongside the representative man (the king and the saint).[10] Through his secret decision on the questions posed by life and the external situation, each one shares in making a mark on the face of his time and of posterity (*Vom täglichen Leben in der Geschichte*).[11] "Day by day occurs the confluence between this external

---

[6] 16:40.
[7] 52:128.
[8] 52:23f.; 54:7.
[9] 7:298.
[10] 9:203.
[11] 18:124–27.

event we call history and an inner event from souls, and the faces of
the peoples change in an irresistible manner that is scarcely open to
investigation, under the influence of decisions that their individuals
make."[12] Thus the concept of representation, without losing its qualified sense in the king and the saint, becomes a universally binding
category: first, because each man ought to live, "not on the basis of
conditions as they are",[13] but on the basis of fundamental principles
that stand above time; and secondly, more clearly still, because there
must be individuals and groups of individuals in history who visibly
represent transcendence and administer in the name of all the office
of the mountain, of the height, of the light. On the basis of the spirit
of representation and of the effective power of prayer and thought,
a division between active life and contemplative life is legitimate—
even in the face of modern history.[14]

"Often that which is greatest in history takes place almost unnoticed, through an inner change, a yielding of the soul",[15] or also when
the soul summons up its courage. Reinhold Schneider never wearies
of lifting the veil from the chamber of the hidden man of prayer:
as Moses, supported by Aaron and Hur, decides the progress of the
battle through his pleading, [Ex 17:10–13] like the dying, praying
Tilly ("sometimes the course of the world turns around in a quiet
chamber, while the armies struggle against each other on the field of
battle"),[16] so is each one who throws his heart into the battle before
God. "One cannot separate work from prayer any more than one can
separate work from faith." "Once again, we experience that it is not
really *we* ourselves who pray and who ought to pray: time and all of
life burdened by guilt turn in us to God—how much hesitation there
is here, what resistance the flesh puts up! Prayer is the great transition
of historical life into eternal life. This is why it is the one who prays
who accomplishes history."[17] Who could fail to think here first of the
women who bear in an excellent manner the office of suffering prayer
alongside fighting men![18] A long essay presents them in a sequence

---

[12] 18:125f.
[13] 18:127.
[14] 18:172–78.
[15] 9:279.
[16] 24:44, 53; 18:91, 156f., 175; 51:49–61, 114f.; 76:22; 114:3–14.
[17] 51:54, 59f.
[18] 9:39f.; 13:108; 62:125; 71:12.

from Hannah to Mary to Helena, Monica, Bertha, Olga, Elizabeth, Hildegard and Clare, stopping for a long time at Bridget and finally passing on to Catherine, Frances of Rome and Joan of Arc.[19] Then we have those saints who devote themselves totally to contemplation for the salvation of the world, as Teresa and Thérèse understand this; and finally we have the poets, thinkers and shapers who create holy images over the din of daily life, in their responsibility. Silence is the origin: "the silence of Stratford", "the silence of Petit-Couronne",[20] the silence within cathedrals,[21] silence that reigns "before the beginning of a tragedy and again at its end".[22] Were God not in the still, small voice, it would be impossible to perceive him in the great storm and fire of history.

But the soul is "given a reference point", "sent" in the sphere where it must prove itself: its unity with the body makes it historical in the external sense. "The body ties the soul to history; it is only its unity with the body that gives the soul the possibility of proving itself and of returning to God victorious under grace."[23] "The bodily existence calls the soul into the historical course of events on earth, where it is not at home."[24] "Christ took on the body of man, that is, he decided to become history."[25] And this union with the weak flesh is its nailing to a cross. So "Die Seele an den Körper" (The soul addresses the body):

> Beloved cross, which lets me prove my worth,
> let us embrace each other forever
> and not be afraid before the gloomy gate!
>
> Transfigure me, so that I may transfigure you!
> When I arrive among those who have been perfected,
> I shall call you too up into the eternal life.[26]

Through the body, the soul is ordained to the powers of the world; the body is its history, and so history becomes its body. "For the soul, history is only the medium of its sanctification; history's struggles and demands and its theater overshadowed by the tempter are assigned to the soul so that it may be purified and perfected, so that it may be-

[19] 136:166–207.
[20] 9:401f.; 18:251–56.
[21] 18:245f.
[22] 18:254.
[23] 83:76.
[24] 91:29.
[25] 62:56.
[26] 69:53.

come a sacrifice for all, so that the kingdom of God may triumph. The ultimate seriousness of the state and the fatherland has its base in the demands they make of the soul, demands that serve to perfect it and thus to praise the Lord."[27] The world that opens up here is essentially that over which it is installed as administrator (Gen 1:28–29), that is, a field and a vessel for the soul's power. Every action —and action is history—is the activation and extending of power. The elevation of the being of the soul above the world becomes a "capacity", power, vis-à-vis the world. This means in principle that Scheler's fateful system is overcome: the spirit is not powerlessness vis-à-vis the dark depths of the mighty world of the instincts, for the primary power lies with the spirit. This is what Schneider is aiming at when he begins *Macht und Gnade* (1940) with a chapter entitled "Die Rechtfertigung der Macht" (The justification of power), and he achieves this when he begins *Die Nacht des Heils* (1947) with the programmatic pages about "Die Macht des Bösen und die gute Macht" (The power of evil and the good power). But in each case a condition is attached to the truth of what is affirmed: that the power of the soul be set in its relationship to the eternal God and in its transcendence over all that is created and, indeed, over all that can be created, in its immediacy to the God of eternal grace, since the soul is called to see him face to face in heaven and to follow him here below. This is the doctrine of the *unicus finis supernaturalis hominis*, from which Church Fathers and high Scholasticism interpret the essence and the countenance of man, carried through with absolute logic. Like everything in the creation, the soul, too, is a symbol of the eternal Spirit, and so all its power can be only a symbol of the eternal power: good only where it is the intentional and determined expression of this eternal power, and evil where it demarcates itself off from God's power and opposes this as an arbitrary power. But since the body and history as a body offer an infinite number of empty spaces into which the soul's power can pour itself, these spaces become a temptation and, after the fall, the location of the demonic hostile power.

Only God possesses genuine, archetypal power—not the soul. "Absolute power dwells beyond the earth, history and man; by recommending himself to it, man acquires a share in it, although the

---

[27] 51:7.

power entrusted to him is subject to the history that has made it possible."[28] Seen from the viewpoint of the world and history, the power
of man is per se *neutral*: it takes on the label of positive or negative,
good or evil, graced or demonic, only through man's decision whether
he will subject himself to God in faith and love or be his own ruler;
whether he makes use of the highest force of faith[29] in order to learn
the true power (the power to become children of God, which God
gives to those who receive him [Jn 1:12],[30] and "much greater force
is required for the suspension of the self than for the gathering of
any kind of property at the service of this self")[31] or chooses to be
powerful for his own self. It is out of the question "that power could
be evil". But "God has given a part of his power to Satan", since it is
not without God's will that man is tempted. The evil power works in
the world under the superior power of God. And "man can become
powerful between the two powers that are so unequal. To become
powerful means acquiring a share in one power or the other. For man
is not powerful because of his own self; he must, as it were, join one
current or the other and allow himself to be charged with power by it.
Where he turns his mind, he will find help; the power he addresses
will bear him. To become powerful means that man works on his
fellows in the forcefield of the power he has chosen."[32] In both cases
"the mystery" holds true that "power cannot be possessed but only
administered."[33] The one who wants to possess it is already evil, for
"God's power is love itself", and it is not possible to get possession
of love. But God displays his power in the one who loves him and
gives him a share in the administration of it. The kingdom of God
in the world is nothing other than this power of God that portrays
and diffuses itself in those who are obedient. "What is power? God's
commission to share in the government of the earth; it cannot be
one's property but is something held in fief and is at the same time
a terrible testing stone. God demands the righteous administrator."[34]
Those "who want to administer power must in a certain sense have
died; they must have 'got rid of their earlier self'. They must be born
and reborn for their office, called and chosen. They must stand in the

---

[28] 70:137.
[29] 9:83.
[30] 70:138.
[31] Ibid.

[32] 91:10f., 15.
[33] 91:17.
[34] 51:108.

purifying power of the office that comes from above and impels upward, the power that overcomes the personal dimension."[35] For it is
only now that the full basis of the concept of office or of representation is established: the one who has power on earth is essentially one
who represents and presents another, and his most personal dimension consists in effacing himself in order to allow the outlines of the
other to appear. The relationship to God (in faith and love) always
involves both stripping oneself of power so that God's power may appear and a mission in which the self becomes a bearer and a banner of
the divine power. Faith, as the gift of oneself to God's perfect power,
is the primordial power in the world. This possibility exists; Philip
demonstrated it, as did England of old: "Reverence clothed itself in
the garment of power and yet remained what it ought to be."[36] "The
great achievement of life in history is trust in the reality of what one
believes and action on the basis of this trust."[37] What is true of the
archetype it depicts must also be true of this: it is "a power whose
innermost life is love".[38]

Man's true power, as God intends it, is power derived from the
relationship to what is ultimate, to the goal of grace, that is, power
in subordination to the one who reveals God's eternal power in the
world, Jesus Christ ("from now on, genuine power was a fief received
from Christ"),[39] and in union with the Church that has received his
commission; but as in the case of Christ, this is a power that enters the
sphere of darkness and of the demonic powers to take up the struggle
against them and to extend the power of God on earth. Thus everything depends on *the discernment of spirits*: What power speaks out of
them, the upper or the lower; what gleam lies upon them: the heavenly or that of the abyss? We can call this picture of the world Augustinian, for the resolute transcendence of its ethics is Augustinian,
springing over all inner-worldly criteria ("the virtues of the Romans
as glittering vice") to evaluate everything according to the two ultimate criteria, *caritas* or *cupiditas*, the orientation toward or away from
the supernatural goal: the power to give or the power to seize. A second Augustinian characteristic is the understanding of the kingdom of
God in agonic-dynamic terms as the unending confrontation between

---

[35] 51:110.
[36] 9:170.
[37] 26:89.

[38] 51:129.
[39] 81:19.

the *civitas dei* and the *civitas terrena sive diaboli*, both of which are inextricably intertwined until the end of time. A third point, perhaps more Ignatian than Augustinian, is the art of the discernment of spirits in concrete situations ("of the two standards"), which is demanded ever anew in specific situations and is kept alive only through watchfulness and prayer. This means that the Thomist view, which considers the power given (one can also say "lent") to man by God as such, and independently of the use made of it, fades into the background. Schneider is not a philosopher but an interpreter of history.

In the lectures *Weltreich und Gottesreich*, the fundamental Augustinian tone emerges clearly, indeed, this Church Father himself is put at the head of these lectures,[40] also with his exhortation not to despair because of the citizens of the kingdom of heaven "when we see them carrying out their business after the fashion of Babylon, something earthly in the earthly state: they cannot and should not detach themselves from the kingdom of the world." It is the correctness that is all-important; "All that happens presses over to the other side."[41]

> Hallowed be thy name: these words stand over all love, to lay claim to it and to transform it. There is no mercy, no justice, that is not included within this commandment; there is no true power on earth that is not made to feel utter dread by this commandment. Those who ought to trust in one another must discover each other in this world; those who enter into an alliance ought to utter it, for otherwise their alliance will dissolve. For they need the protection of the Lord, and the only protection of their alliance can come from the Third one whose name is to be sanctified. The sword rests in the fetter of this terribly serious word. This word stands at the beginning of art; every poem, every building, every image ought to be its echo. It decides on every single work of human hands, whether it serves sanctification or not. But the peoples, too, live for the sake of sanctification. But your Son began the great work.[42]

That which cannot be interpreted at least in an explanatory sense on the basis of the soul's intention (and not merely in keeping with an objectively irreproachable substance) as making toward this goal belongs to the hostile kingdom.[43] Schneider speaks repeatedly of the two

---

[40] 71:7.
[41] 71:8f.; 70:33.
[42] 23:17f.
[43] 83:86f.

kingdoms,[44] of the "struggle between the good seed and the bad",[45] "between the city of God and the city of earth",[46] in the most formal terms between the old age and the new, between the age of sinners that is passing away and the coming age of the redemption, in a moment of encounter that irrupts in an incalculable manner and precisely for this reason always endures, making a total demand of all watchfulness and power of decision.[47] But this waiting attentively for God's moment is not an eschatological existence in the sense that it would dispense one from the moment and the commission of history:

> Thus all the saints looked up to the signs that God showed in heaven; these signs allowed them to recognize their commission, which was determined most precisely in the hour allocated to them. As warriors of the kingdom of God, they were historical appearances in the true sense. All that each time supplies is initially images, and often images of the most terrible kind; these images imperiously demand an interpretation; the interpretation can succeed only to the extent that the images are set in relation to the light of the world.[48]

"It is only on the basis of the revelation that falls to our lot as history that we can understand history."[49]

This criterion is applied to the history of peoples: the greatness of Spain, no matter how heavily guilt and inadequacy may weigh down upon it (as upon all peoples), is this: "Confronted with the question whether it is permissible to purchase earthly power at the price of the salvation of the soul, rulers and poets, the saints and the conquistador burdened down with guilt all concur in the answer that eternity is worth more than all earthly kingdoms; it is the highest destiny to give away kingdoms in order to spread the light of the truth and to share thereby in establishing God's kingdom in souls."[50] But this criterion applies with equal force in the sphere of intellectual life, above all in that of art. Schneider often develops in detail a theory of *light* as the criterion of genuine or false art; this light is the gleam of the relationship upward or downward, the confirmation of the work by grace or the demon, that unutterable dimension that reveals the ultimate kind

---

[44] 52:86f.
[45] 70:32.
[46] 18:159.
[47] 81:14f.

[48] 81:16f.
[49] 52:104.
[50] 18:231.

of beauty and pours ultimate nobility over the work.[51] This is why this criterion forbids every separation of aesthetics and ethics, "since the form succeeds only where the gift of grace in the shaping of it unites with the ethos that is its equal in rank. Without the ethos, tragedy would dissolve into floods of images, the novel would become a river without any banks, the circle of the short story would remain unclosed, and song would be blown away."[52] In the short stories about artists (such as "Das getilgte Antlitz"), the work always becomes the judge over the artist.[53] We see in the light radiated by the work where the master's spirit belonged; Schneider will construct what amounts almost to a history of literature in numerous essays on the inseparably ethical and aesthetic principle of discernment.

The concept of the tragic existence has lost something of its melancholy through the flowing of the earlier interest in tragedy into an Augustinian idea of struggle, into a striving toward salvation on the part of the whole of history. Where the element of grace becomes the criterion to such an extent, the confrontation of the "soul" with the powers of history can finally be measured only against the descent of Christ into the world, his struggle and death, his mysterious victory on the Cross. If the light of Christ is called "grace", and the world that does not receive him but rather rejects and kills him is called "nature" (as it in truth appears when he comes), then one must of course speak of a "contradiction", but this "contra" is once again dissolved in the struggle of the Cross to become a genuine elevation and bestowal of grace on nature. The Christian soul, as it sets out to live and to work in the *civitas terrena*, must be prepared for the same Pauline "contradiction of two laws",[54] one of which rules over a kingdom of guilt that has turned away from God. Schneider often comes close to asserting, in the sense of the earlier dialectic, that collaboration in the earthly kingdom means that one becomes guilty out of necessity; in such passages, to be guilty seems to be a quality attaching to action within history. But Christ did not become guilty when he acted, nor did his Mother. The Cross can be called tragic because the ultimate contradiction is fought out to the end in

---

[51] 18:212–16, 217–22, 232–38, 273f.; 21:6; 34:116–19; 35:20; 62:54; 91:120f.

[52] 52:154.

[53] 34:120.

[54] 9:83.

this suffering, but the Incarnation itself cannot be called tragic, for the human nature of the Son does not stand in antithesis to his divine nature. Here everything is decided. It is not Being that is tragic; the tragic has a boundary. Schneider knows this: "Tragedy ends in the presence of humility, as it ends in the presence of perfect love",[55] and the fullness of man and of his possibilities extends far beyond the sphere of the tragic.[56] "So few tragedians have ended as tragedians: after suffering death again and again with their hero, their heart softened, and a presentiment came over them of the peace that spreads out on the far side of guilt."[57] One can indeed speak in a Christian sense of a tragedy of existence, for "historical life is incurable, but it strives unwearyingly in the direction of salvation; so essentially dangerous is its greatness, so deep its suffering, so terrible its division with its own self, that it presses with all its might toward the shore where peace is. Tragedy is not a cycle; it is the deadly breakthrough into the eternal ordering."[58] "The tragic element under grace: this is the experience of the West."[59] For "history is the history of our salvation: the tragic history, full of grace, of our return home."[60] Only in "the strictest Christian sense" may the Christian existence, including that of the saints, be called tragic now—no longer as the individual case of a universal tragic constitution of the world.[61]

> The Christian stands in a thoroughly dramatic, indeed, tragic relationship to the world: he must represent in the world something that is not of the world. The truth into which the life of the Christian is to enter has been crucified: it cuts across the course of the world and man, and yet it addresses the course of the world and man, and these are related to it; the Christian has experienced, and will continually experience, that to the extent he genuinely tries to do the truth, and the truth acts through him, he will become a tragic person; the truth that is life in eternity can take on the form of death in time. The same is true of the historical image of the Christian, in whom those values are the highest that count for the least in the world or are hated by it. Thus it is not correct to say that Christianity has abolished tragedy through the proclamation of grace.[62]

---

[55] 13:97.

[56] 13:105.

[57] 52:68.

[58] 52:65f.

[59] 52:147.

[60] 29:56.

[61] 16:19.

[62] 112:22f.; cf. 92.

Nevertheless, this Christian (and perhaps intensified) tragedy is not an inextricable contradiction. In the death on the Cross lies the victory, the explosion of the contradiction. This is no natural law but the miracle of grace. And the world stands upon the miracle of the Cross and the Resurrection. The tragic net has been opened. "This drama, which is concerned with the salvation of man's soul, is no tragedy but rather a mystery play."[63]

Right

Man has power, and he exercises it in history. Has he a right to do so, and, if so, where does this right come from? The consistently Augustinian perspective will establish "*the justification of power*" (this is the structurally decisive first chapter of *Macht und Gnade*), the right to power, on the basis of man's transcendence into the eternal dimension. The question posed depends on this transcendence: "The assertion that power needs to be justified cannot initially be demonstrated to be true, since it holds good only if man is subject to criteria that lie beyond this earthly life, and it loses its force if he sees his highest goal in the earthly realm and its fulfillment."[1] A distinction is made next between external expansive power and force and the internal power of the spirit and of thought. The attempt is made to justify the external power, the sinister dynamic of which is taught by all of history, on the basis of three values. First, the religious value: Portugal and Spain conquered their colonies in the name of Christendom and thereby committed almost unavoidable cruelties that bring the use of power into the gravest *krisis*, into the "shadow of an indissoluble contradiction".[2] Second, the ethical value: in the name of duty, as Kant and Fichte formulate this, the kings of Prussia exercised and administered power, but the "ultimate ethical requirement was basically impossible to meet". Third, the cultural value: the only "attempt at justification that is still taken seriously today, although it is the most problematical", "also the only attempt at a justification that has no martyrs to show for itself".[3] In other words, the mere appeal to higher values to justify the exercise of force does not suffice in any of these cases.

---

[63] 81:22.
[1] 18:7.

[2] 18:12.
[3] 18:13, 15.

Alongside this, there exists the internal power of the spirit, its relationship to the eternal; even its struggle for the higher justification of external power belongs to this internal power and has shown itself to be such in the course of history. The attempt has continually been made to shape the external reality out of the power of the highest internal reality, that of the ideal. And yet, the higher the ideal of the one who justified it, the less was it capable of becoming historical reality, and the highest image remains that of the one who loses out for the sake of the ideal and demonstrates through his death the power of the spirit, thus—paradoxically enough—justifying the power that was used in the name of the spirit.[4] "Thus power is finally justified; not because the justification succeeded de facto but because it was only under the spell of power that the heaviest struggle could become necessary, the struggle in which men sacrificed themselves and bore witness in their failure to that which is definitive."[5]

This solution of the problem of power may have been suggested by the present reality of Germany at that period. It sees only the rift between the brutal power of coercion and expansion and the internal power of the spirit, and the utterly ferocious settling of accounts with the Hitler era in *Der Mensch vor dem Gericht der Geschichte* (Man on trial before history, 1946) shows this clearly. But this does not exhaust the whole of Reinhold Schneider's thought, for there is also, at least in a few hours of history, a valid portrayal of the power of the spirit in external power—naturally with the accompanying paradox that the authorization to administer external power proceeds only from the genuineness of one's relationship to God. If one calls the organ of man's relationship to eternity his conscience, then everything depends on the "extent of the consciousness of responsibility" on the part of this conscience: "A different decision will be made by the conscience if man feels himself responsible only for his soul, only for his people, or for humanity; if he limits his responsibility to the temporal sphere or dares to extend it to eternity."[6] Whenever he acts, he ought to aim at the ultimate breadth, keeping in view the common good of humanity as a whole and their eternal salvation as well. Then the conscience can develop to a genuine form that sets its imprint completely on the fabric of power. This will succeed all the

---

[4] 18:16f.

[5] 18:17.

[6] 77:9.

better, the more the powerful man remains conscious that the true power remains transcendent and that all he can do when he acts is to relate to this power. The right lies in man's relation to the One who has right in eternity. "The right was visible at every hour—not in human beings, but above them."[7] And in *Lothar*: "All that remained was renunciation; the striving toward the unattainable right, not this right itself."[8] "So all that was given on the coronation day in the Lateran was a fleeting image of the order that was sought, an image, so to speak, that once again rendered the right present to men but did not give it to them."[9] In *Verwaltung der Macht*: "The crown of the earthly king is only a reflection, a tiny splinter of the immeasurable power that irradiates out over the creation."[10] "The right from which all rights proceed rests above men; it does not have its foundation in man. Man lives on the basis of right, but right does not live in him. It endures and is not dependent on us."[11] We have only approximations: "The conflict of powers ought never to come to a reconciliation, because right is not in man but above him, and the one who is highest is indeed closest to the right but is not himself this right."[12] But this means that a drop of injustice is mingled with all earthly justice, increasing proportionately as this justice presents itself as independent, absolute justice. At the sixth station on the Way of the Cross, Schneider prays: "Since injustice rules, under the protection of force, over what belongs to God, and your exalted innocence is judged by earthly judges, perfect justice will not be reestablished again until you ascend your throne as judge: all the righteous of the earth share in the judgment that has been pronounced on you, and they will have to bear their responsibility for it. Pure justice will no longer appear, but love can prevent injustice."[13] This points us back to the Cross as the ultimate form of justice: God creates his justice in the world when all are put in the wrong vis-à-vis him, when their justice is revealed to be injustice in relation to him, and he takes upon himself all the injustice in his atoning death.

Let us pause and ask about the theological meaning of these ideas.

---

[7] 9:271.
[8] 11:137.
[9] 11:144f.
[10] 51:107.
[11] 101:45.
[12] 9:210.
[13] 29:29f.

Reinhold Schneider's dualistic system (which is already revealed by the titles of his books: *Macht und Gnade, Dämonie und Verklärung*) does indeed possess an intense dramatic excitement, but it tacitly presupposes the characterization of man and his essential situation, which as such are the object of the struggle between heaven and hell. The concluding theological description of man's position presupposes this philosophical description of man—no matter how true it may be on the other hand that this philosophical description remains per se impossible to achieve completely and transcends itself to become the theological description. Thus, although it may be correct to say that the zone in man that is the object of the struggle between grace and the abyss is provisionally "neutral" vis-à-vis both, so that man's "power" can still bear the sign either of grace or of rebellion, this does not mean that it does not belong to man's "nature" to possess a power *of his own*, since this concept is indispensable as an inherent characterization of a spiritual being and is a "very good" potential, when considered on the basis of the creation. Man's power is not only a relationship to God's power; it is, to begin with, a quality of his being. Man's social nature means that there exists a natural legitimacy of the state's power, or better, of the state's authority, which belongs to man's essential dignity and can indeed be misused but cannot simply be abolished. Precedence (*praelatio*) is a concept that belongs to the order of creation, with its first justification in the fact that living intellectual beings can be the origin of one another and thus have to give "increase", education and guidance: "Bodily paternity permits us to measure every other person who is an origin; in some manner, every authority shares in the paternal office."[14] In accordance with this, "the laws are not simply the coercive powerful expression of the will of one who possesses authority but forms and channels in which the original authority communicates life to its members."[15] Through sin, of course, a shadow has been cast on the "natural law" that is as deep as the shadow cast on the nature of man himself, which falls into guilt, misery and death. But no matter how profound the degenerations of the "primary natural law" (that of paradise) may be supposed to be in the "secondary natural law" (corresponding to the fallen condition), they do not justify us in hopping over man's essential structure, both

---

[14] Richard Hauser, *Autorität und Macht* (Heidelberg 1949), 373.

[15] Ibid., 377.

in his individual aspect and in his social and political aspect; the state, too, whose coercive character has been made necessary by the fall, is per se not evil but rather good. It is also conditioned by guilt and is thus the eloquent expression of guilt; it is administered by guilty men, and its apparatus of power entices the sinner to misuse it in a demonic fashion. But the punitive authority remains, if not a primary expression of the Creator's will, at least a secondary expression, as we find expressed with perfect clarity by Paul in the Letter to the Romans (13:1–7) and Peter in his First Letter (2:13–17).

Schneider always sees the individual who is furnished with power: the person of the ruler; he sees him as the representative of the infinite Person of God in the world. But as such, he is clothed with a worldly authority that is established through man's social nature, and this authority *as such* is also a reflection in the fallen world of the will of the Creator. As a historian, he always begins with the individual and sees the one who holds power: this is why, when the question of the justification of power arises, he does not discuss the application of the apparatus of power within the state but turns at once to the dubious and dangerous tendency this power has to expand. But before speaking of a war of conquest, indeed, before even speaking of a defensive war, one ought seriously to speak of the police—the very etymology of this word would speak volumes. The punitive force of the state could be legitimated on the basis of the paternal and domestic punitive authority, and the sword willed by God could provide the legitimation for that protection of order against outside attacks that finds its minimum in armed resistance. As we shall have to show later, Schneider is no naive pacifist; the fact that he rejects every form of war under modern conditions is another matter altogether. The fact that it is difficult to draw the boundaries for the legitimate use of power is no objection to the necessity of the existence of this power. And the fact that the clash of these systems of law is painful does not permit one to pass over essential factors in silence.[16]

---

[16] Such intellectual short circuits were always the danger of Protestant theology, which was influenced by nominalism, as Richard Hauser has shown in masterly fashion: the essential structure of authority was suppressed in favor of a merely positive power, and indeed the essential creaturely structures as a whole were suppressed in favor of a purely theological-supernatural table of values; the enthusiastic sectarian groups passed over in silence the ordering of the fallen world, of the "old aeon", in favor of an ethics and politics conceived purely in New Testament or eschatological terms, by replacing the analogy of nature and the

But Schneider provides Christian thinking about the interpretation of history with a salutary corrective against a purely abstract thinking in terms of the natural law. His reflections begin where the natural law thinker has already had his say. The word of the gospel must come, not to abolish, but to fulfill: to reveal in the Cross and the Resurrection (after death) the ultimate meaning of what had been the Creator's ultimate intention. One can indeed speak in abstract terms of a "harmony" between nature and the supernatural, but the mystery of the Cross can never be built into a synthesis as a "harmonious" element, and where there is a clash between the demands made by the fallen social order and those made by the gospel's commandment, the result certainly *can* be a relationship of statement and antithesis. This contradiction will not be unavoidable in every individual situation; but it will be necessary, where an "order of natural law" is to be thought out to its logical conclusion or lived in the concrete world without consideration for the word of the gospel. The reason for this accords most profoundly with Reinhold Schneider's intention: If the natural order is not simply a positive will of God as the lawgiver but is a law imprinted on the essence of the created nature itself (a law that as such reproduces God's intention), then the law that has been changed by sin does not float like something innocent above the individual who has become guilty, regulating his life from now on. Rather, the natural law is nothing other than the legal character of the concrete fallen nature in its social aspect. And if this nature is handed over to the attack and the lordship of the devil "before" redemption (but in view of redemption), then this applies in the same way to the structures, which are nothing other than the concrete presentation of the life of human society—and this does not prevent something that appears here in a demonized mode from being good per se, just as good as human nature. Indeed, one can ask whether the "authorities and powers" (*exousiai*) of scriptures, at least in some aspects, are anything other than these demonized social structures, the concrete universality of fallen human nature in itself and in its historical actualization. And since man has only one single supernatural

---

supernatural with a paradoxical contradictory unity: a static unity, since it constitutes itself from the deadly antithesis of the levels; a dynamic unity, since the one dissolves its own existence by being absorbed into the other. But the eschatological impatience must coexist with the patience of the gospel, which commands that one hold out in the sheerly impossible situation "between the ages".

final goal, and the supernatural God of grace and redemption gives him the ultimate, directive meaningfulness of his existence en route to this final goal, the social structures here on earth can never give a complete meaning and value to human existence; their earthly and natural character must necessarily remain open to a realm of grace, that is, they must depend on the positive revelation of the will of the God of grace and of judgment. Here lies the complement to the doctrine of the natural law (which Richard Hauser, too, has urgently demanded) in the direction of the historicity of the state, which is the genuine concern of a social and political situation ethics, something that up to now has been taken up only hesitatingly and from the edge of the problem; in Hauser's view, Leo XIII, too, passed by the central question,[17] and he sees the outcome of this omission in a passivity on the part of Catholics in relation to the unceasingly changing situations of history (a passivity suggested by the doctrine itself), instead of an active share in shaping the changing situation on the basis of genuine ethical and religious responsibility. The aim of Reinhold Schneider's entire historical work is the formation of such a responsibility. In the confused situations of history, the principles of the natural law do offer general parameters but not concrete solutions full of substance. The immediate decisions on which the good and ill of the peoples depend cannot be made without looking at a perspective that goes beyond this world: as decisions of humility or of pride, of piety or of godlessness.

For Schneider, power is not evil per se. If it were demonic as such, as he was inclined to suppose in his younger days[18] (a position he explicitly revoked),[19] then the Christian conscience and activity could not make use of it. But we have the example of Christian rulers who are saints: we have power as the expression of mildness and goodness, we have Louis of France, Philip II, Maria Teresa.[20] We have power as a sharing in Gods governance on earth.[21] We have a desirable trans-

---

[17] Hauser, *Autorität*, 384–406.

[18] Cf. 7:35f. or 11:31f.: "It is the essence of power that it splits and turns against itself, like some hellish beast whose parts separate from one another, only to fall upon one another and devour one another."

[19] 51:116; 91:48.

[20] 62:103f.; 18:257ff.

[21] 51:108, 111; 101:88.

ferral of power to the statesman.[22] His office is so much something coming from God that the "great renunciation" of power under the pretext of purity is desertion. "Indignation at the spread of the destruction has no justification in the mouths of those who make the renunciation. For they are not willing to pay the price that is rendered by the others. This is why they must accept that their sphere of life becomes narrower and narrower, and the governance of the world must be left to the criminals."[23] The price cannot mean (as Schneider had formulated it earlier on) that the one who acts necessarily incurs guilt. Naturally, not even the most pious king will establish the kingdom of God with his rule. He will have to make allowance for the refraction that exists between the spiritual and the worldly realms: "God's order is refracted through the medium of history, which stands under the curse of sin."[24] To stand at the point of this refraction, without behaving contrary to either law: this, of course, means standing close to the Cross. "The kingdoms collide with one another. . . . The one who fights with the darkness is overshadowed by it, and yet it must not be allowed to stain his soul. Thus the Christian unfailingly ends up in front of the Cross in history."[25] To stand under the Cross means that one enters the judgment of grace as a sinful man and that one is laid bare in guilt before that One who bore all guilt for us. And yet Mary, too, stands under the Cross, the representative of humanity and the proof that it is possible to live without guilt on earth, even without being God. And John stands beside her, linking her to the visible, official, authoritative Church. Only, there is no more distinction made under the Cross between guilty and innocent, since the One who is most innocent of all pays the penalty for all guilt. Thus he who is without guilt seems himself in solidarity with all the debtors—and the Son's refusal to make any distinction passes over to his Mother and, through her, to the Church. From now on, thanks to her, it is possible to stand in history, in the sphere of human and social guilt, without isolating oneself, in a mysterious act of distinction made by God, but also in a mysterious coredemptive fellowship before God.

---

[22] 51:115.
[23] 91:12.
[24] 62:108.
[25] 51:113.

Yet all this remains still abstract and is insufficient for the realist of history. The burning concrete question posed by Schneider is this: Concrete history applies force, but the gospel forbids the use of force —does not every Christian who intervenes actively in concrete history, therefore, become guilty in relation to the gospel? This syllogism reveals an ultimate problematic of right and power. Reinhold Schneider believes that this syllogism holds water, in the face of the fifth commandment and of the words of Christ. And he believes that the simple word of God, "Thou shalt not kill" (nor do anything that leads in the direction of killing), need only be applied in practice to remove the terrible nightmare from humanity. Other, equally simple facts initially speak against this apparently simple position. If the use of force were inherently evil, how could the God of the Old Covenant have commanded it on such a large scale (with inexorable harshness, as the case of Saul and Agag proves) and have used it himself? There exists, at least in a preparatory period of salvation history that had an educative character, alongside the animal sacrifices (and the idea of human sacrifice to God, which is at least touched on in the Old Testament), the permission and the command to take life as a symbolic gesture that will give glory to God. It is certainly true that the New Covenant has transferred the fleshly symbol to the spiritual reality: Does this not mean that the fleshly symbol has been superseded? But although the words of the Sermon on the Mount relating to individual behavior are clear, they do not speak unambiguously of the order of the state and its requirements, at least not according to traditional exegesis and praxis.

But this is to describe only half the truth. The New Covenant is a spirit, a yeast in history, which "does not rest until everything has been leavened"; its inner power works through all ages, and its ultimate logic will have come into force only on the Last Day. Insights that will one day break out of the womb and emerge clearly as demands develop in a mysterious maturing process, and one cannot say how much of this process is due to the natural development of humanity and how much to the gospel seed that sprouts in individuals and peoples. A few centuries ago, humanity was ripe for the insight that slavery is incompatible with human rights. Today we see the dawning of the day when responsible humanity will be ripe for the insight that bloody war contradicts its present adult state and is no longer an appropriate means to resolve questions and conflicts of the humanity that has become indivisible and takes charge of its own self; this is the day when the best men begin to be ashamed of war. Very earthly economic and political reasons may have contributed to the emergence of this insight, but it is nevertheless the Christian seed that sprouts in the human conscience and leads to this decision, which is mature today. This decision contains a conclusion from premises that have existed for a long time, and yet it is difficult to pin down the precise location of these. It is not that the human individual has become more perfect today or that Christian principles in social ethics have won the victory over natural instincts, as a shallow humanitarian faith in development would like to portray it; no, natural necessities of history have brought the human conscience to the point where a Christian requirement finally appears practicable, indeed, urgently demanded in the social sphere. Only, it will be necessary once again to make a sharp distinction here between the ethics of the consistent Christian, the saint, who practices nonresistance and "turning the other cheek" out of the fullness of Christian insight into the Cross and the law of its fruitfulness, on the one hand, and, on the other, the political ethics of the people—the non-Christian peoples, or those that have again become largely de-Christianized—who can never be compelled to accept such a first-class ethics as a whole and whose decisions can be made only under consideration of all the political, social and economic circumstances as well. But between both, sharing intimately in both and interested in both, stands the Church. And it is in her that the question ought to be posed most acutely of all; it is here that there ought to lie the conscious point of exchange between the spirit of the gospel and of the saints, and the spirit of today's humanity, in the sense that humanity would be strengthened in its perception that it can no longer resolve conflicts through war and that such a solution is increasingly to be seen as immoral and unworthy of man. And this is true not merely in a relative sense (because *today's* conduct of war, through its excessive destruction and the cruelty of the means employed, goes beyond the measure that was tolerable earlier on) but in an absolute sense, just as the insight into human rights and into the freedom of the individual makes slavery appear absolutely immoral. Thus this is not solely a question of the opportuneness of the rearmament of a people, or even of the difficulty of concrete decisions in this transitional period in which ultimate antitheses between worlds begin their confrontation, and the aggressive armament of the one power calls forth a defensive armament of the other. What is meant here is a breakthrough of the world conscience, which announces itself in Schneider's work (as in other works, too, those of a Romain Rolland, Bergson, Péguy) and which is envisaged and demanded by Schneider out of the highest Christian ethos.

Thus there is a heavier burden today than ever before on the Christian conscience, but basically on the citizen's conscience, too. That which is intolerable—war—is nevertheless being stirred up with new means. That which had been rejected—slavery—is practiced anew through modern technology and the modern state. The closer one seems to come to a solution, the farther does a contrary current drive one away from it.

Ought we perhaps to say (with Romano Guardini) that the Word of God has itself suffered this descent, this refraction from a pure and, as it were, supraecclesiastical form that did not in the least reckon in the Sermon on the Mount with such a refraction and has become a word that has experienced rejection, has taken on the form of the Passion and become the word of the Church? If this is true, then we ought never to appeal from the second form to the first; all we ought to do is to look reverently through the second form into that dazzling original purity, yearning painfully to be purified in its direction, without ever leaving the second form behind us. We should then see something like the incarnation of the Word, its taking on the dimension of the Church, and only gnosticism would refuse to follow the Word as far as its crucified form. Then St. Louis may well defend his kingdom in his time with sharp weapons and go into battle against the Moors;[26] one may venture a word in praise of the life of the Christian solider;[27] a prayer for victory in battle may not deserve condemnation, and even a sword may be blessed;[28] the death penalty may be defended as "a marvelous possibility of expiation", as "the most human institution": "The guilty man was not alone, and only a few will have omitted to pray when the bell for poor sinners rang out; only a few will have omitted to examine their conscience and to feel that the one who was now making his way to the place of execution bore a part of the guilt of all mankind."[29]

---

[26] 62:108.

[27] 91:141.

[28] 24:40–44; 83:101; 114:12.

[29] 79:28f.

For the responsible Christian, all this means, not a relief from his burden, but an additional burden. It would be simple if he were able to flee from the law of responsibility for people and culture in the world to the exclusive law of grace, the powerlessness and defenselessness of the Cross. He must stand between both and do the will of God. As yet, he lives under the law of the old aeon, for the state is not the Church, and the Church is not the heavenly Jerusalem. Both the state (internally) and the Church (externally) retain a relationship to the Old Covenant and to God's punitive justice, a relationship that is not superseded until the judgment of Christ (as one can see from the Apocalypse). The authority that bears the sword is, according to Paul's teaching, "a servant of God, to carry out his judgment of avenging anger on the one who does evil" (Rom 13:4). Schneider, too, knows this: "The peak of the earthly kingdom is lit up by the ray of judgment."[30] "Thus the earthly kingdom is a protective defense against evil."[31] The gospel with its word about nonresistance is addressed to man in this ordered situation. It must now be listened to in all its radicality.

---

[30] 23:23. [31] Ibid.

RUSSIA—CONFESSION

The Good Thief

"A ship sails out under a threatening sky; the flag flies in the late, pallid light, the cannon points fixedly down, and the waves make almost no resistance to the force that presses mightily onward. The ship does not waver; but only the eye of the one who knows penetrates what lies inside, what lies innermost of all; into the soul of the captain that is lacerated by the rift that is torn. All guilt and all greatness remain a reality that has effects in the soul."[1] This removes a symbol, and a question remains: Can the rift be healed, can the guilt be taken away? This was not yet possible in the Iberian world; the rift was the Being of the world itself. All that existed was the image and the dumb, representative form. After guilt has changed from an ontic category to a historical-temporal category with a beginning and a development, one must ask the question: How can existence come back from guilt, which is its untruth, into the truth? Because the historical Cross of Jesus Christ now stands in the point where the rift is torn, it is only from there that we can await the answer: through God's grace, which however is linked to the act whereby Jesus takes upon himself the guilt of the world, bears it and confesses it before the eternal Father. And because the man Jesus Christ makes confession, the form in which man will receive the grace of truth becomes a sharing in his admission of guilt, a share in his confession. And because Christ confesses the entire sin of the world, and every man stands in history and is in indissoluble solidarity with all that happens, the confession of sin has always both aspects: it is wholly personal, and it is wholly historical-social.

As a counterweight to the vision of historical guilt, three new fundamental concepts appear with tremendous force: truth, conscience

---

[1] 9:552.

132

and confession. These three are inseparable from now on and form the equipment with which Reinhold Schneider attempts to encounter and to do justice to the essence of history and the requirement it makes. In *Camoes*, existence was incurable: the truth lay in the image that transfigured it without transforming it in its real being. In *Philipp*, the truth of existence was that form which it generates from itself in its death, indeed, when it is dead, in an act of transfiguration: the innermost reality in the Escorial was only the Cross and, before it, a heart that had poured all its life-blood into its task; the truth lay in the death of existence, and the representation meant the death of the person. As late as in *Innozenz*, guilt towered above the guilty man like a doom: as the contradiction inherent in the dichotomy that had grown up in the course of history between the Caesarean form and the Christian substance, between an unconditional imperial claim and its link to a conditioned reality. But the silent burial of the guilty heart could not be its redemption. The truth corresponding to this is not an image, a form or a doom, but only the living "Thou" of God, which meets it and bestows grace upon it. And so the first chime of the clock of redemption rings out, namely, the insight that, not man, but God is the truth. But he is the revealed truth, that is, the truth that is opened and given as grace. The organ with which man perceives the truth is the conscience, and the form in which he receives it is the confession of sin. This means the overcoming of the Protestant dualism: for the truth is no ideality that is related to the crude reality only in an external, forensic manner. The truth is the grace that makes its demands of the real guilty heart and inexorably wears it down. This is expressed by the words of the starets in *Alexander*, words that from now on contain the whole soul of Reinhold Schneider: "*The truth displays no grace. It is grace itself.*"[2] And Alexander says: "It judged me without any accusation. It was the accusation itself."[3] Grace and confession emerge with perfect simultaneity, and the unity of both is the truth of the Lord. It is now that image and representation receive their soul; truth dwells in both art and ethos and fuses with both to become the one Catholic form of life: a service of the person that has become the soul's transparent admission of sin, the confession that has taken on a permanent existence and that now as a whole is an image in the

---

[2] 110:110.   [3] 110:113.

Church, light on top of the bushel, the city set on a hill. The missing piece could be supplied only by that country that was the antipodes of Iberia just as much as of the rational, psychological-empirical England: namely, the formless Russia, homeland of the naked souls, of the sinners who make their confession without restraint, of the solidarity passionately grasped in guilt and in grace. Thus Reinhold Schneider's West comes to its completion in the triangle between the Escorial, the Tower and the Kremlin, with a provisional midpoint in Potsdam; the fourth point will be Rome, while the Athens of the classical thinkers will not be a structural support. Finally, Vienna will come on the scene; the Scandinavian North remains a sporadic presence. Schneider's West is the Christian West, which always bears in itself the classical inheritance in one way or another.

Russia is the Good Thief. "The fettered man becomes free again, in a certain sense, when he says: 'What is done to us is done rightly'; these words denote the one single deed that was still possible for him —for no one is going to take him down from the cross; his guilt is demonstrated, his sentence irrevocable. But now he bows before the verdict—and in the same moment, he is exalted above all that can be imagined; God says to him, 'You will be with me in paradise.'"[4] Where there is no more hope, in earthly terms (and where Camões and Philip, too, and even Innocent, begin, where every true doctrine of man must begin), the miracle, the leap into salvation takes place through the grace of the confession of sin. The fact that this is the last deed in the thief's life, something he does in the moment of his physical death, is not the essential point; what is important is the end of every earthly hope, the hanging on the cross beside the Lord as he makes confession of sin, the will to throw everything into the word of confession but without being able to give this word the weight of a demand: all this is the symbolic situation for historical man in every moment of his existence, something he can put into action through the grace of the Lord. Just as guilt was a historical path taken in the past, so confession is a historical path leading back behind the origin of guilt: a reversal of direction, taking up and rescuing the time that has decayed: and this means that it is grace, a participation in God's eternal time. "Oh, how terrible it is to greet one's own life like a

---

[4] 88c:14.

boat one has missed!"[5] But grace offers to the one who confesses
the possibility of getting back what cannot be retrieved. "Alexander
says passionately: I must get back to my own self. From that point, I
must attempt to unpick my life like a garment that fits badly."[6] This
is the path back to the place where things began to go wrong, back to
the clandestine guilt. We find this already in *Las Casas*: "We cannot
avoid going back to that point on our path where we deviated from
the right goal, even if this means that we would have to wander back
along almost the entire path of our life; perhaps that has been the
meaning of my life, and perhaps this is why I had to come back to
the place where the cross stood."[7] And in *Taganrog*: "You must take
hold of the truth at the place in your life where you lost it. I believe
that you know the place very well, but you do not dare to enter it."[8]
"It is dangerous and painful to follow a guilt back into its origins—as
yet, this work has scarcely begun. But one thing is certain: there is no
greater misfortune than a guilt that is veiled and denied. At the place
where it is hushed up, the path diverts into total ruin; from then on,
the spirit can no longer be heard."[9] This makes it also clear that one
cannot pray without confession and, therefore, cannot take up the
attitude of contemplation that moves the world and history: the beginning of prayer as the praise of God, *confessio Dei*, is the confession
of sin, *confessio peccati*. This is a "self-encounter" as encounter with
one's own guilt,[10] but this can take place only where the entire act is
embraced within a comprehensive act of forgiving grace: that is, it is
self-encounter within the encounter with God. This is the difference
between confession and psychology: the latter is unacquainted with
any grace and therefore lacks all criteria for the assessment of guilt.
The desire to confess outside of grace could lead to an even deeper
burial of guilt.

But now comes the decisive point, which Russia (and up to now
only Russia) knew: one never becomes guilty in isolation. Guilt exists
in the presence of God but also in the presence of his world: guilt
is historical, in a double sense, since I share in the guilt (and this
means, to begin with, that I become guilty in a very real sense) of all
the world when I commit a sin and that I must share in the work of

---

[5] 110:156.

[6] 110:123.

[7] 12:78f.; cf. his confession, 12:143ff.

[8] 65:32.

[9] 91:143f.

[10] 91:47.

expiating the guilt of the world, not as if this were a guilt belonging to someone else, but as my own guilt. "My guilt has become a reality in the world, and all the chaos outside is merely a magnified image of the confusion within myself."[11] This is why the confession necessarily includes more than a limited empirical consciousness would be able to confess as definable personal guilt. By sinning, man steps into a river that comes from far off, and through him this river swells into an illimitable breadth and future.[12] This is why there also exists a guilt on the part of a people, but this cannot be neatly detached from the guilt of the world.[13] Once again, it is *Der Mensch vor dem Gericht der Geschichte* that expresses this most urgently. Thus confession takes on its social dimension; not only because the individual receives new tasks and strengths for the fellowship through being purified but, on a much deeper level, because it is completely impossible for him as an individual to submit himself to the judgment of grace without at the same time involving in a mysterious manner the fellowship with which and because of which he became guilty and which fell into new and alien guilt through his guilt. And if guilt is in its most profound essence the lack of love, which creates isolation, so that there is in the deepest sense no fellowship in guilt, then the paradoxical fellowship in guilt becomes a true fellowship within the act of confession.

Appeal is made here to Dostoyevsky and all the great Russian authors who have achieved "the overcoming of tragedy" from this standpoint: the guilty person admits before everyone the deed he has covered up and thus becomes everyone's brother.[14] This is the theme of Tolstoy's *Power of Darkness*.[15] But it becomes clear in the act itself that the one who confesses was not alone in his courageous deed either: just as the fruit of his act is social, so too is its origin: "No sinner arrives at salvation without the help given by his brothers."[16] The one who confesses reconciles himself to God, but this takes place through the Church and therefore also thanks to the Church; if he has confessed, then he has essentially carried out the expiation—for the venture of this deed and the courage needed for it are the highest possible achievement of expiation[17]—and thus the fellowship *must*

---

[11] 29:15.

[12] 12:149.

[13] 51:4.

[14] 91:146.

[15] 60:6f.

[16] 91:148.

[17] 12:110f.; 91:57.

take him up too.[18] Much Christian composition, above all folk tales, lives (without really knowing it) from this idea, which is conceived with clear awareness among the Russians. Let us listen to Alexander once again: "My guilt is not a property that one locks up, something that I can do what I like with. It affects everybody. It must not remain hidden."[19]

This applies in an eminent sense to that person who must guide the history of the fellowship in a representative manner, the ruler. His conscience, his guilt and his confession are social and historical in an outstanding manner, and the highest realization of a confession would be that of a leader who confesses in the name of his people his personal guilt, since he senses the historical devastation that comes from this guilt. England's tragic ruler Henry VIII failed to do this: "He was not the kind of man who looked into himself and asked himself why he did things. In the depths of his soul, contradictions piled up that he never investigated, never put an end to, contradictions that one day would poison him from within, without his knowing the reason why he was poisoned."[20] *Czar Alexander* (whose mysterious expiation seems to be confirmed by history) is the opposite example: he confesses that injury to his conscience on which his sovereignty was built up (a sharing in thought in the guilt of his father's murder, since he knew about it and did not intervene), and he understands that "in a deeper sense, everything that happened after this had been futile."[21] For the Sermon on the Mount does not excuse us from the guilt in thought that stands at the beginning of all evils. Shakespeare's Macbeth and Brutus are familiar with this.[22] In a homily about Herod's feast, it is shown how this man, who lets things happen and only gives half his assent in his spirit, is implicated in a share of guilt with historic dimensions: "All those who had appeared for whatever reason at the table of the tyrant and enjoyed this, or were retained there through their fear or cowardice, shared in the guilt of the death of the fearless one, the great Precursor on whose traces the future Judge is already coming into view."[23] "It can be simply an act of letting something happen that in some circumstances has the most dreadful consequences. A slight deviation from that which is right in our

---

[18] 91:46.
[19] 110:157.
[20] 9:256.

[21] 65:60.
[22] 77:35.
[23] 60:13.

breast can unleash devastations when its effects are carried over to the whole world. So deadly serious is our life, so sensitive the organism to which we belong, that the most hidden error lays its own claim to history."[24] This is why the confession of the king is so important, as we see in the short story "Der Tod des Mächtigen" where the saint ultimately wrings the admission of sin out of the guilty king of France, Louis XI, as he lies dying; or as in *Traum des Heiligen* Thomas More wants his unshriven king to "Summon up the highest holy courage, tear away the veil from your sin and look it in the face";[25] or as the dying Frederick William I makes his confession in his own way, soldierly and genuine,[26] very close to the Good Thief. Each one of these guilty men confesses a guilt that is truly not diffuse and generalized but a guilt that is most intimately his own, a guilt he knows exactly, a guilt that cannot be pushed off onto anyone else. But there is more than this present in his guilt, and this is why the absolution, too, reaches farther; and this is why every Christian hope is permitted to go so far: because the range of *my* guilt coalesces with the range of the guilt of the world. "There remains a hope that we cannot wholly penetrate. If we cannot hope and plead for the damned, how are we then to hope and plead for ourselves! There is only one guilt, the guilt of our innermost heart. Guilt must become visible in the fate of the peoples; then a light will fall on the guilt, and we shall understand its unfathomable origin and be thankful to those who have borne out our guilt onto the theaters of the world."[27]

One motif that continually recurs in Reinhold Schneider's writing is the great symbol for the "historical" confession: in the old fortresses there are subterranean, gloomy dungeons with prisoners who have been there from time immemorial, prisoners whom life passes by, and one day someone must go down and look the prisoners in the eye, opening the prison and reestablishing the truth that is mercy and redemption. So we have John in fetters, above whose prison Herod and his men hold their feast, "the voice of the truth under the vaults, the voice that is not permitted to speak",[28] and in *Las Casas* the Indians who are kept cruelly as prisoners in the belly of the ship, shrieking and wailing during the storm: "It did not occur to me that I was

---

[24] 91:51; cf. 65:82.

[25] 34:51.

[26] 7:162.

[27] 29:39f.

[28] 60:14f.

hearing the voice of my own guilt."[29] And again in *Alexander*: "It is as if a buried man were stirring under Russia's soil",[30] and definitively in the *Große Verzicht*, where the forgotten prisoner from the time of Conradin, his suffering, his reprieve that comes too late, the descent of the guilty king to him, and the exchange between the crown of gold and the crown of straw become the concluding symbol.[31] And with a transformation from the prisoner to the decaying corpse (the image is consciously taken over from Tolstoy):[32] "Guilt that is denied is like the body of a slain man that is buried in the cellar and poisons all life."[33] And in *Tarnkappe*: "These vaults are built on dead men; perhaps on dead peoples."[34] In the heart of *Inselreich* it is Warwick, the secret of the Tower, the man who is a prisoner pure and simple, who is the catalyst for the destinies: "a man who was nothing but a living law".[35] Those who descend are the saints, like Madame de Chantal, who steals down at night to bring the prisoners food and a little light,[36] or St. Leo IX in the short story "Der fünfte Kelch".[37] Three things forbid us from understanding this motif as the meaning of analytic psychology. What is involved in this descent into the hidden heart is an encounter with the "Thou" in relation to whom the soul has incurred guilt; this is an encounter with justice and truth, which ultimately exist with God and which demand a confession in order for the guilt to be remitted. What is involved is the clarification and cleansing of the spheres of history, and in this sense history truly participates in the judgment of the world, which is the judgment of God and of Christ, just as sacramental confession participates in this judgment. One of the greatest examples of this is Newman, who bears the burden of centuries throughout his long, slow *via dolorosa* of the truth, untangling the threads that were knotted in the wrong way and annulling Henry's decision through the decision he pays for with his own pain, through his life, which is as transparent as water and crystal and is in its totality admission of sin and confession. Here the personal element becomes the historical element, and vice versa.[38]

---

[29] 12:99.

[30] 110:121.

[31] 108:272–80.

[32] 70:135.

[33] 91:54.

[34] 111:12.

[35] 9:244.

[36] 27:17.

[37] 34:26.

[38] 71:113.

It is "man's nobility that he can confess guilt and that, purified in the confession, he raises himself above the guilt".[39] This is because man, as one who recognizes, is spirit; but one who recognizes must also confess, he must bear witness to the truth,[40] since the truth of being a lie is in the guilty man. Not theoretical knowledge but the concrete conscience is the highest in man,[41] for this is the organ of the real truth, which is not a proposition but a person, not an insight but a living being and doing. It is only these triumphant insights that will permit Schneider to appear before his own people as an undaunted issuer of demands. The "crown", which hitherto floated above the earthly reality as an unattainable ideal, now descends into the nobility of the soul: the conscience, which knows the truth and takes hold of the truth in confession through the grace of the truth, is the true kingship of man.[42]

> And only the conscience, which with most audacious courage
> takes its stance and deliberates before the eternal throne,
> administers aright and becomes like right itself.[43]

Thus the conscience becomes "the element that gives form to life and to art",[44] because it is the organ of the truth for both these. This means that the Portuguese metaphysics of the images is definitively recognized to be inadequate. The image is the subsequent reflection of the inner truth: this is the content of the narrative "Das getilgte Antlitz".[45] Now the solution is: "I will be the voice of truth alone."

> The truth wants to reveal itself to us in struggle
> in the reflection of formed images,
> if a life presses on after the truth in difficult years,
> then the images of this life, too, will become pure.[46]

From now on, the entire struggle is devoted to the lived truth; no sacrifice is too high for this, especially not the sacrifice of one's life.[47] In the short story "Die Wahrheit, Erzählung nach einem russischen Dokument", fate compels mildly and terribly to ultimate truthfulness, not only to the true attitude of mind,[48] whereas the Russian *Elisabeth*

---

[39] 83:28.
[40] 91:45.
[41] 76:19; 78:8f.; 80:7.
[42] 91:49f.
[43] 98:71.

[44] 91:91.
[45] 34:113−74.
[46] 69:35.
[47] 35:54; 78:10; 79:23; 81:72; 84:12.
[48] 94:162−78.

Tarakanow understands the truth as a mere external legitimacy and surrenders her heart to the craving for power, which pulls her down into the abyss.[49] The essence of Christianity is that the truth is a deed, "that the only one to come to the light is the one who does the truth" and that "there is no possibility of understanding Christ except by carrying out his word."[50] And God is the truth because in him "there is no boundary between his love and his word."[51] "The presupposition of genuine knowledge, of a true and just judgment, is the Yes of love, for it is only this Yes that reaches to Being. Everything that exists reaches down with its deepest root into the foundation of love, of true Being."[52] Since there does not exist any second concept of truth, aesthetics, too, must have its origin here: the first axiom is "that what is perfect is true".[53] The legend of Genesius (the actor who converts in the course of his play and then becomes a martyr) "perhaps expresses the highest mystery of the stage: the mystery of the truth takes place visibly-invisibly before the affected spectators": a heart is changed and draws other hearts into its own transformation.[54] *Die Wahrheit vom Menschen in Calderons geistlichem Theater* shows the application of this principle.[55] Art enters upon the highest service, that of truth and grace; on this basis, beauty receives its share in man's nobility.

> Thus the power of the light that is sent
> spreads out in images, and the word will take hold of them
> when word and truth are deeply rooted in life.

> Art, thanks to renunciation,
> touches the deepest misery: time will bring it to maturity,
> but only a heart can enkindle men's hearts.[56]

The Left Cheek

The Russian penitent confesses in the presence of his brothers, but since his guilt is the guilt of all, he also confesses for his brothers. "There is no crime committed in the world without everyone sharing

---

[49] 15.
[50] 51:39.
[51] 29:51.
[52] 112:36.
[53] 52:28.
[54] 52:41-46.
[55] 52:47-55.
[56] 35:58.

in its guilt; no crime that does not demand expiation on the part of each one." "As sin is one single sin, so this single sin is the sin of all; no misdeed occurs without our flesh and blood, our rebellious, arrogant spirit sharing in it."[1] "But after Christ walked on this earth, and the entire guilt of mankind was concentrated into the terrible guilt in relation to him, and he took upon himself the mighty impetus of this guilt and shattered it",[2] the possibility of vicarious atonement exists: through taking the blow that is meant for him, through breaking the iron regularity of the law of blow and counterblow, through the mysterious miracle of suffering. There is the Christian deed that is posited against other earthly deeds. But the ultimate fate of the world is not decided on the level of deeds. The trial of strength between these deeds will intensify, and the earthly force will not refrain from resorting to violence. Here is the turning point that decides everything: Will the Christian deed arm itself for the counterblow with the boxing glove of earthly force, or will it recall the path of Christ and take hold of the highest possibility he gives it, the possibility of sacrifice, which demands the highest courage and the utmost degree of energy? "The highest value was always summoned to sacrifice itself, because only sacrifice is able to overcome the world's most vehement resistance."[3] "For that which is mightiest is also that which is the most silent, and violence will run away from you if you surrender yourselves totally to it. Today and tomorrow the spirit is not working, but on the third day it will transform everything from within."[4] And this is why "the sacrifices of the pure and the sufferings of the purified are the only hope of a generation weighed down by debts it can never redeem."[5] Where the deed was radically wrong, all that helps now is suffering.[6] And because vicarious representation exists, it suffices that some should take this suffering upon themselves, that some should go through the fire in the name of all.[7] But those who are active cannot be active effectively without the willingness to suffer.[8]

This is the great Russian teaching about nonresistance, which Reinhold Schneider here makes his own.

---

[1] 62:33.

[2] 62:34.

[3] 52:68.

[4] 94:51; 62:68.

[5] 51:7.

[6] 69:21.

[7] 62:86; 70:78.

[8] 83:9.

Tolstoy and Dostoyevsky are among the few who have dared to conceive of a radically Christian ethic in this epoch of negligence and of dawning catastrophes. Tolstoy said: Love your enemies, and you will have no more enemies. Dostoyevsky was the herald of the universal love that took on form in the person of Jesus Christ; he developed the doctrine of the conscience that has Christ as its litmus test and decides in the presence of Christ, according to a law that cannot be tied down in formulations, fearlessly and regardlessly, whether or not a deed is permitted, whether it is ethical in the only valid meaning of this term: in the sense of the imitation of Jesus Christ.[9]

But this imitation leads to the Cross, into nonresistance, into suffering. And since the saint of Assisi agrees, it is here that "West and East meet."[10] Reinhold Schneider is never more eloquent, never more aglow, than when he glorifies the names of these sacrificial victims. Let us mention first the protopresbyter Avvakum, who became the protomartyr of the Old Believers "thanks to his unheard-of ability to suffer and endure" and ultimately to die at the stake;[11] the Old Believers in turn were the instigators of the sacrificial deed of Czar Alexander.[12] It is not for nothing that Leskov's *On the End of the World* was given a place in the "Abendländische Bücherei" with an introduction by Schneider: this is the glorification of that "holy modesty" which "endures everything God imposes on it", "the wisdom of a suffering without resistance, which is basically the strongest faith";[13] not for nothing is the *The Way of a Pilgrim* praised.[14] The image of holy audacity, which penetrates unarmed through the hostile weaponry in order to do her work of faith and of love, is Veronica: "Even the armed men yield before this love. It desires nothing; it does not utter any contradiction, it only wants to help."[15] In her footprints follow those saints who let themselves be sent out defenseless to wild tribes that had no faith:[16] Abbot Augustine, Otto of Bamberg, but also the idyllic Isaac Walton,[17] to whom Schneider devoted a short story of his own ("Der Edelstein"),[18] and his greater brother Thomas More ("Der Traum des Heiligen");[19] the Pilgrims of Grace who went out

---

[9] 112:91f.

[10] 112:41.

[11] 18:114–23.

[12] 65:51f., 61; 69:34.

[13] 102h:7.

[14] 112:39f.

[15] 29:29–32, 30.

[16] 18:32–38.

[17] 11:55–81; 9:372f.

[18] 94:67–79.

[19] 34:37–55, 42.

to meet the king with a desire, not to fight, but only to make known the truth through their existence and their word.[20] Las Casas wanted to convert the Indians "with the means of the faith alone, and in a certain sense without giving consideration to the state";[21] Friedrich Spee ("Der Tröster")[22] exposes his breast to the superior power of human and demonic forces; Captain Renaud in Vigny's *The Military Necessity*, also given an introduction by Schneider, has suffered all the tragedy of a military man and ends in nonresistance with his bamboo cane (instead of a rifle).[23] St. Sebastian, pierced by everyone's arrows, is the precursor ("I see his kingdom dawning at a sacred distance, / and I am his herald without protection or defense"),[24] and the Children's Crusade is the tragic realization of this (to which Schneider often refers) in the midst of an age of the world dominated by power.[25] Schneider adapts even the Siegfried material to the idea of nonresistance (in the *Tarnkappe*): when the hero falls unarmed, this is the expression of his turning from the pagan to the Christian sphere. But it is the image of Daniel in the den of lions that Schneider loves best. The Romanesque relief in Wurms portrays this with unexampled intensity, and Schneider himself expounds it with deep emotion: the saint among the wild beasts, including those in human form, as hired soldier, man of prayer, man of sacrifice, savior.[26] From this point, Schneider's nonresistance extends to the cosmos that fell through man's sin and has been caught up against its will into violence: he has the Franciscan compassion with the suffering animal but also with the cruel animal, and he suffers even when plant and stone are ravished by man. It is logical that he speaks against the murder of tyrants and that he condemns the heroes of July 20 (who acted in good faith) in his commemorative speech.[27] They have become righteous through their tragic end and because they looked upward to God's eternal right.

Once again, to set limits on this cutting logic of the gospel is to expose oneself to the suspicion that one is limping on both sides (the "Catholic *both* . . . *and*" has always appeared as a compromise in the eyes of the Augustinians, who think things out to the end, and who

---

[20] 18:79f.

[21] 12:70.

[22] 34:195–226.

[23] 102i.

[24] 35:71.

[25] 26:85; 71:34f.; 112:77.

[26] 70:79–85; 112:33ff.; 114, picture 11.

[27] 76.

include Luther and Karl Barth). But Catholic, that is, universal truth can exist only where all the truths are together, even those that are apparently incompatible. In order to be faithful to this proposition, we must give them their place as indispensable partial elements in a more comprehensive framework.

To begin with, one must not forget that the hours of the Cross were not the entire meaning of Christ's life but only its goal and its end and that he took care not to enter the hour of darkness on the basis of his own judgment. On the contrary, he preserved his life, withdrew and hid himself, in order not to glorify himself by bringing the hour too soon. The Christian, too, and the Church are meant to live, not to enter martyrdom unless the Holy Spirit explicitly summons them to this. Then, in the decisive hour of suffering, they are not to seek to protect themselves from the passion with worldly instruments of power—Peter's sword!—but equally, up to that hour they are not only to watch and pray but to "sell their mantle and buy a sword" (Lk 22:36). Reference has been made above to the question of "war and the Bible". But one must consider another point too: the state —which is not the Church—has no eschatological goal: the human beings who form the state will rise from the dead, not the state itself. This means that the laws it follows cannot be governed primarily or exclusively by the law of the Cross, which finds its justification at Easter from beyond this world. If one wishes to tie the state down to the formulae of the Sermon on the Mount, one will almost in-evitably open the door to a concealed millenarianism, desiring to see at some time on the earth, at a future date, what can be seen only in heaven. This is the reverse side of the idea of progress that was men-tioned earlier. This is why we are told by Sebastian: "I see his king-dom dawning at a sacred distance", a kingdom "where holy humility bends its brow and right and faith wear rulers' crowns".[28] It is indeed true that Schneider only describes the future expectation of the Old Believers, which he does not share;[29] but we do find the expectation of a humanity that "in all-embracing responsibility" no longer makes use of the power that is given to it and thereby becomes "the body called to transfiguration beyond death".[30] "The deed that has not yet

---

[28] 35:20; cf. 98:92, 95; 37:141; 107:57.   [30] 91:40f.
[29] 65:40.

taken place, the new power in thinking and acting"[31] belongs to the
future. "One day someone must come, one day someone will come
. . .",[32] or, as Ignatius says in prison, "Neither today nor tomorrow,
but on the third day".[33] Thus the "Stimme des Joachim von Floris",
too, is heard, and the mythical level is projected onto the historical
level:[34] we hear again and again the myth of the soul that has fallen
down into its destiny and must free itself again from the realm of
the harsh "law" and of "power". In his interpretation of Grillparzer's
Libussa, Schneider writes: "History in the real sense begins with the
entry of the supraearthly into the earthly sphere, when what is pure
has descended into the world of men and becomes turbid; in the deepest sense, history begins with a falling-away."[35] Prudence takes the
place of wisdom, "Libussa's gift as a seer is to be useful to the state",
but what is holy disappears and dies, withdrawing again into its own
pure sphere. The same motif is the basis of the drama of *Siegfried*: the
mythical primal unity of Brunhild and Siegfried, which belongs to
prehistory, is made turbid by Siegfried's second, traitorous irruption
into the circle of flame under the form of Gunther; in the impure
world of the Wurms relief, the hero dies and Brunhild returns into
the sacred fire. And if it were not for the fact that Kriemhild (the representative of the Christian dimension vis-à-vis the myth), according
to the saga, must be a woman filled with hatred who cries out for
revenge, then Siegfried's atoning death could have pointed the way
to a better time for the world.[36] It is indeed possible to interpret the
myth as eschatological even in the strict sense of this word (rather
than as millenarian): "There rests on that day the reflected splendor
of the first and the last days",[37] "the crown gleams with the splendor
of a holy time that has passed away and that returns, with the splendor of the first and the last days".[38] But this brings us back to our
earlier observation that the earthly orientation of the state passes away
in the heavenly orientation of the "kingdom of God".

But is all this an absolute objection, to which no answer is possible?
Or does not Reinhold Schneider as historian know well enough that
society has an immanent regularity; can we not summarize all that he

---

[31] 98:91.
[32] 112:38.
[33] 94:51.
[34] 35:64.

[35] 55:47.
[36] 111.
[37] 55:64.
[38] 55:58.

wants to say in the assertion that the one who bears responsibility for the state—and his decision includes that of all the citizens as well —must prefer the commandment of the Lord to every natural consideration, where it is a question of a Yes or a No? And is he not right to hold that the "Catholic *both . . . and*" has repeatedly been a mantle to cover the cowardice and Pharisaism of the Christian?

> In the one half, the Cross asserts itself, while the law of the Old Testament holds good in the other half; religious conduct consists in an unceasing alternation between these two. In the same way, there is an alternation between the order of salvation and the order of power, trust in grace and the claim to a natural right, as if there did not exist the harshest antitheses between these. . . . But if we call ourselves Christians, we can do so only as disciples of Christ, by seeking in all conflicts to follow the gospel as the first commandment.[39]

And yet: the Lord himself does not destroy the Old Covenant but fulfills it; he does not want to see those who belong to him only on the cross but also fighting in life; nor does he want the situation of bloody martyrdom, to which only the individual can be called by the Holy Spirit, to be forced on the generality of his disciples by those who hold the reins of society, for otherwise these rulers would presumptuously lay claim to the prerogative of the Spirit. And this would be all the more wrong where the majority of those who are to be guided by those with responsibility are no longer able to think in Christian terms, still less in the terms of Christian heroism. So nothing is left but to bear those "harshest antitheses" through the ages; as we have already said, it is only these antitheses in their tension that fully characterize the tragic situation of the Christian. Christian ethics here below remains something that cannot be completely achieved, in a position between the "natural law" colored by original sin (or the "existence in Advent") and the Christian law, which always at some point remains eschatological for the state as such (not for the Christians in the state).

This becomes even clearer when we widen our panorama and recall that the question about power and weapons is only one section from a much larger context. Not merely the structure of public power is "demonized" through original sin but all the spheres of fallen na-

---

[39] 112:79.

ture as well; the first of these we must mention is eros, which Reinhold Schneider seldom mentions and scarcely discusses. The lethal
poison sits in eros no less than in power; indeed, eros is perhaps the
most dangerous place where divine power becomes demonic, egoistic
power. It is surely only rarely that a Christian blessing has emptied
eros of the last drop of poison, in the concrete sphere of concupiscence. And what about the possession of earthly goods? Will not man
attach his heart to them, as the Sermon on the Mount puts it? Ought
he not to practice nonviolence here, too, and give his mantle to the
one who steals his coat? Are not all the structures equally "infected
by the plague" of concupiscence: possession, eros, having power at
one's disposal? And is not Christ's remedy for them all something
much deeper than mere nonresistance to an external superior power?
Christ's nonresistance is directed, not primarily against his enemies,
but *to the Father*: his essence is the total availability for the Father's
will and therefore the refusal to hold fast to anything in the world,
the provisional character of every use made of something, the revoca-
bility of all that he does and plans. Redemption comes, not from the
Cross as pain and tragedy, but only from the loving obedience that
expresses itself therein. And Jesus Christ has given this, his innermost
disposition (which had also been proclaimed before the Church and
in words that stand over the Church, in the Sermon on the Mount),
expression in the Church in a *state of life*, in that ecclesial form of life
that is permitted to take the counsels of the gospel as the basic form
of its existence. What Reinhold Schneider describes as nonresistance
certainly finds here the place where it is fully realized: in the refusal to
have goods, eros or power at one's disposal, a refusal made for the sake
of total availability to God, in a life that oscillates between paradise
(the true primal state before history) and the Cross (the true *eschaton*
of history), a life that becomes the representative idea of Christian
and human existence within the Church and, through the Church,
within humanity. For according to Thomas Aquinas, this state of life
is nothing other than a representation permitted for the sake of the *totality*: simultaneously an image to which one looks up and a vicarious
representation that works and atones for all. Thus Reinhold Schneider's earliest inspiration is wholly true, wholly ecclesial. The vision
of *Camoes*, of *Philipp*, of *Hohenzollern*, even of *Fichte*, was that genuine
action that has an effect on history can only come from a heart that
has died to the world (but that lives through love).

The dream was and remains a king, one who guides men's destinies, and who at the same time in his heart obeys God without any
resistance. But here there comes into play the "tragic law" that state
and Church are two separate things, that the "state of perfection"
as a *form* is bound to the Church (although this does not mean that
the *substance* of perfection, namely, selfless love, need not be aimed
at by everyone) and that the ruler who is bound by the laws of this
earthly world is, according to Paul's words, a "divided" man (1 Cor
7:34) just as much as the married man who remains bound to the
laws of eros: "The king ought to have had the experience of being a monk and to rule with this experience." But even if he "uses
the things of this world as if he were not exploiting them" (1 Cor
7:31),[40] he will never be able to be "without care" (1 Cor 7:32),
"without care for the morrow" (Mt 6:34), and he will never be able
to turn the palace of government into a monastery. In Christ's ecclesiastical foundation, the sphere of that pure representative existence
(from the "first day" before history to the "last day" after history)
remains a circumscribed sphere, which one cannot spiritualize as one
sees fit. And there is no way of reintroducing the mediaeval ordering,
which distinguished the king through a quasi sacrament of anointing
and thus elevated the "holy kingdom" in a manner similar to that
in which marriage makes husband and wife in their flesh an image
of Christ and the Church—this was an ordering that bound Church
and state indissolubly together. "Faith" and "knowledge", "revelation" and "reason" have become increasingly autonomous (cf. First
Vatican Council, third session chap. 4: DS 3019). Precisely this ought
to delight Reinhold Schneider, because it means that only fragments
are left after the disappearance of the temptation for the Church to
take hold of the secular sword. And yet, precisely for this reason, now
is the time when the walls of monasteries are opening up and the form
of religious life is changing from its foundations upward: because it
is more deeply than ever conscious of its social and thereby of its
historical function and begins at last to understand its representative
position also in the sense of a genuine responsibility for the world,
without drawing arbitrary and timid boundaries between monastery
and world, Church and world, and without asserting any incompatibility between obedience, which remains its essential form, and gen-

---

[40] 37:82.

uine responsibility and the power to make decisions. How could a Christian ever bear responsibility other than in obedience to God, to Christ and the Church, indeed, precisely out of the force of this obedience? And so, unnoticed, the image of the *nonresistant* man, that is, of the obedient man, takes center stage once more, as the image of the one who has his position in the life of the counsels but must solidify his effective power so that he becomes a model for the rulers of this world and those who bear responsibility. It is he who continuously holds his "left cheek", his availability and his vulnerability, to God and to the Church; where the Spirit in a particular situation tells him to do so, he will not withdraw this cheek from the earthly foe. The swords cut through him most sharply of all, and yet he will be a possible man in the coming age of the Church because he is formed by Christ.

The Thief on the Left

It is only where we have the confluence of confession as a social and historical power, of the state of being chosen for responsibility for others, of nonresistance and of suffering as vicarious representation for all that the form of the other thief, the one on the left, emerges out of the darkness of its past—mysterious, mighty and demanding. This figure never ceased to occupy Reinhold Schneider; here he is once again, this time more deeply than ever, following in the tracks of the Russians, in the passionate interest in the salvation of his brother—of all brothers. This motif appears already in the essay on "The Thieves without the Lord" ("Die Schächer ohne den Herrn"),[1] suggested by a crucifix that was destroyed in the Flemish revolt in 1566, alongside which the other two crosses had remained standing, unharmed:

> Now even the repentant thief was lost . . . and how lost was the cross of the blasphemer! The mediator had disappeared, the center was empty; in vain one thief looked up to the heights, while the other turned his cramped body to the earth. Like the redeemed, so the damned, too, ought to have their place in God's ordering, the sphere of which also contains hell. Total silence is the reply to the hope of the one thief and

---

[1] 18:262–66, 263f.

to the blasphemy of the other. And if God does not exist, how empty would be the pathos of those who deny God!

After the War, a whole homily, *Der Andere*,[2] is devoted to the thief on the left, under the general title *Sein Reich*: "The Savior, who came for all, in order to save all, has a man who is lost as the companion of his sufferings." The "dreadful decision" about man is made on the Cross: whether he is saved or totters, breaks down and collapses. "Let me repeat: it is a cross, and not even the one who denies it frees himself from the cross of this one death of ours, this salvation of ours." And again, in the *Sieben Worte des Herrn*: "The man who denies is crucified too, for there is no escaping the cross", and for this reason: "Hoping against all hope, we should make sacrifices and struggle against the cross that is without grace, and against its power."[3]

The Russian element is that the Christian in his Church cannot set himself against the others as a party, the party of the saved. This is the entire wisdom of Leskov's Father Cyriacus, and it is in keeping with this that he forms his mission among the pagans. The Lord died both for those on the left and for those on the right. Were the Church a party, she would put up an earthly resistance; the fact that she does not do so strengthens the Russian in his solidarity with those on the left; and he would not have the strength to suffer for all as he does unless there existed the hope "that all will be saved".[4] Reinhold Schneider agrees: "Our misery is so great that it is impossible for one single individual to be helped. It is only possible for all to be helped."[5] He opposes the incorrigible egoism of the West in these words: "It will scarcely be possible for us to gain the salvation of our soul if we forget that this is the salvation of all."[6] And again: "It will scarcely be possible for a soul to be saved if it is concerned only with its own salvation; it will scarcely be possible for a people to do justice to what it is meant to be if it sets its goals without consideration for the unity of the world."[7] It is never a question of the Church as one part but always of the world—but always in such a way that this world is confronted with "the uttermost seriousness of decision".[8] "At every hour of history, Christ's message is for *the world*. Since the

---

[2] 57:10–15, 14.
[3] 88c:16–20.
[4] 89:10.
[5] 83:104.
[6] 83:90.
[7] 77:10.
[8] 62:30.

appearing of the Lord, the whole world has a right to redemption."[9]
This is why a Christian prayer can never be anything other than universal: "Prayer is always for all, for the whole world and its salvation,
for which He sacrificed himself."[10] And just as prayer, according to
the Lord's commandment, *must* embrace all, so hope *may* embrace
all: "We cannot give up the hope that even those who use their last
strength to turn away from you die within the circle of salvation and
that you find ways to the lost and build bridges where we see only
gulfs."[11] And he addresses Our Lady of Sorrows: "Even those who
did not recognize the truth in your Son are allowed to come to you.
All the dead lie before you."[12] In the text *Über den Selbstmord* (On
Suicide): "And so we do not give up the apparently lost members of
the one life. It is possible that one who is tortured throws himself
over death and lands in front of God's throne."[13] He prays to the
Lord: "Let not one soul be missing!"[14] For "how could we bear to
see that one of our brothers was missing, one whom we might love
and embrace with the love of God?" "The creation will not recover
from the fall of one of its members into the abyss. Everything that is
created, the whole of creation, is to return home to the Father through
Christ. The time is lost if it no longer knows this path of the return
home for one single creature."[15] "As long as a man is deeply moved
by Christ, he cannot resign himself to the perishing of one single
member of the creation. . . . This is why there can be no consolation
for Peter's pain at the loss of a single one of the sheep entrusted to
him."[16] "The Christian life is a life for all, the beginning of reverent
and warm participation in Jesus Christ's work of unification. This is
why the Christian cannot keep silent about the danger that one soul
could be lost."[17] "If one soul falls into the hand of the enemy with
full, as it were, visible certainty, then God's kingdom is lacerated, and
no one is able to measure what this occurrence means for eternal life,
but also for life on earth."[18] But "grace can come out of all guilt;
perhaps this is why there is so much guilt in the world."[19] And thus
the divine hope always has a social dimension: "If we cannot hope

[9] 62:142.
[10] 114:5.
[11] 29:55.
[12] 29:58.
[13] 79:39.
[14] 82:52.

[15] 112:38f.
[16] 51:72, 73.
[17] 62:84.
[18] 92:42.
[19] 12:181.

and plead for the damned, how are we then to hope and plead for ourselves! There exists only one single guilt."[20] "We can only pray that he awaits us on the other shore after the terrible crossing of the river—friend and foe, waiting for all of us, all of us."[21]

The unity of guilt means that the brothers each become guilty in relation to the other, as this is described by the Letter to the Romans in the verses about election and rejection: but the one "rejected" is always a function of the one chosen and exists for his sake, as in the "drama about the salvation of Egypt", where Pharaoh is a function of Moses; the hardening of Pharaoh's heart is the cause of the height of Moses' mission. This is *one* destiny, one cloud: " 'On the one side the cloud was dark, and on the other side it lit up the night' (Ex 14:20). Here we have the ultimate dimension of this destiny: the mystery of darkness is also the mystery of light."[22] God and Satan do not have the same power;[23] rather, the power that God has bestowed for a time on Satan works to the advantage of those whom God has chosen. But the one "chosen" likewise exists for the sake of the one rejected: so that grace may leap over the gulf separating them, through the blow the one rejected receives from the one chosen.[24] Thus Stephen and Paul stand over against one another; More tells his king that they belong together in the same way,[25] and the same is true of all whose relationship is that of persecutors and persecuted:

> We are united for eternity
> and must come to God hand in hand:
> when I kill you, I ask for your life.[26]

Thus the author modifies the inscription on an old sword of judgment: "When I lift this sword, I wish eternal life for the poor sinner." In the Letter to the Romans, the election and rejection of the persons leads into the election and rejection of the peoples (and was only a preliminary image leading to this), viz. the Jews and the Gentiles, and then the synagogue and the Church, and then again the Church for the sake of Israel, so that Israel as a whole may be saved. Each people takes the place of the other people, so that *all* may learn to fear and that all may be saved by the same grace, after they have been handed

---

[20] 29:39.
[21] 123:229.
[22] 52:103.
[23] 91:10.

[24] 70:41.
[25] 34:54.
[26] 69:29.

over to the same disobedience (Rom 11:1–36). Nothing is so social, nothing so intimately linked together, as these elections and nonelections in the sphere of the revelation. This goes so far that even the heretics have their place in the New Covenant: "Even those who rebelled had a commission and a mysterious right—though assuredly not the commission and the right that they took for themselves without permission. They had a word to say that gave new life to ardor; and they had a right to a response, but this right was not always respected. And with this right, and this ministry full of suffering, they have a claim to the Church's active interest in the salvation of their souls, to the unceasing prayer of the Church."[27] And if the light ones and the dark ones stand beside one another in this way, both with a commission—in utterly different, indeed, incommensurable ways— then it is less difficult to see behind all of them—the light ones and the dark ones—the one Son of all men who performs penance for all.[28] Indeed, one sees him precisely in the dark persecutor, for in his act of persecution he leads to Christ.[29] And there exists a still deeper mystery between them: "Sometimes expiation is made for the one called through the guilt of the one rejected."[30] Or as Francis of Paola says about the dying king in the *Tod des Mächtigen*: "There are holy men and women who have atoned for the errors of their brothers through their suffering and perseverance; and it seems that there are also men who experience all the sin of the world and the power of evil and bring this to birth in their life and their guilt; they, too, suffer for all, and we must all atone for their guilt and offer God a satisfaction for the terrible insult that such an existence is."[31] This is a genuinely Russian idea, which does not forget the social dimension even in the terrible isolation of the wicked man. The destinies of men do not stand juxtaposed to each other like private properties; there exists a communism of grace, so that destinies represent one another, as is shown in the story "Die himmlischen Wohnungen".[32] The destinies of the peoples represent one another in this way too, as we see in the destiny of the Jews.[33] We do not have an overview, "yet all the notes we hear stand on the invisible musical score of the great harmony".[34]

---

[27] 81:27.
[28] Ibid.
[29] 112:54.
[30] 12:93.

[31] 67:77.
[32] 94:7–19.
[33] 88c:38.
[34] 81:36.

It suffices for the believer to know that: "By believing, we take up a share in responsibility for everyone and for everything; we cannot profess faith in Christ without sharing through prayer and work in the redemption of all men. Since the message is addressed to the world, one who renounces the world cannot be a hearer and bearer of the message."[35] A faith that neglected the universality of hope would already be a faith that produced impoverishment and resignation and that tended in the direction of sectarianism.

Russian Christianity will never base this hope on the paltriness of guilt (as Western liberal Christianity would tend to do) but only on the grace of God and the unlimited effect of the suffering of our brother Jesus. For it is in relation to him that all have directly incurred guilt: "We have all condemned you; we have denied you in our life, with our words and thoughts."[36] All of us stand around the Way of the Cross: "and the Son looked with his mighty glance into the shy eyes of every single one who stood along the way".[37] Nor is there any debtor who does not die in the face of the one who bore his debt:

> Those who die far from you, in gravest sin,
> and turn their face from you even in death,
> they die nevertheless before your face.[38]

Christ is not only the Lord over all the world who lays claim to all lives and to all peoples, the Lord of the entire creation[39] ("his endeavor excludes no soul, no creature, no thing, no being");[40] it is through his work of redemption that he is king and inherits, along with the world, all its sufferings, its death and its guilt, so that this becomes his property. "In the last hours, you yourself became pain; you yourself are in the depths of every pain."[41] In the state of abandonment by God, he suffered on behalf of all "the believing despair, the despairing faith",[42] and from then onward he is present in all misery, even that which is farthest from God.[43] So Leo IX prays among the corpses on the devastated field of battle: "My God, whither have you summoned their souls? Have you received their suffering gra-

---

[35] 83:89, 90.
[36] 29:9.
[37] 35:60.
[38] 69:32.
[39] 83:88f.

[40] 91:64; cf. 112:15.
[41] 88c:5.
[42] 88c:33.
[43] 81:90.

ciously? Has it become their salvation? And even if they should have died in sin, nevertheless their suffering was true until the bitter end; basically, they have all suffered for you. Their pain has brought them closer to you; they have become like you, and you will see a hidden resemblance."[44] For it is Christ himself who prays along with us the words: "Forgive us our trespasses."[45]

The unbounded character of the power of Christ's suffering gives the good man his advantage in principle vis-à-vis the evil man. Through Christ's suffering, Satan was thrown down from heaven, from eternity, onto the limited earth, and his rage is so great because his time is short. "Satan has fallen from heaven; he is no longer what he once was."[46] "The hatred of the abyss will never fall silent, precisely because this prince is judged and no longer possesses anything; all he can expect is this temporal dimension."[47] This was why hell was so agitated when Christ was on the Cross, because the dark powers "sensed the end of their kingdom".[48] Through the essence of the judgment of the Cross, where the one condemned without resistance is the infinite God, while the accuser is the evil that has lost its power and has been reduced to temporality, the eternal decision has been made, and history is the reflection of this. "Basically, all has been decided, and yet everything must be won by struggle from hour to hour."[49] In regard to the judgment, confidence must be dominant, for the judgment is the shadow of grace; and God no longer judges without also bestowing his blessing.[50] The poems in *Die letzten Tage* proclaim "God's punitive patience"[51] and say that the "fear that shudders lethally through us" will "be grace's final fire of love".[52] *Die neuen Türme* sings even more boldly:

> Then will his word light up this time,
> and the damned will be messengers of blessing,
> and those rejected will be his children.[53]

But hope is to remain what it is: a confidence in grace, not a desire to know and see completely the paths of God: a confidence in the boundlessness of grace and a sure knowledge in faith that in the pres-

---

[44] 34:29.

[45] 23:43.

[46] 62:31.

[47] 51:66.

[48] 29:22.

[49] 51:66.

[50] 62:13; 34:31.

[51] 66:15.

[52] 66:32.

[53] 69:41.

ence of God, evil is untruth, nonbeing, the self-consumption whose smoke rises up for ever. The "unhappy spirit" is addressed as "Death of your own self, fire of guilt that is stoked by guilt!"[54]

> But that which is nothing draws its life from nothing.
> Those who believe, see how death takes death's scepter away from it,
> and the abyss becomes subject to God the Lord.[55]

A Christology reminiscent of Soloviev crowns the whole: Christ, who has had the total experience of the world as God and man through his descent into the world, the Cross and hell, wins the entire creation as his body—and it is precisely for this reason that it is murder when the members of the one Body "have mortal conflicts with each other".[56] The beams of the Cross reach over all boundaries, and the "overwhelming superior power of love's suffering" draws up all the peoples to the heart of Christ.[57] In this power is made known "the superior power of love"; through this, "hell is overcome again and again";[58] finally, Christ is all.

> One and only fire that kindles the spirits,
> sharing out the rays in order to unite them,
> consuming the world in order to raise it up.[59]

---

[54] 66:28.
[55] 66:30.
[56] 98:90.
[57] 35:51.
[58] 35:56.
[59] 69:33.

GERMANY—PENANCE

Turning Around

When he returned home with the booty of the North—historical guilt and historical confession—the author found his native land in the worst possible situation: the fire of despair and destruction, which he had once sensed in advance as a presentiment on behalf of others, had now become universal. The country was ruled by intellectual suicides who always carried their poison around on their persons. "Surely no worse fate can befall a people, and thereby the world, than the rule of a man who is secretly resolved to destroy himself, whether consciously or unconsciously. There is virtually nothing that can stop him from generating death. Those who meet him fall into his trap; those who celebrate him praise death without wanting to."[1] The author follows the rise of the terror from year to year, and he warns (as long as his voice is permitted to be heard) in strong sonnets that often recall the force of George's indignation (*Jetzt ist des Heiligen Zeit, Die neuen Türme*);[2] he sees the vehicle rolling without brakes into the abyss; he sees that the fire of anger and revenge has already been kindled everywhere, and when this really begins to blaze, he accompanies his fellows into the flames (the sonnets *Apokalypse, Die letzten Tage*).[3] He does this out of the strength he has received from the grace that has existed in the downfalls of history; again and again we meet the Pauline verse about the fire of judgment that consumes the work of straw but saves the worker as if through fire (1 Cor 3:15).[4] He does not want to describe but to help; this is his only desire to such a degree that he applies less aesthetic care to the form of the work in order to be present everywhere with his word; where the

---

[1] 79:21.
[2] 35; 69.
[3] 58; 66.
[4] 66:16; 69:52; 63:8.

ruins pile up on every side, he no longer seeks any beauty other than
that of truth and of love. This allowed him to give his voice literally
the strongest echo in Germany: "When other words of human consolation stood clumsily before the greatness of the suffering and often
seemed to be mere pious phrases, his words and verses penetrated,
opening for men's hearts the sphere of an invisible reality in such a
way that it became more perceptible than all brutal power: the sphere
of the living God."[5] The service that Reinhold Schneider was able
to perform for contemporary Germany in its hardest hour bears witness that he was profoundly in the right and that he truly belonged
to the present moment; the German people must never forget this
service, which he carried out as a believing Christian and Catholic
but equally as a man of knowledge, one who had looked into the
abysses of historical guilt and of the historical path back to the truth.
All the help that he could offer was to point to the truth of grace,
which demands and includes the truth of confession, of insight and
of repentance. What he had learned was at once demanded of him
as the most urgent message to his age. The only hope of salvation
left was in the penance that turns around and makes confession. The
bombs had opened craters in the fields and in men's souls: things that
had been utterly hidden rose up in the light through the judgment of
heaven, and only something small was demanded, namely, the confession of what was public in any case. The penance, and almost the
new work itself, lay in this and in the consequence of insight and
repentance. All that counted was the grace of truth. Nothing should
be hushed up, nothing glossed over; one must look the inexorable in
the face and bear the birthmark of disgrace as a grace; nothing should
be forgotten, but rather everything should be recalled exactly—when
one had sinned, how often and since when; one should not side-step
in any direction but stand firm under the judgment of truth: this was
now the only path of transformation. It would not be a process of
nature but grace that comes from the endless treasury of the Cross.

The people are now to do what the individual does in sacramental confession. They must begin by seeing their "Führer" and taking good note of his figure, not forgetting him—they must see his

[5] Heinrich Kreutz, S.J., "Macht und Gnade: Zur Werkgestalt Reinhold Schneiders", *Stim-men der Zeit* 140 (1947): 241–58.

facelessness,[6] how the word rotted and perished through him, how
he corrupted every silence and contemplation.[7] Then they must consider his collapse into the abyss,[8] the end of a continuous, unstop-
pable collapse, of a cataract of all good things and all values.[9] In this
revelation of the abyss, each one should recognize the demon as a reality and learn to fear him as a power[10] that also has the force to take
possession of a people and use them as a body.[11] This mirror ought
to allow everyone to recognize anew what it means to be guilty and
not to deny the fact "that guilt can occur only where there is a context".[12] No one should dare to deny his share in guilt. Even one who
does not believe in original sin, even one who is not conscious of
any dark deed, should not hold himself excused: one "who believed
even only one single time in the right of this powerful man" is not
pure in thoughts or attitudes.[13] "No one, no spiritual and no secular authority, has any right to anticipate through a surface decision
from above the question of the internal participation of the individual, thus suffocating the conscience."[14] Only One on earth is without
guilt: and it is precisely he who took all guilt upon himself. The act
of shifting the guilt from one's own shoulders is a sure sign of guilt.
The closer one stands to the truth—the saints are the closest—the
more willing is one to recognize one's share in guilt. And there is no
distribution of guilt that would relieve the individual of his burden,
no chance to point out that others are guilty "too".[15] Not even the
young people who feel themselves to be victims and want to have
nothing more to do with the past that they themselves did not shape
can extricate themselves from the noose. In the future, they will be
the people that *have* this past: one cannot be a German without a
historical inheritance.[16] The urgent appeals to young people make
the demand that they bear witness to a responsibility vis-à-vis history by sharing in bearing and expiating the guilt, contributing their
help to the process of clarification and purification in such a way that
the past can take its place in the new reality as something good, some-

---

[6] 52:1ff.; 61:8; 69:25.

[7] 51:8; 52:120.

[8] 69:14.

[9] 61:14.

[10] 52:5; 61:29f.

[11] 70:102f.

[12] 91:43f.; 61:9.

[13] 61:21.

[14] 61:44; 91:26f.

[15] 51:144.

[16] 51:143f.; 52:79ff.; 78; 98:50.

thing cleansed and sifted. Each one must represent his people.[17] Nor
is the word to the mourners, who have lost everything, soft: it is
as radiantly hard as grace itself. It points into the truth of guilt but
also into the blessed truth of penance: it is here that the message of
nonresistance (against the God who sits in judgment) holds true with
unlimited force. Only out of the defenselessness of the hour, out of
its patience, out of bearing that which is unbearable, can the new
strength grow;[18] out of the risk of meeting oneself without lies can
the new truthfulness in relation to the historical task grow. Reinhold
Schneider is aware that these words are "undesirable", but no one
will prevent him from speaking them.[19] He has the courage not only
to demand that all make confession but to do what used to be called
"public *culpa*"—he confesses in the name of all;[20] he himself goes
ahead of the others with the example of the historical confession that
he demands of his *Alexander*. The absolution of the individual has a
retroactive effect on his life; the absolution of history redeems the
centuries from their curse. And because it is the hour of the social
dimension,[21] man is prepared today to recognize that he cannot atone
for himself without history: he must include the historical element in
his own confession of guilt, and he must take on the historical task
in his own good resolve.

The present day is an objective confession in its entire form: the
inside has turned outward, and the fruit that ripened long ago is born
at last.

> Now what is hidden becomes true. The wicked word
> spoken by a long-decayed mouth takes on form.
> A curse on the watchmen, who heard it sluggishly!
> A curse upon us, who have destroyed ourselves![22]

But the involuntary revelation of guilt is already the situation of judgment. Thus it is the last time of all—the chance to change the judgment once more through a voluntary confession. And as the penitent
calls on the Holy Spirit, so that he may see his guilt in the light of

---

[17] 52:82f.; 76:20.

[18] 51:15; 79:14; 80:5, 12; 52:92; 54:11; 69:45.

[19] 80:7; 83:27; 91:43.

[20] 91:134; 91:142ff.

[21] 80:6f.

[22] 69:46.

God, so the new penitent appeals to the "strong spirits of high-minded days", the old men of prayer at the origin of the people and of their history, to "bear witness" to this inheritance in the light of God in such a way that it may present itself to the eyes of his contemporaries in the way that God intended it,[23] in a vision that shows the falling-away. In the light of this affirmation, it is now a question of seeing the negation from the beginning, as it swells through the ages: the "contradiction from the outset",[24] the ancient German nihilism that breathes already through the sagas and the Nibelungen,[25] the congenital German desire to be like God.[26] In the course of this confession, *man* must appear *on trial before history*,[27] just as history must appear on trial before the judgment of the Christian man, for naturally, this claim can be made only by the Christian, not in his own name, but in the name of Christ. The decisive question for the German spirit is that of its attitude to Christ. *Die Heimkehr des Deutschen Geistes* (The return home of the German spirit)[28] can only be a return home to Christ. Only Christ, who is the Spirit (2 Cor 3:17), can test and discern the spirits, "whether they are from God; for many false prophets have gone out into the world. By this we know the Spirit of God: every spirit that confesses that Jesus Christ has come in the flesh is of God" (1 Jn 4:1–2).[29] Thus the historical responsibility of the creative spirits is emphasized very forcefully, and the contrary assertion (which often suited the Germans) that the levels of art, of thinking and of intellectual creation lie above the level of power is attacked as a betrayal of the Spirit.[30] Time has disclosed the ultimate consequences of that dualism which was Schneider's own starting point and which he then struggled hard to overcome; the German disproportion to reality has borne every evil fruit. The farther aesthetics and ethics, ethics and politics once stood from one another, the more inseparably are they now bound together. The ethical and political aspect of all intellectual aesthetics must be brought to light. One cannot build anything further on something that is unfinished. The work of insight is the basis of the new mission.

---

[23] 69:47.

[24] 88c:41.

[25] 112:58.

[26] 62:110–15.

[27] 61.

[28] 54.

[29] 54, cf. motto.

[30] 52:23ff.; 51:3.

Insight

It is a thankless task to give a sketch of Reinhold Schneider's critical achievement here; all one could offer would be a scaffolding of judgments and evaluations, and the effect of such an assemblage would inevitably be pedantic. One should read the work and see for oneself the weight of his words, above all *Dämonie und Verklärung*.[1] One thing is astonishing: that we find nowhere in Schneider's total *oeuvre* a thorough confrontation with Luther and the Reformation, which had been the starting point for Hugo Ball in his "Kritik der deutschen Intelligenz" and the "Folgen der Reformation". In the early years, this is the tragic counterweight to the Roman ordering of the empire; in the later years, he always begins with the "consequences" themselves, in the age of Weimar and Idealism. Schneider himself begins here; he has deep and indelible experience of the "consequences". But the historian Schneider has good reasons for paying so much attention to literature, for it was here that the point of deviation lay that drew the spirit away from its responsibility within history. The author who would have had to utter the innermost element of history[2] landed alongside it in the Weimar era.[3] For Kant, the historical is "something quite indifferent, which one can treat as one wishes".[4] And Fichte says: "Only the metaphysical gives blessedness, not in the least the historical—all it does is to make one intelligent."[5] Thus this whole epoch passes by the historicity of Christ and of his Church too, diverting their essential substance into a suprahistorical ideality. Lessing already does this, introducing the Faustian ideal, "the unease of the eternal process of becoming", with the ideal of eternal seeking, because he cannot accept the absoluteness of the truth of Christ within history. *Lessings Drama*[6] fills out the picture by showing that there is no more place in this worldview, with its explicitly bourgeois character, for a king and for the divine ordering that is posited with him, for genuine tragedy, or thereby for a reconciliation that is more than compassion. "The drama presupposes a total decisiveness in relation to the last things." "It is strange how this mighty, clear

---

[1] 90.
[2] 9:395.
[3] 7:288, 298ff.

[4] Quotation, 54:1.
[5] Quotation, 54:38.
[6] 54:17–28; 100.

spirit ends up in indeterminate, vacillating contradictoriness."[7] The
subsequent effects are fatal: "an onward rush of that which is essentially bourgeois, of the moral as opposed to the ethical, of demands
made by a political class, a refusal to be open to the totality of the
powers of earth and of heaven—this is what is communicated to the
historical drama of the German classical period."[8]

There does indeed live a feeling for the transcendent in Weimar
and in Königsberg,[9] "the belief that our Being and action must be
determined on the basis of the spirit"; but the genuine transcendence
is missing, as we see most clearly in the lack of a serious concept of
evil (something that remains present in English and Spanish drama
and in the English and the French novel).[10] Thus man no longer genuinely stands between heaven and hell. In the critique of *Faust* (*Fausts
Rettung*,[11] *Im Schatten Mephistos*),[12] in which Schneider summarizes his
entire assessment of Goethe, and in the critique of *Wallenstein* ("Wal-
lensteins Verrat"),[13] the chief objections are recapitulated. *Faust*, constructed on ultimate contradictions and giving feeling priority over
truth, retains a corrupting ambiguity in its denouement: Goethe does
indeed save himself *from* Faustianism, but he thrusts the German spirit
into Faustianism through his work. He believes in grace, but this does
not become truth in Faust, who remains closed until the last. Nothing
of repentance and rebirth can be seen; thus the suspicion remains that
Faust is saved, not despite, but because of his blind error. Here too,
the ordering of the imperial court remains a nebulous fantasy: it is
not sufficient to generate a genuine action, let alone a tragedy. Only
the figure of Mephisto is wholly alive; and what does it mean, when
all the strong words come from the father of lies? Nothing else than
the prevention of every encounter with oneself on the basis of truth.
But Schiller's highest dramatic work likewise remains in a hopeless
ambiguity: it is a question of treachery vis-à-vis emperor and empire,
but this is committed by a great man, and the great man enkindles
ecstatic admiration and love in the idealist Max Piccolomini. Wallenstein wants to overthrow the emperor or "to shake the power that sits

---

[7] 100:19, 23.
[8] 100:26.
[9] 52:62ff.
[10] 52:147–49.

[11] 92:8.
[12] 63; 92:5–13.
[13] 92:13–33.

calmly and securely on the throne, resting in its obsolete sacred possessions, firmly established in custom". His words are self-deception,
high words are at the service of naked power; but "it is the author,
in the form of Max, who admires the hero or accompanies him with
quaking and lamentation; indeed, he changes himself into Wallenstein
and always begins to speak out of him when the hero feels compelled
to accuse himself." [14] Wallenstein is not in the truth:

> He is too bad to be good, too good to be bad, too cunning to be able to
> call himself a dream, with too much imagination for his artifice to be able
> to make him happy, too selfish and at the same time too self-contented;
> he is voluntarily and involuntarily untrue to his own self, and thereby
> —to reverse Polonius' words—untrue to everyone; he thinks where
> he ought to feel and feels where he ought to think; he does not take
> on himself the political guilt, the guilt of world history, for which he
> unquestionably must bear responsibility, but takes on in a certain sense
> a "beautiful" guilt, guilt in relation to the heart; . . . he always equips
> himself with a gesture that is pleasing.

Thus he deceives himself even "en route to his last sleep . . . as Faust
deceives himself before his own open grave. He is Faust's true relative", [15] one who prepares the way for historical chaos. And it may
often seem "as if Wallenstein's puzzling figure were walking ahead of
our people . . . with a similar significance and power of seduction and
expression in the political-historical sphere as Faust has in relation to
religion and thought". [16] Here, too, the antithetic power, the emperor,
is not truly alive: the tragedy of the rebel does not take place in the
force-field of the imperial ordering. And as the empire of the past
finds no one to give it form in Weimar (there is a weaker, epigonic
form only in Grillparzer, and even there the bourgeois level is seldom
transcended), so the present day, the revolution, is not mastered. [17] In
Schiller's many letters "there is very seldom a word about the historical events of the period. As far as is possible at all, no mention is
made of the collapse of empires, military campaigns and battles and
the threat of new clashes of the powers, the change of forms of the

---

[14] 92:22.
[15] 92:26.
[16] 92:29.
[17] Goethe: 52:31–34; 63:42f.; 91:130f.; Schiller: 50:95; Schiller's renunciation: 52:7–16.

state, or the names of the men who are involved in the action; a proud and mighty will persistently pushes the political-historical into the background." Schneider does not in the least overlook Schiller's high values and always finds words of reverent acknowledgment for what is noble in Schiller—his ethical sense, the endeavor to grasp the dimension of universal history, the struggle for the noble element in the image of man, the example of restless creativity.[18] But he prefers to turn to the Romantics when it is a question of mastering the historical situation through the spirit.

Schneider no longer turns to Fichte, to whom the blessed life seems attainable at every point in time without any connection to history,[19] or to Hegel's God in the process of becoming, who justifies that which is becoming and that which exists at each moment and in whom "no barrier of death separated the theater of world history, where the spirit 'is in its most concrete reality', from eternal glory",[20] but turns instead (despite all his reservations) to the old Schelling and his decisive turning to history, even if the battle between revelation and philosophy has not been fought to its finish in Schelling. Schelling knew that "The real substance of Christianity is nothing other than the *person* of Christ. Christ is not the teacher, as people often say, or the founder, he is the *substance* of Christianity." His Incarnation, his dying and his Resurrection are the meaning, not only of history, but also of the creation.[21] And now the tradition of the nineteenth century—which is our own tradition and which we cannot throw overboard, for otherwise it will come back unasked and unseparated —is investigated in search of true helpers. Here everything is indeed "open and fragmentary; the Germans lack a solid house." "But perhaps the less glorious names can give the German people much better help."[22] Not Hölderlin, whose tragic relationship to Christ Schneider portrays with reverence, while the guilt for this is laid on the shoulders of the Christians, the guilt for the scandal that the poet found in the Church. For Hölderlin turned decisively away from the people and its history, "feeling that his great task was the healing of nature, the rediscovery of a sanctification that had taken place and that continued to exist in secret. His tragic fate was that he did not

---

[18] 50:95, 106.
[19] 54:33ff.
[20] 54:48.

[21] 54:60f.; 62:67.
[22] 91:131; 90:69–98.

see the one basis of sanctification in the relationship of Christ to the
creation, in Christ's life on earth and in the sacrament",[23] no matter
how much he circled again and again around these mysteries until
the end of his life. He knew that sacrifice was necessary, to make
expiation for the godless present age (*Empedokles*); his sacrifice, the
achievement of his life as a poet, remains pure and exalted; and yet
this cannot oblige us to accept what he proclaims, since the same un-
godly disruption cuts across his proclamation. He sought unity with
all his powers, but it could not be found on his path: there is no path
leading from the classical gods to Christ. "But perhaps it would be
possible to begin from Christ and find a relationship to the powers
of the ancient world, whether these have now been overthrown or
continue to work in their place."[24] The picture of Novalis becomes
full of light; through all the fantasy of Romanticism, Schneider sees
genuine history shimmering into view in *Ofterdingen*: Italy as the theater of a great chivalrous war, the pilgrimage to Jerusalem, the Orient,
the open sea, and once again the business of empire at the court of
Emperor Frederick II—and all this on the basis of the descent into
the realm of the dead, into that which is both earthly and heavenly:
"The one who has gone down into the grave will truly be powerful
as the shaper of the world and of history."[25] Even if everything in
Hardenberg's historical image remains fragmentary, nevertheless "the
ascending lines, which must meet in the crown, become visible everywhere."[26] At the imperial court, according to Tieck's narrative of
the supposed continuation, "the greatest splendor and the true great
world appear. The German character and German history are made
clear. Henry talks with the emperor about government, about the
empire—obscure speeches about America and East India. The attitudes of a prince. A mystical emperor". But all this is given its place
around the Church as midpoint: "The Church is the house where
history dwells", says Novalis, and Schneider continues: "Just as there
is no salvation outside the Church, so there is no history outside her,
no action before the Judge in the expectation of eternal life; nor is
there any binding and ordering in the highest sense outside her. Only
those who are summoned together by Christ become one, become

---

[23] 90:83.   [25] 90:109.
[24] 90:94.   [26] 90:110.

a people in time for eternity." Naturally, "Christendom or Europe" is only a "drunk departing glance" won from the poet's death wish, and yet he is right: "Only religion can awaken Europe to life again", and his highest dream, "the reconciliation of thought, and especially of the German spirit, with the Redeemer", remains his most serious bequest.[27] History and the poet's responsibility before history are the basis of the poetical ethos of Arnim (*Die Sendung Achims von Arnim*);[28] his work never took on life among the people and remains question-able as poetry, but in its ultimate intention it can still provide orien-tation today; in "Gräfin Dolores" we have the will "to make posses-sion of all that hitherto belonged to the noble houses", introducing a new, chivalrous way of thinking and living; in the fragment "Die Kronenwächter" we have the endeavor to replace the rigid tradition that clung tightly to the old world of the empire by the free crown working in the present day. Arnim fails; he was too lonely—"the whole people ought to have helped its poet, ought to have shared with him in the work of poetic composition." In the same way, the talent of Uhland (*Ludwig Uhland*)[29] was not adequate for his historical mission; yet it is his greatness that he "recognized and described the poetical as a historical power", not only by taking the aspiration of the people seriously as poet and literary historian, but by refusing to separate in his own person and lifework the poet and the politician: "The ethical existence of the people and through the medium of the people is a concern the artist cannot renounce and great art has never renounced; here, art and politics that are conscious of their responsi-bility are united in their historical hour." This same point sheds light on the picture of Chamisso (*Chamissos Geschichtserfahrung*)[30] and on that of the darker Platen (*Platen*),[31] both of whom look deeply into historical existence from their stance of restraint and melancholy.

But the ultimate criterion for the fulfillment of a poetic mission and for its fruitfulness in the fellowship is not the thematic dealing with historical material but the preservation of the poetic existence in the inseparability of poetics and ethics, in the force-field between God and the abyss, between the transfiguring light from on high and the demonic fire from below. Schneider remains faithful here to his

---

[27] 90:111ff.
[28] 113:133(7)–148(22).
[29] 113:159(33)–177(51).

[30] 18:290–301.
[31] 18:39–45.

decidedly transcendent methodology: over and above all the immanent criteria for good and bad art (he does not deny these, but they
are not so much what concerns him), he asks about the last weight on
the scale of eternity: it is here that the one is justified, while the other
is found to be too light. He derives the right to such an evaluation
from the gospel, which promises the Christian the possibility of the
discernment of spirits, the sense of smell for good and rotten fruit.
And where we have the possibility, we already have the necessity; a
Christian must at least have this discernment as *one factor* in his consideration and evaluation of works of the human spirit. In Schneider,
harsh decisiveness in the act of judging goes together with great reverence and reserve; his Yes and No can cut like a sword, but he never
gives up what he has rejected; he leaves the last word of judgment
to the Lord and entrusts the unsuccessful fruit to him. The flames
of ruin flicker around Kleist (*Kleists Ende*);[32] when faith is lost, the
victory falls to hatred (in *Hermannsschlacht*), to the demonic force of
the destructive eros (in *Penthesilea*, against which *Käthchen* stands only
as a dialectical opposite number) and, indeed, to the conscious abandonment of eternal salvation (in *Findling*, "the hatred of the one who
has decided in full consciousness for damnation, in order to torment
for all eternity the one who had insulted him"), His world is without
grace: "In him, German Idealism already failed completely; the values this posited turned to ashes in the flames of the demonic power,
which consumed even the Prussian form, the education and vocation
to a state."[33] Kleist reveals the "incurable *krisis* of the Prussian form":
"its excess and this heart that was never sober" are most deeply alien
to Prussia. "His work became the challenge issued by the heart to the
rigidity and narrowness of the Prussian form of life."[34] Brentano (*Die
Wende Clemens Brentanos*)[35] is set in a way paralleled perhaps only by
Droste in the midst of the force-field between heaven and the abyss:
in the period of his brilliant, Dionysian creative power, he remains
turned to what lies below, going so far as to abuse art, love, marriage and life in a demonic game; "the profligacy in Romanticism",
of which Steffens spoke, can be seen in him; the great turning to God,
which is carried out in full seriousness, can no longer save the poetic

---

[32] 90:131–65.

[33] 90:147.

[34] 90:133f.

[35] 19, reprint in 97:9–44.

work. He came "onto the market place at the eleventh hour, tired out by his journey and timid indeed, but with humble prayer"—but his word has burned up in the meantime. Lenau (*Der Katarakt. Das Schicksal Nikolaus Lenaus*)[36] could not do other than captivate Schneider through his melancholy and through his sensitivity to the suffering of nature, which revealed itself to him through this melancholy. The poems about Niagara Falls reach the heart of this sentiment about life, the thirst that the heart and the world have to be destroyed. The pain entrusted to him could have turned into grace; but the Cross, which he does indeed see, is removed and made inaccessible through veils of doubt and unbelief; the verse epics get tangled in problems he has not mastered, and his attachment to his friend's wife makes his life too meaningless and mendacious; he must fall into the power of the night. Schneider devoted the longest time to the study of Droste (*Zur Zeit der Scheide zwischen Tag und Nacht. Der Lebenskampf der Droste,*[37] *Erworbenes Erbe. Zum Gedächtnis der Droste,*[38] "Magie und Glaube. Annette von Droste-Hülshoff"),[39] for here there is no simple either/or that can cut through the knot that is tied inextricably between earthly powers that draw the poet down and the yearning for heaven that purifies her. The realm of Droste is not only an "intermediate kingdom, since day and night mingle with one another, and this is more than day and night", it is "the terrible double-faced quality of nature with its two faces; the second face is near, and perhaps there slumbers a vocation to mysticism in the woman at her solitary prayers",[40] but her "mysticism" remains broken by the necessity to seek access to the heights through the forces of nature and even through the experiences of decay, of melancholy and of guilt. The powers of nature, the dead, the patrimony of the ancient family are burdensome realities, "the special color that gleams in her world came from the abyss, just as there is no enmity between knowledge about the depths and the encounter with the demonic, on the one hand, and the transfiguration of the earthly, on the other", as long as the poet keeps making toward the light.[41] She does not spare herself in any way; she puts up the hardest, almost hopeless struggle, and yet faith always salvages itself and comes through to the Lord in whom everything is created, even

---

[36] 20, reprinted in 96:7–48; 54:70f.
[37] 22, reprinted in 97:45–88.
[38] 99.

[39] 91:65–80.
[40] 91:76.
[41] 97:55f.

the guilty heart and the dark nature.[42] She is the lonely fighter from an ancient family to whom it is congenital "to be in the forefront of the intellectual struggle": "the intellectualization of chivalry was one of her great achievements."[43] Gotthelf stands close to her, like the peasant standing near the nobleman: "Free from the dangers of German Idealism, as only very few poets of the nineteenth century were—one might almost say that only Droste had this same freedom—but in a very lonely position, he saw the coming destruction, which clothed itself in the appearance of happy achievements. He knew about the clear truth of evil and of its historical power—once again, it is only Droste who is near him there." And it is the consuming care for his people that generates his tremendous work.[44] The "*spiritus familiaris* of the one who changes horses in midstream*", the darkest poem of Droste, stands face to face with Gotthelf's "black spider": in both, the demonic power of evil has become a form, the transformations of the world through the hidden pact.

Two guiding images of particular significance arise now. Schneider is capable of distinguishing here between the structure and intention of the work and the questionable quality of what was produced; but it is already much to have wanted and begun something great. No one has survived the fight with the dragon so purely and piously as Freiherr von Eichendorff (*Der Pilger. Eichendorffs Weltgefühl,*[45] *Eichendorff: Seine Ahnung und unsere Gegenwart*);[46] he "experiences the entire enticing sweetness of the world, the powers of the deep want to hold him fast in the power of beauty." "But there is something invulnerable in his soul, . . . in all the danger, he has remained a child." This does not prevent him from being manly, with an "unconditional truthfulness that did not accept that a shadow should fall from the artificial world of art on the conduct of life, or that one could reduce in the least the seriousness of ethical responsibility by appealing to art."[47] The glory of nature is a promise of eternal life to the carefree wanderer, but he always remains watchful and sober in his song and his love. So he looks into history, into the collapse of his social class brought about by the Revolution, into the castles that are going up in flames

---

[42] 91:78–80.
[43] 99:11.
[44] 92:33–44, 35; 70:102f.
[45] 21, reprinted in 96:49–81.
[46] 113:149(23)–158(32).
[47] 21:6.

on every side: "Everything points with a bloody finger to a great, un-avoidable disaster. We are born in struggle, and we will die in strug-gle, overcome or triumphing. For a ghost of war will form itself out of the magical smoke of our culture (*Ahnung und Gegenwart*)." When he becomes active as official, scholar and poet for the restoration of Marienburg, when he finds "archetype and copy in the mentality of the spiritual knights" and, on the other hand, also leads his heroes into monasteries and lets them end their days as men of prayer, what he is concerned with is not a Romanticism remote from the world but contemporary history. He and his kindred spirits (Chamisso, A. Grün, Droste) "save what could still be saved by bearing the noble form and manner out into life from the castles where it had been formed and by keeping it unharmed in life",[48] with the presentiment "that perhaps it is only the man of prayer who can make the decisive contribution needed now."[49] Eichendorff was a great man of prayer. "The mystics have liked to speak of the spotless glass that is wedded to the light without losing its own substance: such a purity shines out of the last prayers of the poet."[50] If there is one voice with which the people ought again to become familiar, it is this voice.

Finally we have Franz Grillparzer ("Der Einsame",[51] *Im Anfang liegt das Ende. Grillparzers Epilog auf die Geschichte*).[52] As a boy, he would have liked to become a priest and monk but was struck by his fa-ther's unbelief as by a flash of lightning, losing the Catholic faith—and thereby prayer too—forever. Since he does not meet with recog-nition, he must live a life that reckons with isolation. But his art, in a secularized form, remains a priestly art, just as his themes re-main indissolubly bound to the old imperial order; he wanted to give his imperial tragedies to the people, as Shakespeare had given his nation the dramas about kings. He possesses deep insight into the essence of the crown and the transformation that the office brings about in the one who is crowned; even the contrasting picture of Ottokar is formed with superior knowledge about the true motifs

---

[48] 21:17, 15.

[49] 21:18.

[50] 21:27.

[51] 18:203–11.

[52] 55, reprinted in 90:331–75; introduction to *König Ottokars Glück und Ende*, 102m; cf. 51; 89f.

of history; here "for the first and only time, the internal essence of the empire has appeared on the German stage in the image of a great, colorful action."[53] In *Libussa*, the poet sets his sights on the highest goal: the essence of the historical is to become visible as myth, in the tragic dualism of the prophetic-female element and the male element that demands power and property, in the unavoidable descent of the pure one into turbidity, in the expiatory purification that passes through death and sacrifice, with an eschatological perspective that must necessarily remain ambiguous, incipient, uncertain in Grillparzer.

The names of the later poets and artists are not mentioned. Marée is not mentioned, Stifter very seldom, Rilke and Hofmannsthal only occasionally; Paul Ernst is greeted in an aside.[54] The rest is silence. Enough has been done for the examination of conscience. Apart from this, the Germans are surrounded by the greatest images, which are to permit them to evaluate their own work: by Greek tragedy, by Dante and Calderon,[55] and repeatedly by Shakespeare,[56] to whom Goethe too looked up as the unattainable ideal. Only that which is highest and purest can help us: through looking on it, we shall be healed, and the insight and the resolve will come to maturity that we must make a deep incision into the body of our own tradition in order to remove what is poisoned. The warning voice has done its work; will the warning be heard?

The Work

Criticism may be only one part of the new work of construction, and Schneider always intended it this way. His own work contains the elements of a radical Christian *poetics*—only what is inexorably true has some prospect of being able to put down new roots—and after a decade of "service as a Good Samaritan", which divides up Reinhold Schneider's work into small and tiny fragments, it begins to come together again in large-scale works conceived as providing ori-

---

[53] 55:33.
[54] 18:25–31.
[55] 87; 52:128f.; cf. n. 16 above, p. 69.
[56] 51:103–17; 77; 79:29f.; 91:81–92, 105–15; 98:77 (sonnet to Shakespeare), 1021 (edition of *Henry IV* with introduction).

entation after the War. After he unexpectedly entered on the task of addressing the German nation, all that he had inherited, from *Camoes* and *Philipp* up to the experience of the collapse of Germany, could be used meaningfully for the new construction.

First, the *poet*. Like the Portuguese, he has to clothe in images that unwieldy reality.[1] It is not words alone that he must provide, but gestures, deeds that can be perceived in rapid succession, images so pregnant with substance that they break out beyond themselves in a double direction, pointing back to the origin from which they derive and to the deed to which they are to give birth. A new evaluation was made of the oscillating realm of images, which had been separated from its origin and had become its unclear cipher, so that it no longer put on any pressure for realization in history—this was the danger for the Germans. The image must mediate between the God whose word it is and the man who is to realize this word. "Christ, in whom everything is created, bears the creation, man and thereby also the world of images to which the artist is directed."[2] This is why "no image is possible without transcendence, no human face can be understood except in the way it is determined by its relation to the face of the God-man, either turning toward him or denying him."[3] Images by themselves are nothing, and they "demand in a peremptory manner to be interpreted; the interpretation can succeed only to the extent that the images are brought into relation to the light of the world."[4] But this light makes the demand that one enter time; for, like the images, so the deeds of history belong to Christ: if his word can be mediated through the poet to the present generation, then this generation is summoned to action. "A word that does not compel us to ask: 'What ought we to do?' is not worth uttering; it is not a word in the real sense, no echo of the eternal Word that was in the beginning, that bears the world, in which everything is created." But this Word was also "crucified by us", so that we "must become crucified to it, if it is to become strong in us".[5] Thus art becomes a function of faith in both directions: it is "creative, active faith",[6] which cannot avoid listening to every worldly word so that it can hear the divine word and obeying the divine word in every worldly

---

[1] 55:21f.
[2] 91:78.
[3] 91:122.

[4] 81:17.
[5] 62:60, 61.
[6] 91:125.

situation. Now the poet, as one who listens to God and creates on the basis of his service of God, enters the circle of those who represent the truth: like Philip, he dies to himself and lives out of faith, in order to give birth to the form. Only on the basis of Christ, who as the Word of the Father is a Person and is intensely subjective life as the message of Another, is it possible to understand the paradox that the Christian artist must be completely submerged in the work, in the idea, which is never himself, and that nevertheless a claim is made on his entire personal existence and vitality for his activity of creation. The biography is not meant to give information about the work, which must speak for itself[7]—and yet the poet's life can help to reveal what spirit breathes in the work, the spirit from above or the spirit from below. A life that did not reveal the will to accept responsibility, to politics in the classical sense of the word, would not be capable of giving birth to responsible art. Both aspects come together in the concept of representation.

It is not possible to compel the Christian author to leave the fundamental requirement of his existence—to be in the world as one who is not of the world, to be dead to the world with Christ and to be hidden in God—so that he can carry out a Christian commission.[8] The commission exists and can be accomplished only under the shadow and likeness of the entire Christian commission. "The composition reproduces the image of life, not life itself; just as on the heights of faith the only one to win life is the one who has died and been reborn, so one can say of art in its place that the only artist to achieve the image of life and of the world is the one who has detached himself from the world, indeed, has died to it in a certain sense, and then has reentered the world in freedom, without being bothered by its gods."[9]

> Thus the power of the light that is sent
> spreads out in images, and the word will take hold of them
> when word and truth are deeply rooted in life.

> Art, thanks to renunciation,
> touches the deepest misery; time will bring it to maturity,
> but only a heart can enkindle men's hearts.[10]

---

[7] 112:9–13.
[8] 18:53.
[9] 90:108.
[10] 69:35.

And if nothing was so much desecrated in the years before the collapse as the word and its truth, it follows that the first requirement of the one who creates intellectual form is elementary reverence for the word and for its validity in life.[11] "Man can give man nothing higher than his word. And the word is the pure, appropriate echo of inner truthfulness; it is the whole man."[12] When the pure heart becomes the source of the word, it receives its force in return.

> There exists a word from which you cannot escape:
> you must perform it, but its performance is death.
> This is the misery far above all misery,
> which must begin unswervingly from within.[13]

After all this, it is logical that the word as *drama* is at the center of the new poetics; the decision of the conscience is portrayed here as a decision in favor of the truth about the world, as a decision that directly summons to action. "No other form of art can do what is expected of drama: it is an essential characteristic of drama that it summons to a Yes and No, that it brings to an end an intellectual, mental, historical process, that it does not merely reflect."[14] So the hour of drama has certainly come today. Drama is not a period piece, which provides a thesis and is linear; drama reflects the world, and is therefore spherical and self-contained. "The presence of the idea is something living and indwelling; the completed state as something closed is constructed from the toughest antitheses", and the "passion for the truth" fights its way "through all resistance, like a consuming fire" until it reaches the solution, which need not be earthly; for the real truth is not produced within time but remains eschatological: the drama has the same delta as history itself, namely, the Last Day. "The fire breaks out in the last act: the judge is present: that which is earthly is shattered on the rock of the truth. Drama is the radical carrying-out of the truth." Truth can (and ultimately will always) have an agonic and tragic character, since "truth does not offer protection or safety or peace with the world: it demands a passionate struggle; it demands that the sheltered spirit be willing to die." Precisely "the life of the Christian who truly wants to be a Christian cannot be surpassed in its measure of painful tragedy."[15] And because the Christian author of

---

[11] 52:17–22.
[12] 78:12.
[13] 98:69.

[14] 100:27.
[15] 112:21–26.

drama is called to the place where truth is necessarily the realization
of history, and he cannot separate his existence from his work, Ibsen
is correct to say: "The act of composition means holding the day of
judgment on oneself." "For he has in himself the world that submits
to the truth as its judgment. As he stands here today before the judge
with all his characters, so will the world one day stand before the
judge."[16] But the possibility of making the truth present like this belongs almost exclusively to the future: "The dramatic-tragic substance
of the Christian life and faith has not yet found its exhaustive expression; this may in large part be due to the fact that in the period of the
highest creative power of the English, the Spanish and the French,
the drama, misunderstood as 'theater', was not acknowledged by the
Church."[17] And this is perhaps not only because of extrinsic reasons
or prejudices but because theology's form of truth (the "system") did
not have any adequate place for the agonic-dramatic form of presentation of the truth or of its realization in creation, revelation, the
gospel, and the history of the Church and of the world. Unamuno's
message, cleansed of all its abstruse exaggerations, remains unforgot-
ten: Christianity is agonic. "The dramatic form, which makes present
the collision of the powers and the decision of ultimate human freedom that is offered in this collision, could supply solutions that cannot be expected from any other quarter."[18] This is why he hopes
that yearning for a "meeting between the Church and drama". "It
could take place only when the essentially tragic element of Christianity, the antithesis between world and truth, the question whether
one must choose the truth or one's life, found its embodiment on
the stage out of the power of the WORD."[19] Everything comes together in this poetics: the original dualism between art and history
(in *Camoes*) is not simply abolished, for "the stage is not a 'pulpit'
and can never be one";[20] but the image becomes the judgment on
history, which can find orientation in it: this is a judgment of grace,
because in Christ, to whom image and history belong, all judging is a
function of redemption. The theological-aesthetic double meaning of
kharis becomes clear here, too, in an unusual manner, namely, in the
sense of the event of grace, just as the meaning of judgment as grace

---

[16] 112:24.
[17] 112:25f.
[18] 101:91 (postscript).

[19] 112:26.
[20] 100:27.

lies in sacramental confession, and the drama becomes a confession
on the part of history, which is to be led by the image of confession
to the real admission of sin.

But it would be one-sided to exalt the drama above the other forms
of art. We know from *Camoes* and from Unamuno that the agonic dimension of life is antecedent to all external action, that it is a condition
and ultimately a suffering: life's contradiction of itself, the necessity
of accepting life as it is and of bearing in piety the excessive burden
without rebellion against God, without breaking out of the society
one belongs to, without bitterness and hatred. It is sufficiently indica-
tive to note which dramas Reinhold Schneider selected and provided
with an introduction when he began to build up his "Abendländische
Bücherei": above all *Oedipus at Colonus*, which "makes us shudder at
our own existence", "so monstrous in life". "It is the living suffering,
in a sense the life that has decomposed, that is divided in itself", "the
giving of form to life's internal contradiction":[21] and yet the one who
suffers in pious acceptance. Milton's *Samson Agonistes* and Molière's
Misanthrope are chosen ultimately for the sake of the condition they
portray: the former is the great threnody over the humiliation of the
one chosen, "the tragedy is much more a lament than an action; it is
the most serious, the most passionate dialogue with God", "the purely
religious poem, as it was for the men of the classical period".[22] The
latter is the insight that a pure man has no place among his fellows,
that untruth is a state of existence in the world and that it "laughs"
everyone "out of the room" who refuses to bow down to it.[23] Byron's
Cain is a lyrical portrait of a condition, a kind of existential analysis
that (as Camus has shown in *Homme révolté*) bridges the gap between
the Christian mystery of original sin and the problematic of Dostoyevsky, Heidegger and Sartre: the melancholy of the existence that
already knows sin but does not yet know death, the existence that runs
ahead into death with Lucifer's help, tasting to the full the abyss of its
nothingness and precisely thereby becoming a murderer: this belongs
to the fundamental supporting pillars of European drama. Only then
comes the sphere of culture and of the state: Grillparzer's *Ottokar*, the
pure imperial drama, Goethe's *Natürliche Tochter*, "the highest drama
of state that belongs to our literature", Shakespeare's *Henry IV*, the

---

[21] 102f:5f.
[22] 102d:2f.

[23] 102e:9.

graced possibility of a genuine king on earth. The rooting of tragedy in its existential state, its essence as lamentation, shows its connection with lyric poetry; from Greek tragedy to Spanish and Shakespearean tragedy, the innermost, holiest room is left open for lyric poetry (of the chorus or of the tragic person himself: the greatest example is that of the three women in *Richard III*). But epic has the freedom of accompanying both, bridging in itself the distance between condition of things and event.

Reinhold Schneider then began to make clear in works of his own the Christian poetics of which he was the spokesman: between 1948 and 1952, six dramatic compositions joined his epic and lyrical works. *Der Traum des Eroberers* and *Zar Alexander*[24] are dramatizations of the first main episode in *Inselreich*, the tragedy of William the Bastard, and of the short story "Taganrog": the kingdom of sin and the kingdom of the expiatory confession meet more harshly than ever for their symbolic duel, urging the spectators in the form of drama to make a decision. Irreproachable in their intensity, tempo, intellectual scope and contemporary urgency, they are the equal of the highest works of Schneider's inspired early period of composition. In the Nibelungen drama *Die Tarnkappe*,[25] Schneider seeks to reconquer the material of the German tragedy of the old literature, and the material of the myth of Schopenhauer, Hebbel and Wagner (which the author knows out of an innermost perception and kinship), for a Christian interpretation. This succeeds when Siegfried crosses the threshold of Christianity and accepts his death out of the expiatory nonresistance of the Cross; another spirit breathes through the world of the tragic myth as such: Siegfried is indeed guilty, since he breaks out of the original virginal unity of two in one with Brunhild, the bearer of the mythical element, and breaks into it again treacherously with the symbol of falsehood, the cloak of invisibility—this is his "descent" into the realm of history, falling-away and sin. But this is interpreted at the same time as a necessary guilt, as the unavoidable impurity of all that belongs to history, indeed, as the descent of the divine into flesh, as humility, as a symbol of Christ,[26] in such a way that Christianity in the struggle for victory seems to blend itself to the point of unrecognizability with the symbol of the German-Idealistic pan-tragedy.

---

[24] 110.

[25] 111.

[26] 111:52f., 63.

Der Kronprinz, Der grosse Verzicht and *Innozenz*[27] belong to the group
of problems of ecclesial existence, and we shall deal with these below in the section on Rome. In a formal sense, *Der Kronprinz. Politisches Drama* is directly linked to Goethe's *Natürliche Tochter*: it is the
translation into the present day of Goethe's problematic of the nobility's form of existence in the age of the French Revolution, made
sharper by the Christian-ecclesiastical question posed about the relation between the nobility of family and the nobility of priestly or-
dination and of the sacrificed heart: a question that presupposes the
world of thought of the Escorial and of Potsdam; it forms as well
the immediate preliminary study to *Große Verzicht* and to *Innozenz
und Franziskus*, which brings us to the innermost heart of Reinhold
Schneider's world. The extended form, laid out on a large scale in
the manner of a fresco, reminiscent of Gobineau's *Renaissance*, oscillates here between epic and drama. One will have to evaluate all
these realizations on the basis of the table of values of the poetics
that was sketched at the beginning of this section; above all, one will
have to ask how an existence that has been made utterly transparent
(in the face of the last judgment) and is already *decided* corresponds
to the laws of historical drama with its concealment and its *decision*
that must always be made—but this is what is demanded by the final paradox of Christianity. There does not seem to be a remotely
comparable achievement anywhere in today's German literature: the
entire sphere of history is opened up—from the concrete event into
its hidden background—and this leads to the forward thrust to the
ethical decision in the heart of the present day, inexorably in the way
Christ intends. The *kairos* in which these works stand is tremendous,
and it is grasped by the author both intuitively and with conscious
reflection: he knows what must be said; he knows very exactly why
it must be said and that no one but he is called to say it. He works
in this like a beacon visible for miles around, compelling even those
who contradict him to find their criterion in him and measure their
distance from him. It is here that we find orientation and stimulus
for Christian literature in the responsibility demanded by the present
moment.

Behind the dramas stands the lyric poetry; perhaps not always free
of thesis and abstraction, but in many places so transfigured that it

---

[27] 101; 108; 138.

becomes the truest poetic expression: where the flames of indignation and the demand made burn everything down, so that the naked word is all that is left standing, the word that writes on tablets of iron—but also where the naked soul sings its song between the note of melody and the transfigured flight of departure. The span between George's poem of time and Eichendorff's poem of prayer is held open and filled with substance. Alongside the splendor of the sonnets, such tender forms like the "first part" of *Herz am Erdensaume* succeed, with "Morgen", the "Magisch Abend", "Vollendung" and "Mantel";[28] but the light of the tranquil life in eternity also breaks through in the strict form, beyond all the sadness of existence and of the present day that he has experienced as suffering.

> So let me be free for the transfigured days,
> since the late fruits ripen here and there
> in the shadow of the leaves, fruits I do not care
> to lay hold of, and scarcely dare to bite into, in my dreams!
>
> I feel the sun going down on the hedge,
> its reflection in image and glass; the birds flutter
> from branch to branch, and late lights brush over me
> in the twilight, which I can easily bear.
>
> What an excess of time that I did not bear,
> does it not make the entire soul burn with thirst!
> O lamp of the world in the life imposed on me!
>
> The bird's departure seems scarcely light enough.
> How wonderful, before the garden whispers,
> to fly off through the branches as a ray![29]

---

[28] 82.   [29] 98:86.

The Church

ROUEN—THE GLORY

The Commission

The kingdom for which Reinhold Schneider fights is the kingdom of the light that breaks in from on high as grace. The light is not empty and abstract: it is the holy God, whose Word became flesh in order to bestow on the kingdom of light truth and presence in the world. The space and form of this presence is the Church. She is the unheard-of unity of the lightning flash that irrupts into time from on high and the stabilized form of this same higher dimension as it spreads out in time. She is the "summons to come out" (*ek-klēsia*) and the "institution directed inward", a dying to the world and a mission into the world, and this makes her both the redemption itself and the place where the fighting for the sake of this redemption is keenest. All the upward momentum that characterizes Reinhold Schneider the man must cease its soaring leaps; but at the same time, the entire rupture between the upper and the lower dimensions, in which he stands, must open up here in its most tragic form. He is always concerned with man. Just as Schneider did not speak about the state but about the ruler, so he does not now discuss the Church but the man who stands in her and is formed by her, and once again, this is the representative man who stands at the top of the building, so that the rest of it can be measured against him. But whereas there is only one person at the top of the state, namely, the king, there exists in the Church, thanks to a necessity of her very being, a double hierarchy, that of holiness and that of ministry. The saint is the exemplary person in the Church, thanks to grace; the pope is the exponent of her holy form in time. If both were a priori identical, then the Church would be identical with Christ (in whom person and office, holiness and work absolutely coincide); her external action would be infallibly divine, and an increase in the form would be a direct increase in holiness. This would mean the abolition, not only of original sin, but of creatureliness as a whole. The dualism of the two hierarchies, that of subjective holiness and that of objective holiness,[1] gives the Church the opportunity to follow her Lord in the humility of his descent: since John and Peter exist for one another (love renounces what is its own and submits to the office, while the office knows that it serves love—each allows the other precedence), the Church's existence is perfected in an act of transcendence beyond herself to the unity that is Christ. The Son is the representative of the Father; the one who sees him, sees Another; as Person, he is the Word; as one who bears responsibility, he is one who obeys; as light, he is transparent. The following of the Son leads into this mystery portrayed by holiness and office together: they can always be distinguished from each other, and yet they form an inseparable fellowship. It is only at this point that the form and the soul truly meet each other, and the strictest representation becomes identical with the most relaxed love and gift of self. Only now does a midpoint capture the whole span between the Spain of Philip and the Russia of the starets: in the presence of the person of Jesus Christ, Ignatius, the protector of the West (where the form is at its most explicit), and John, the patron of the Eastern empire (the empire of love), grasp each other's hand. In the form, Ignatius aimed at love; the only love John knows is a testimony, a humble renunciation that enters into the form.

For Schneider, the essence of ecclesial existence must infallibly disclose itself in the convergent relationship of the one who is raised to the honors of the altar and the one who sits on the cathedra. Both stand at the incomprehensible point that is simultaneously within history and above history: in history, because both are men who struggle between light and darkness, men to whom the destiny of the kingdom is entrusted in a manner that goes terribly beyond their own capacities. And above history, because they are the Church, voluntarily or forcibly expropriated into the inviolable realm of Christ's lordship. The decision they now make is already decided a priori at the place where they struggle: they struggle, with the strength given by decisiveness, to achieve the decision.

The Church of the office will have a geographical-symbolical place: Rome. From this place, the Church even enters the force-field of sec-

---

[1] On this, cf. H. U. von Balthasar, "Le Mystérion d'Origène", *Recherches de science religieuse* 26–27 (December 1936, February 1937).

ular history. It is essentially impossible for the Church of holiness to possess such a place; here, one city can stand only for all the places of holiness, which are its equal in value. Instead of Rouen, we could have Assisi, Manresa or Lourdes. Rouen is chosen here because France remains the country of great saints and because among all the saints it is the destiny of Joan—precisely as Schneider sees her—that remains the most expressive.

> The peasant girl from Domrémy experienced the purest tragedy it is possible to conceive of, one that perhaps has never been repeated. For with her, that which is perfectly pure has entered history—into a sphere foreign to itself—so that it can work among men, giving them the fire that they themselves could not generate, and be destroyed by them. Joan received a commission from God, carried this out and became its sacrifice; one cannot demonstrate any guilt in her, and the human trepidation that took hold of her in the hours of her deepest distress and indescribable abandonment (without totally overwhelming her), as well as the natural quality, the freedom and joyful superiority with which she met the most dangerous and cunning questions of her judges, only serve to make her image more alive—they do not tarnish it in the slightest. Thus there is surely no more moving phenomenon in the whole history of the West, so excessively rich in suffering and tears, than the martyr of Rouen. All the suffering of genius is outshone by the halo of pain worn by this saint on whom her contemporaries and the succeeding generations poured all imaginable disgrace, but who yet was inviolable and (so one could think) could not even be tempted.[2]

The first characteristic of ecclesial holiness is overwhelmingly clear in Joan: she herself is a commission, a mission, the burden of a responsibility that holds spellbound the one chosen and makes demands that go as far as his blood. Others are left with their freedom, but not he; others have a choice, but not he. The space into which he is directed to go is demarcated: this task (and no other), this particular grace, to be used in this way. The saint "is a power that reigns in the space assigned to him", in a "relationship of a particular, unique kind, comparable to an office established once and for all and equipped with great authority, similar in its own place to the office that St. Peter continues to carry out in the Church."[3] The mission makes the saint

---

[2] 18:149–55, 149f.
[3] 62:69.

a power in history: "It belongs to the essence of holiness that some-thing hidden and deeply personal coincides with a historical mission: the marvelous history of the saint's soul flows into the great history."[4] Many are handed over to their people in a kind of solemn vow, so that they can be their protector and representative before God, and this "consecration is performed only once, the solemn vow is made only once".[5] This is the case with Boniface and the Germans: "From now on, the existence of the Germans had an inseparable relationship to the work of redemption, which had been inserted into history",[6] and with Louis and the French: "Under St. Louis, the French people uttered their last word about God and history."[7]

> Thus all the saints looked up to the signs that God made to appear in heaven; these signs allowed them to recognize their commission, which was determined with total precision in the hour appointed to them. As warriors of the kingdom of God, they were historical phenomena in the true sense, since they met a public or a hidden challenge, made atone-ment for a public or a hidden guilt, invoked grace through their entire life on the place where grace was most bitterly needed, and gave God the glory where too little glory was given him. In the mighty struggle of the kingdom of God with its enemies, whose name is "legion", each individual warrior receives an objective, unique task.[8]

Through the office of grace (charism) entrusted to them, the saints are the concrete powers, the real symbols of the kingdom of God, its "ideas" and at the same time its "mighty forces", under the lord-ship of the highest idea and omnipotence, namely, Christ, who as a concrete Person is the truth. They are the kingdom, which must shine out at this point in history—as once under Tiberius. "If the light has been extinguished, then a man must go into the flames. The commission of each single saint is to take up and to master one par-ticular concern of his period in time on the basis of eternity and of his knowledge of Christ; by filling the temporal with the eternal, he exalts time and history to the praise of the Lord; the saints yearn for time to praise the Lord."[9] "Their relationship to historical life, to the decline and to the conversion of the peoples, is so deep that at

---

[4] 62:22f.
[5] 62:73.
[6] 62:72.

[7] 62:106.
[8] 81:16.
[9] 26:80.

some places we ought perhaps to infer the presence of saints without knowing about them—just as astronomers infer the existence of an unidentified heavenly body." [10]

We have already spoken earlier of the historical power of prayer: nothing is more active than contemplation. Here this proposition soars up to form another thesis: "Mysticism leads to action", [11] be this the foundation of Orders that are given their place in history or, as with Teresa, apostolic activity in hiddenness for those who are active in the Church. The innermost point is set in motion in such an endless manner that it appears to be at rest: the strength of the rotations can be measured only on the periphery. The center and prototype of history is Mary's *fiat*: it is here that "the meaning of the world" is decided: "Precisely for this reason, everything that happens afterward must resemble the sacred event of Nazareth." [12] The word of decision is "spoken in holy calm and certainty; the highest moment of history is also the stillest." [13]

> The greatest is reserved to the Virgin
> who descends with a judgment there is no escaping,
> she who is the tent of the heavenly lightning flashes and the star of time.
>
> Her swords shatter the powers,
> and the world changes. The Mother's glory
> trembles and weaves that which is transient. [14]

Mary's office of grace embraces the whole breadth of the Church, of the entire kingdom. She is the real potency of the Church. The Beloved Disciple stands very close to her, the virginal man entrusted to her at the Cross, the friend of the Son. His commission is love, concern for the Mother-Church, concern for holiness in general terms. "His is the first Marian spirit" and thereby ecclesial spirit; he "is the priest in the state of the highest grace"; he "is the teaching itself"; [15] the embodiment of the proclamation that is lived and performed.

But if a commission is exposed, as a city on the hill, then so is the life that serves this commission: it is expropriated for the commis-

---

[10] 81:73.
[11] 62:82; 16:38–40.
[12] 70:122.
[13] 62:43.
[14] 98:75; cf. 98:97 and the essay on Mary in *Pfeiler im Strom*: 136:155ff.
[15] 62:44f.

sion and must emerge naked, holding out in God's storm. "The saint
stands in the front line, with the responsibility for all the warriors on
his conscience, their nameless suffering on his soul. Just as even the
hardest stone on the peak is crushed under lightning, storms, frost
and heat and runs down as black-green rubble and debris over the
steep slopes with their gorse bushes, while much weaker formations
manage to retain their form in the valley, so too the leader is ravaged
by a suffering that cannot be measured. A silence lies upon the pains
of the peaks."[16] Other criteria are applied: "What appears up there
to be a very great offense has scarcely the weight of a trivial mis-
demeanor here below. Something that awakens bitterest remorse up
there, a pain that sets the whole life on fire and changes it, is scarcely
felt at all as suffering and reproach down below, in the sphere of much
blunter pains."[17] The laws of such an existence are reversed, "since
only half the life of the saint lies in the light of the earth, while the
other half is turned to that which lies beyond this world."[18] But one
should not presume to think that there is no connection between the
suffering of the peaks and the darkness of the lowlands: the chosen
one is to bear the light of his certainty into the twilight, extending
his operation from his own self into others; he is to be strong there
and is to win the victory where the power of a man does not reach:
in the others.

> Even if the saint himself were to win the victory, this does not yet mean
> that his army is victorious: this knowledge is his hardest and most per-
> sonal burden. His image and his deeds fight on; his foundations are to
> build walls that provide a shelter, so that the struggle can be carried on
> with greater certainty. But he himself, as he looks out from the eternal
> clarity over the ranks as they storm onward, fall and flee, will be invoked
> even there by those who are losing the battle: he will struggle with his
> prayer, and he will suffer.[19]

He will suffer because his work and his commission do not stand
firm against the storms of history. Francis of Assisi "had founded
something perfectly pure, by the fact of his living it, but all human
work gets spoiled. Every will that enters the temporal dimension is

---

[16] 107:237.
[17] 16:8.
[18] 26:93.
[19] 107:237f.

thwarted: precisely this is the plan of grace."[20] "The foundations of the saints have taken on the color of the earth to a greater or lesser extent; all human work has been perverted, even when it was a work blessed by grace."[21] And Ignatius says in prison: "I have not failed to perceive that the works seldom resemble the founders and that the world tends to corrupt the fire without which it cannot live, instead of blazing up through contact with this fire."[22] But Spee knows the answer to this, which of course imposes on the founder a new burden that goes beyond all measure: "Even if only our master Ignatius has lived, the Order endures and is justified for all times, even if none of his disciples is like him—indeed, even when every one of them sins against his founder, as is certainly the case."[23]

The life of these expropriated ones now becomes a struggling, suffering, perishing existence in the souls of all who are entrusted to them. It is the highest peaks that irradiate this mystery most clearly: Francis of Assisi, the most severe of the saints, who stands closest to Christ,[24] made himself a rule and canon in an unparalleled manner: above all words and interpretations, he casts his indestructible light and imprints a burning sign on all who follow him, as they falter and fail. Beside him stands Ignatius,[25] who lives out his commission (like his Master) on a level higher than Scripture: in Manresa, he fights the contest through to total despair, until he knows every objection of the serpent, every "in vain!" and every "nevertheless!". The seducer whispers to him:

> You are willing to bear your own suffering. Will you also bear theirs? There are men among them whom you love with your special love, you love them for the sake of the third One. But is this love less painful? Or more painful? It will be the same as with a tree that has spread out its roots in a wide circle. Now one root after the other is damaged, and the tree will feel this, as if the trunk itself were affected. And as the tree is dumb, so you too must be dumb. Only very few have any idea of what is in your heart.[26]

---

[20] 26:74.

[21] 26:29.

[22] 94:47.

[23] 34:212.

[24] 26:27, 30f.; 61:39; 52:154; 69:22; 70:13; 81:89.

[25] 107:219-28; 28; 34:187f.; 62:64; 94:34-52.

[26] 28:38f.

The mysticism of Teresa of Avila makes her soul totally *quadammodo
omnia*, but in the sense of salvation history:

> She had been placed in hell and had experienced the nameless torment
> of the damned in body and soul, when she was squeezed in the narrow
> space of hell; she had been lifted up into the light and had been permit-
> ted to sense something of the bliss of the elect. United in a mysterious
> way to all the heights and depths of the realm of the soul, its earthly
> and heavenly dimensions in all their extension, she joined in living the
> lives of countless people who had never met her; she felt the terrible
> convulsion of the division in faith as her most personal destiny and was
> never free of the distress of her own age.[27]

And the one who truly knows the "dark night", John of the Cross,[28]
is ultimately convinced of the social meaning of his suffering, when
layer after layer of his self opens up and falls away in the darkest
dungeon. When he describes these darknesses, Schneider goes back
into his own origins, in order to purify them and to pass beyond
them: the "nothing" above which the fantastic castle of Portugal rose
up need not be the "nothing" of a secular despair: it is left behind,
thanks to the experience of the saint in his dungeon: "He lived as if
at the bottom of the sea, no longer accessible to men and indifferent to everything they might contrive against him. Only now did he
sense with trembling that the freedom from possession is more than
possession, that values are transformed in the innermost depth of life
and that what men called 'nothing' became the highest good."[29]

But the dark fire that burns and widens the souls of the saints is
not kindled by God alone: the pyre of Rouen is an eternal beacon.[30]
The saints burn in a social sense, for the Church: but they also burn
because of the Church, because of all the sinners in her, and care has
been taken to give visible expression to this truth again and again
in the life of the saints. Their fellow Christians—often the official
representatives of the Church too—are sluggish in hearing the word
addressed to them but zealous in displaying distrust and open rejection;[31] the bribed judges are incapable of discerning the spirits and

---

[27] 16:41.
[28] 34:57–112; on the saint's night: 28:27–43; 16:32; 82:16; 88c:34f.
[29] 34:82f.
[30] 81:27.
[31] 16:20.

look on the divine as the work of the devil. They kindle the fire under the witch and adore what they have burned only when it is too late. The commission cannot aim at anything other than this, for the meaning of world history is a struggle. "Struggle is more than development."[32] And if the saints perish again and again thanks to the rigidity of the form that has turned itself into a god, this is not because they struggled against the form, still less because they had received a commission from God to struggle against it, but only in order to give evidence, up to the end in the flames, of their fidelity and their loving obedience to the Church. We see this in Francis, who bowed down before the priesthood in the very depths of his soul, and in Joan of Arc, who "took up arms, not against, but for the order of that age, and fell in this struggle",[33] to say nothing of Ignatius, who becomes a kind of rubbish pit for all mockery and all suspicion in the Church herself and finally sees his work abolished by the popes: "We are the refuse of the world up to the present day."

The place of disgrace remains the place specially reserved for those who are given divine commissions: this is the disgrace of Francis Xavier, who dies before the gates of China, seeing himself abandoned and betrayed by his companions,[34] the disgrace of Elizabeth in the new *Innozenz*, who must turn aside from her children out of obedience, the disgrace in the *Abschied der Frau von Chantal*, who is not spared from walking over the body of her own son, as he lies across the thresh-old, so that she can follow the vocation to enter a convent,[35] the disgrace of Benedict Labre, who becomes the public laughingstock of the educated clergy of Rome,[36] while his soul experiences the passage through the dark night in a manner more historical than any other saint, in connection with the approaching terror of the Revolution: "Who sacrifices himself today? Who sacrifices himself for a man like the Abbé? . . . Surely you must realize that falseness is taking hold of men and that not even the Church is putting up a resistance to it."[37] This is truly the disgrace of Christ, who is ashamed vicariously for the men who despise God, and the saint shares in this by being ashamed for the Church that is so very far from living in accordance with what she really is. He is ashamed for the Lord in the presence of

---

[32] 18:154.
[33] 18:152.
[34] 34:175 ff.

[35] 27:34 f.
[36] 34:227–55.
[37] 34:244, 250.

the Church, and he is ashamed of the Church in the presence of the Lord. But the disgrace is in him, the worst of all sinners, for when did he genuinely fulfill his commission? Only grace has the ability to raise him up above himself and to show him the victory and the transfiguration as its work—it is not his own work, yet an incomprehensible indulgence fuses him with it.

The Encounter

Not all saints are called to penetrate into the external sphere of history: many turn the spokes of the wheel invisibly. But if the call is made to go out, then there occurs the most mysterious thing known to the world's time: the hour of God coalesces with the hour of the world: the saint, who is totally open to God's demand, hears in this the demand of history too. Many have spent long years in allowing Christ to take on his form in them,

> so that they only emerged very late with external deeds, their confession of faith or foundation, the execution of a historical decision: the fact that such a deed became possible, that the hour demanded it, must have been determined in God's plan; but the man must prepare himself for this and keep himself in a state of readiness. The summons of history is not awakened by us; but if it comes, then perhaps it is only the one who strives for sanctification who can understand it: only such a one will make the distinction between the promises and threats of the world and the unconditional command of Christ.[1]

Which spirits ought the saint to have learned to discern if not those spirits that decide the course of history? And when men must make historical decisions but are not themselves holy, ought they not to make use of the saints for the task of discernment? It is necessary for Reinhold Schneider to ask these questions, since he has recognized from below the transcendence of the state's values and from above the historical potency of a holy existence. It is impossible for the encounter of these two to be anything but the key and nodal point of all history. The one who possesses power looks the saint in the face and, through him, looks the truth in the face: power and grace stand eye to eye; the history of the world holds its breath. The

---

[1] 70:88.

bridge *could* be built, the internal conscience that looks to God could come to an agreement with the external ordering; in the encounter of two representatives who look into each other's eyes, who are in dialogue as men and understand one another as men, the ineffective abstractness of the relationship between nature and the supernatural takes on a concrete dramatic quality in which the world turns, as on a hinge.

This encounter took place once and for all when the eternal truth in human form stood before Pilate.[2] But where everything was the answer of the truth, Pilate poses the question of truth. He looks straight at it and does not see it. He looks aside, into emptiness. On his side, the encounter ends with his verdict. Only indirectly, from beyond history, is it possible to see that he himself was the one on whom a verdict was uttered, the one judged, the one saved in the very act of being found too light. The encounter takes a tragic course, in a turning aside; and the one who has power is overtaken by the judgment of grace only in the death on the Cross—where he confirms in writing (as one who himself has power) the power of the all-powerful God —and this place is invisible. Alongside the Lord, who is the truth, stands his friend and precursor, likewise in fetters, eye to eye with Herod: and this encounter is a copy that corresponds faithfully to the archetype. The truth is proclaimed and makes no impression, the one who proclaims it must pay the penalty of his life for doing so, but the king's defiance includes the struggling element of fear before the unknown superior power that judges him.[3] The scene remains tragic: Becket stands as conscience before his king, and his brains are spattered over the tiles of the cathedral floor. More struggles with his lord about the truth and about the historical conscience: the gaze of one friend penetrates more deeply into the eye of the other friend, throwing onto the scales the power of earth alongside the power of heaven. But once again, the king turns aside, is unequal to the summons contained in the encounter, takes a short-cut out of the situation and wrenches the destiny of his people out of the circulation of blood that is the Church's grace.[4] "An Anselm of Canterbury stood up to William Rufus, the infamous son of William the Conqueror, and we are surely right to suppose that there stood behind the bishop

---

[2] 70:23–30.
[3] 62:88–91.
[4] 34:37–55.

an army of praying people who supported him."[5] A final urgency
is the encounter of Bonaparte, with his arrogant declamations, and
Pius VII, silent and defenseless:[6] worlds that are predetermined never
truly to meet one another.

But it is not only the tragedy of the Lord's encounter with Pilate
that must live on in history but also the grace that comes from the
Cross and bestows the sense of hearing on the mighty ones. No matter how hefty the collision of the two worlds may be, both stand
under the lordship of the Cross: the light can force its way through
chinks, perhaps in a situation of extreme distress, and enlighten the
heart of the one who has power. Although each has his own business,
and "it is not permitted to either of them to exchange his own office
for that of the other" so that the king may not lay down his office in
order to enter a monastery, nor the saint abandon his office of prayer
in order to find more time for temporal affairs, nevertheless "the king
should have had the experience of the monk and should rule with this
experience",[7] and the saint should embrace within himself the king
and his kingdom, his cares and his tragedy, in order to bear these to
God—but also, under certain circumstances, in order to throw his
word, the word of a saint, into the world's distress. If holiness is an
office, and the offices belong to the visible Church, then the saint has
his visible place in the relationship between the spiritual realm and
the secular realm: as the personal exponent of the Church, he has a
visible mission in state and history, and no pretext can permit him to
withdraw from this mission. The consequences of an understanding
in real-symbolic terms, that is, of looking at the individual divine acts
of election in a social context, are immense for both. As the king lives
the destiny of his people, so the saint lives to a much greater degree
the destiny of the Church; but as the kingdom of God in the world,
the Church contains in a mysterious fashion the states in herself and
cannot dispense herself from her maternal responsibility. The struggle
of the saints on behalf of the kings is a situation that can never be
bypassed.

So the soul of Las Casas groans and utters its pathetic cry on the
steps of the throne:

---

[5] 37:121.   [7] 37:82.
[6] 102i:64–68.

Oh, if only it were possible to tell kings the truth at all times! Oh, if only the voice of the men whose heart burns for the destiny of their people had a sound of its own, so that it could be distinguished from all other voices! For there are incomprehensibly few who live only as witnesses, in order to say what is true and to what extent the life of men contradicts the eternal truth. And even if a king's ear is made more acute by his ministry as sentry, how is he to know, in all the clamor, whether the man who speaks is one whose word is his destiny or one whose word defines the price at which he can be bought! . . . Human voices cannot answer you; but if you wish to listen, my Lord, then perhaps you will perceive the voice of the one who guides history, who wishes to use you and your crown and your country as his instrument at this moment and to extend his kingdom through you.[8]

The saint is not the one who steers the state but is the conscience of the king—that would put into practice the transcendental ethics that does not use two different sets of weight when measuring. Through his unheard-of cry, Las Casas touched the heart of the ruler—who, of course, was himself almost a saint and was accustomed through much prayer to keep his ear open for the Word of God. Francis de Paola, on the other hand, speaks to deaf ears (*Der Tod des Mächtigen*): Louis XI of France, at the end of a career of guilt and crime, has summoned him, not much differently from Herod's summons of the Lord; he hoped to see a miracle from him, the miracle of a cure. On his journey, the saint warns yet another king, Ferdinand of Naples, and in Rome he reverently meets Sixtus IV. The very existence of the saint is enough to convulse the conscience of Sixtus: "He judges us all without knowing it; what would I not give to have him always standing beside my throne!"[9] Everywhere in Louis' territory, he meets with disorder, hatred, hardness of heart, but he does not stop: "What does it help, if I begin here with individual, small matters—I must get to the king."[10] And so the struggle between the two begins, which will last for years: seldom in words, mostly in the silence in which hardness of heart and stormy prayer, accompanied by excessive penance, take each other's measure. Finally, when the last powers of the king are failing, his resistance, too, collapses: the prisoner is freed, the Dauphin is admitted to his presence, the crown is handed over. The saint must find the

---

[8] 12:151f., 169f.

[9] 67:25.

[10] 67:31.

strength to give a place within his own soul to the king's fear and to his death. His penance lives on for a long time after the ruler's death. Finally, Pope Celestine (in *Große Verzicht*) is taken captive by Charles II of Anjou and captures with his soul with all the king's hardened resistance to God. The blows the king lays on him make it clear to him what his refusal is doing to God himself. The kernel of politics is a conscience that has become visible, and the conscience does not stand alone but is a palpable dialogue with another. The suffering of the saint through the violent attacks by the king serves only to reveal yet more radiantly the power of the spirit. And Celestine, like every saint, is one who speaks in the name of the Church. For the personal struggle is only a conflict between two persons who have both received a commission: a conflict, not about power, but about the grace of their mission. Here, too, through the martyrdom and death of the pope, the closed heart of the king finally opens: he frees the prisoner and renounces his son, who will become a priest and a holy bishop and will do penance for the guilt of Anjou.[11]

The hour of the encounter is perhaps the hardest duel, but alongside this there can exist a continuous, wordless cohabitation in which the missions interpenetrate each other. A saint lives in the kingdom, and the king knows it; they do not need to meet; a deep agreement reigns between them; the king builds on the saint; the saint builds on the king. Philip II can look after the ordering of his kingdom, for he knows that Teresa is praying for him, the holy king. "Philip asked the saint to pray for him, his kingdom and his family, and the holy Mother read this letter aloud to her daughters." He never saw her; this was not necessary, since "she knew that she was united to the king in the preservation of the earthly ordering, which was established from on high, and of its image."[12] Otto of Bamberg rules in a similar way in the empire of Lothair of Supplinburg:[13] in a period obsessed by weapons, he peacefully carries out his nonviolent work, always ready to hasten to the king, when he is summoned, and to give him counsel and help. The encounter of the two office-bearers is so mysterious because one of them, the saint, is the representative at one and the same time of a part and of the totality—of a part, because the Church is not the state, the kingdom of God is

---

[11] 109:112f., 261f.   [13] 11:55–81.
[12] 16:58, 59; 107:268f., 261f.

not the secular kingdom, and yet of the totality, because the Church
is the dynamic working of the kingdom, the irruption of the light of
the world, with a lordship that knows no boundaries. For the king,
the saint is the representative of the "other"; for the saint, the king
is the representative of the same One. Seen from the king's viewpoint, the encounter is an occasion for drawing boundaries and for
conflict, but seen from the saint's viewpoint, it is an occasion for loos-
ening the boundaries that maintain themselves and for the promise
of unity. We are far removed here from the tragic atmosphere of the
early *Innozenz III*, where pope and emperor are caught in the toils
of the common guilt of ancient Roman power. It is not important
that the saint perhaps falls when he bears witness at these boundaries,
compared to the outcome—namely, that the boundary has for one
moment become visible in its nonexistence. "There is no enmity, no
opposition, no division, that cannot or may not be overcome by love;
there is no more urgent task in life than this: to encounter everything
and everyone with love."[14]

The Only One

It is impossible to speak of the saint—of his office as witness in the
Church and in history, of his night, his burden, the crossing over the
boundary between the Church and the world through his committed
action and through his death—without continuously recalling the origin of all holiness, the only One who includes everything in himself,
namely, Jesus Christ. He rules through his obedience to the Father;
he wins the world through his death in which the boundaries are
dissolved; he steps across these boundaries in his struggle against the
prince of this world, whom he conquers in dying. He has overcome
in himself the temptation that arises at the boundary: the temptation
of the king to take hold of the spiritual power, the temptation of the
Church to take hold of the secular sword.[1] He has voluntarily ac-
cepted death into himself and thereby done something that deprives
suicide of all meaning, something that leaves far behind every intentional death:[2] he has proved that the undermost powerlessness is a

---

[14] 37:120.
[1] 81:10.

[2] 79:34f.

function of the uppermost power. His suffering, his trembling from
fear, his dying in abandonment: all this is a form of his power. "God's
power is love itself",[3] and its essence is to refrain from positing or
accepting any boundaries. When Christ dies in the night and hell, in
the realm far from God, this crossing of the boundary from the *civitas
Dei* to the *civitas diaboli et mundi* is nothing other than the ecstasy of
the love that remains itself, and remains at home with itself, as it
crosses over. The same crossing also bursts open the walls separating
"I" and "Thou": the vicarious representative lives the life of the sinner and gives him the life of holiness; both lives are in communion
and form one body; the Head suffers in his members, the members
are glorified in their Head. The "I" of the member is not abolished
but becomes a function of a "Thou". It experiences its own destiny
and senses its own life, but Another holds this destiny in his heart
and suffers in it. All of this is no abstruse metaphysics but the pure
deed of God's miracle, which cannot be derived from anything other
than his gracious will.

The love of God has descended into our lost history, which without him would only have been hell. For the eternal life that he is, we
are a grave. "Your grave is our life, your grave is time. We have shut
you up in the darkness of denial."[4] As long as this No exists in the
world, the incarnate love suffers because of it. "All time is the terrible
time of Christ's suffering."[5] But why did he come, if not to utter his
Yes into the ultimate No? The message from the Father is borne into
the bottomless depth of the grave by the one who descends even to
hell."[6] Hell lies open before him, because no barrier thwarts the path
of the One who is most open of all, who is the love that goes to
the end. The lack of resistance to the infinite will of the Father is
itself infinitely deep, so that all that is finite is included within this
lack of resistance and is absorbed into it. "And the city of God consumes all the cities."[7] It is now that Schopenhauer's philosophy of the
world as appearance is given its final justifying twist: 'appearance'
is now whatever is not understood as a member and function of the
comprehensive life of Christ; and "untruth" is whatever refuses to
understand itself as kept safe in the present truth. All the evidential

---

[3] 91:17.
[4] 29:62.
[5] 88c:44.

[6] 88c:54.
[7] 66:17.

character of existence has its pivot here: "The world may dissolve and flow away like a dream; men's faces disappear while we are still speaking to them, and we ourselves may not wish to recognize our own selves any longer on the paths we once took: but you exist. And since only you exist with absolute certainty, everything belongs to you; it proceeds from you and returns home to you again. You are not only the vine of the community; you are the vine of the world."[8] The abandonment that exists in the world is surely a possibility; in the presence of Christ, it is not a possibility that is destroyed but one that is included with him, an "impossible possibility". "While the most terrible thing of all is taking place", those who are awake "sense that this terrible thing is only apparent; for death does not rule and can never rule."[9] "The great achievement of life in history is trust in the reality of that in which one believes and action on the basis of this trust. Only those who believe this and live out of Christ's kingly power and the kingly power of the truth are unable to be tempted by appearances and cannot be overcome by the demons. They come from the truth and raise the appearance of what is earthly into the reality where it is tested and prepares the way for the Lord."[10] The believer will learn "to honor the heart that beats in every man",[11] learning to hear the one heart beat not only in men but also in animals, plants and stones, like Francis.

> He bent down to the worms, picked them up from the path and set them in a sheltered place, because the prophet had said of the Savior: "I am a worm, no longer a man." He demanded that the brothers should leave a space in the garden free for flowers, for their blossoming reminded him of the heavenly rose that brought salvation to the world. And when he had to walk over rocks, he went with great caution and reverence in the presence of the one who is called "the Rock". He loved the stones, because the Lord had walked over them, and he felt pain when trees were cut down, because the Lord hung on the Cross. He loved the fire best of all the elements, and perhaps he thought of the Savior's words that he had come to cast a fire on the earth. . . . It is as if the full light of revelation and of salvation had fallen upon the earth only with the life of the saint of Assisi; all that exists points back to Christ, and man will experience the greatness of the creation only when he is able to look

---

[8] 88c:50.

[9] 81:70.

[10] 26:89.

[11] 98:89.

from every single point of the earth to the One in whom everything is created.[12]

Thus the saint loves pain, too, for this, more than all the rest, is the possession of the Lord; in his own pain and that of others, the world becomes a homeland, because all pain belongs to the one Heart.[13] And thus a will to suffer can exist—something that transcends all empirical evidence to the contrary—not for the sake of the suffering itself, but thanks to the insight about whom the suffering belongs to. "The greater the pains and the deprivations, the more crushing the cares and the anxiety, the gloomier the mourning, all the more decisively do they wrest this Yes from us. When distress presses hard in upon us from all sides, the only help we can find now is to cry out: I want this pain! For I want to come close to you; now, when I am a prisoner and in chains, I want you. I want to come to you on the Cross, to come up to you! Draw me up! There is no more space on earth."[14]

In the Incarnation, the eternal has become history; in the Resurrection and Ascension, it returns into the eternal and draws temporal history up with it. "Passing through the grave, . . . history has become eternity in him."[15] "When his sacred body ascends, it takes with it in a certain sense the innermost life of the earth, of the creation in which it shares, and when we look after him, it is as if a mighty storm of yearning passed through the creation and all that is transient. For all the transient is opened up to heaven; all creatures and all things are given their point of reference in Christ who bears them; in everything there is a pain that longs for him, a presentiment of his coming."[16] "The words 'I am the resurrection and the life' open for history the gates of eternity; only these words promise the truth about history. In the kingdom of the Risen One, all who share in playing a role in history come into a light that knows no deceit. History is a question; the answer can come only from *him* who is set over history as its Lord."[17] If Christ's historicity has gone to heaven through his Resurrection, then he is no longer historical in the temporal sense: he has been made eternal and is enthroned above time,

---

[12] 26:57, 58.
[13] 66:29.
[14] 70:67.

[15] 62:53.
[16] 62:55.
[17] 83:76f.

and yet he has time within himself, as the one who has lived time and does not separate himself from what he has lived, the one who lives time in his brethren and in all the members of the cosmos, thereby communicating to them something of the eternal substance of his Being. In the Eucharist, this mystery of the suprahistorical historicity of the very basis of the world is realized.

> There the truth without fate continues to rule
> and crowns the sacred chaos of earthly being
> visibly-invisibly in the sacrament.[18]

Through the Eucharist, the basis of every human fate becomes something that has no human fate itself but that has experienced every human fate. Thus the basis of all that comes into being, of every storm and struggle, is the stillness of eternal Being: but in Christ, this has experienced all coming into being. And thus the unfinished world is brought to completion in him.

> Here there is the undying distress of the body,
> which gives birth day by day, century by century,
> to the dreadful fate of the peoples.

> There is no individual member that escapes sickness and corruption.
> But the One who smiles and is admired,
> transfigures himself unconquerably in all.[19]

"I see the creation perfecting itself every day." "The world is perfect." In *Gloria*,[20] all the abysses, the dead and the blind, "who no longer knew the name of his governance", the shattered and the defenseless, praise the same God. They must do so, for he is more intimately present within them than they are to their own selves. The watermark printed on all the pages of the book of the creation is the Cross.

The three sonnets entitled *Geschichte* give the concluding picture: first the vision of power as the beginning of all history: darkly flashing forces of the early period, fighting each other, consuming, stabilizing and then decaying again; then "through the clouds that billow up from land and sea, tossed about by lightning and storm, the Cross appears": unshakable in the surgings until the last day. Now we see the increasing violence that hurls its waves against the walls of

---

[18] 35:48; cf. 69:31f.   [20] 14:50; 58:39.

[19] 98:95.

the city of God, until one night the watchmen make a mistake, the
city succumbs, and only some individual houses remain. But finally,
the superior power from below is only a sign of the superior power
from above: because God could allow the city to succumb, his power
is omnipotent; because the darkness overran all boundaries, God has
both light and darkness in his hand.

> For the beams of your Cross reach out over
> all boundaries, and your praise touches
> each heart that lost its way in the night;
>
> you draw all the beaten peoples,
> through the terrible sanctuary of their pains,
> up to you, in the superior power of your suffering.[21]

A final idea corresponds to this, an indispensable idea. When the Son
of Man struggles against the darkness on the Cross, this is not the
conflict of one party against another. He fights for the souls whose
lost condition he bears, but he does not fight directly with the demon.
The darkness of the Cross is a sacred night; in order to perceive this,
we should not lower our gaze but lift it up. It is a mystery that lies
between Son and Father. And this night, since it is the deepest of all,
embraces all the nights of the lost, explaining and justifying them.

> Around the divine fatherhood there breathes the mystery of a suffering
> to which we can scarcely give a name. Earlier centuries spoke of it in
> the image of the "throne of grace": the Father holds the dead Son in
> his arms, and the mighty Spirit of consolation covers the Father's head
> with his wings. The heavenly Father sent the Son into the world and
> accepted the sacrifice of his suffering. It was not possible to portray this
> mystery otherwise than by having the Father receive a dead man covered
> with wounds (instead of a victor returning home in the splendor of the
> divinity) and showing him to the world, so to speak, as the most terrible
> reproach. When we praise the Father's power and glory, we ought not
> to forget this final point, which we call "pain" in our poor language,
> without making the divine mystery any more comprehensible; a pain,
> which is perhaps the shadow of this mystery, passed over onto all earthly
> fatherhood and to a special degree onto the fatherhood of the one who
> is to give order and command.[22]

---

[21] 35:49–51.   [22] 51:34f.

"No one can gauge the entire suffering of the Son; when we hear the dreadful question of the crucified One to the Father, we have the feeling that the perception of yet another suffering brushes against us, a suffering that has passed through the heights of heaven, but it does not seem that any word is permitted to touch this suffering."[23] "For it is certain that this cry affected the Father in the most terrible way. It may be that the sacrifice above all sacrifices is the fact that he did not immediately open heaven and send down his angel—this sacrifice is no less costly than the pain and isolation of the Son and perhaps even transcends this. So, in the sacred drama of the redemptive deed, there is no more powerful revelation of divine love than this cry of the abandoned Son and the answer of silence."[24] "There is a pain in heaven, high above all the distress of earth; we do not name it, we do not comprehend it; it is perhaps the most venerable of all the mysteries of our faith. When we shudder before it, deep in the terrors of the world, we are marvelously close to the Godhead: divine suffering is the answer to men's distress and guilt."[25]

> Shudder no longer before what is extraordinary,
> and look piously at the ultimate cruelties:
> God suffers with you, you disappear into him.[26]

---

[23] 70:66.
[24] 88c:29.
[25] 88c:55.
[26] 66:8.

ROME—THE MINISTRY

The Office

The office exists for the sake of holiness; the office is temporal, holiness is eternal. But because holiness in time needs an absolute in order to obey and to make the gift of itself in keeping with the mind of Christ—without fear, without reflecting on what belongs to one's own self—the office has been founded and given a divine guarantee. Christ's life in the turbid air of history was totally free of opacity; and although no other life attains the height of his purity, he has the power to pour his own purity into a mold—namely, the office—and to keep it free of opacity in all the subsequent history.[1] How unutterably consoling is this distinction between the office, which cannot fail, and the bearer, who necessarily fails! And at the same time, how unutterably terrible, since the office that has been founded derives from the inseparable unity of ministry and person in Christ! The office is totally pure. The saint purified himself through the office; but the man in the office stands at an utterly tragic place, since he cannot be what the office demands, thanks to its origin, viz. the unity of office and person. If he nevertheless wanted to attain this at any price, he would exalt himself in arrogance and want to be the equal of Christ; but if he wanted to soothe himself for a moment with the reflection that he necessarily must fail, then he would have betrayed the essence and the unquenchable demand of the office. It is easy to say lofty things in abstract terms about ecclesiastical office; it is easy to form a sympathetic and encouraging ethics for priests on the base of the office; but who dares to look the terrible dimension of the office in the eye without wincing? Who dares to sketch without compromises the theology of the man in the office? No one is treated more harshly, more often rebuked and exposed in the Gospels than

---

[1] 26:29.

Peter; he is the man who, despite all his good intentions, mostly gets things wrong, when measured against his office; and he is to know this and remember it because of the way the Lord has treated him.

Reinhold Schneider is no theoretical theologian who would be concerned with the abstract structure of the Church: he is a theologian of history, who is interested in man under Christ's demands in the sphere of historical action and suffering. Just as he does not ask about the state but about the king, so he does not ask about the Church but about the pope, about the way in which a pope, who must administer the office of Christ in a particular historical situation, ought to act. This presupposes a way of looking at the essence of the office that has been entrusted to him, an office that is the criterion for his action; but it will not be possible to detach this vision from the vision of the one who is identical with the origin of the office, that is, the vision of the life and the dying of Christ, who has bestowed on his action and his suffering this abiding form of an official character. To be in office is a specially qualified form and summons to follow Jesus: it is only the Peter who has three times affirmed his love who can be installed in office, not without receiving at the same time the promise that his following of Jesus will lead him to where he does not wish to go: to the upside-down mirror image of the Cross in Rome, through which he is to glorify God (Jn 21:18). Life in office takes on its own stringency, not through the fact that a sinful, unworthy man is instituted into the form of the imitation of Christ (since this is true of every saint and of every believer in general), but through the fact that this man must explicitly assume and exercise powers that belong to Christ. Office means authority, and authority is a form of power. This power can only be a communication of the power of Christ to whom all power belongs in heaven and on earth. But Christ had this omnipotence (which he always possessed) at his own disposal only when the Father bestowed on him "the name above all names" at the Resurrection; throughout the duration of his life on earth, he renounced the full disposition of this and set his existence under the sign of passivity and suffering. Thus the man in office is confronted with the question of whether the office points him to the omnipotence of the glorified *Kyrios* or to the powerlessness of the suffering Jesus. On the one hand, he is to bind and loose, and thereby receive a share in the judicial power of the glorified Lord, who will return to judge the world. On the other hand, he is to be one who serves—all

the more so, the higher he is placed—doing everything out of pure
love and always ready to take the path of the cross and of death. This
tension is already enough to spell death to the officebearer: he is sent
by the omnipotence, in order to administer power in its name, but this
is a power that at every point directs him back and itself returns into
the powerlessness of the Cross, which remains the law for those who
follow Christ on earth. In his exercise of office, Peter is laid claim to,
so that he can be a coefficient cause in the redemption of the whole
world: "As soon as he enters into his office, all beings and things are
referred to his net",[2] and he does not work "in vain".[3] Nevertheless,
the redemption is not accomplished by anything other than suffering
and death, so that every action of power that is performed on the basis
of the Resurrection returns into the powerlessness that is the origin
of all the power of grace, thanks to the Cross and to Holy Saturday.
But there is still more than this: Peter is to pasture, that is, he is to
wield his power of grace in an earthly form—and this is a form that
is not simply alien to the earthly administration of power. As he pas-
tures a Church visible on earth, he necessarily comes into the force-
field of earthly power, and it is not guilt but rather the exercise of his
commission when he announces his authority in this realm of earthly
power and even brings his authority to bear here. Despite this, the
pure power of grace that he administers can never be confused with
the earthly power of dominion that is stained a thousand times by
guilt and original sin. Measured against this, his power will therefore
always appear to be powerlessness, even where it is the reflection of
Christ's omnipotence in heaven, but a fortiori where it is the presence
of the power of his Cross. Thus the first dialectic, which is lethal in
itself, is united here to a second dialectic, of unsurpassable acuteness:
since the power of grace can be exercised even in the sphere of the
secular power of dominion, in order to be continually reminded there
of the testimony of the grace of the Cross. Only the infinite security
of the victor over death and hell could build his Church into such an
exposure to death and hell, in continuous contact with the powers
of darkness that try to overthrow it, not only from without, but also
from within her own structure—and yet, in their apparent victory
over the powerless Church, these powers are made to feel the Lord

---

[2] 91:61.
[3] 91:63.

of the Church, who conquers through powerlessness. It is the security of the Lord, not of the Church; for the Church succumbs to her tragic exposure in a manner that she often cannot connect directly to the mystery of the Cross. But this deeper mystery of the Lord catches hold of the Church as she fails and succumbs, at precisely the place where the gates of hell are getting ready to celebrate their triumph.

The nodal point of all this is the fact that, as was already shown in the first *Innozenz*, the cross of Peter is set up in the center of earthly power, in the Rome of the Caesars, the place where the concentration of earthly power as apparent omnipotence is unveiled as the power opposing Christ's omnipotence. Peter sends greetings from Babylon (1 Pet 5:13), and Babylon is chosen to become the new Jerusalem. The seat of the Antichrist (it is as such that Rome must appear to the apostles in their epistles and in the Apocalypse) is to become the seat of Christ: Santa Maria sopra Minerva, San Pietro sopra Nerone. "Rome, which appeared at one and the same time as the city of the Caesars and the city of the pope",[4] the "dark place", "Nero's house full of cruelty, stricken with a plague by the monster that had its innermost seat in the soul of the Caesars",[5] this was the place where Peter had to bear witness to the "most glorious splendor" (2 Pet 1:17) that he had once seen on Tabor, in order to let it shine out before the peoples. The encounter between Peter and Nero, even if it did not take place physically, is nevertheless "like a conversation", and this is "a word that history speaks to us". "Their conversation would have had to lead to the boundary of this life, where both kingdoms meet: the kingdom that Christ had planted ineradicably in the kingdom of the Caesars and this latter kingdom itself, which could no longer remain what it was. For the kingdom of Christ grew with irresistible force from a seed with divine power, and the most burning of all history's questions had made itself heard: Will there one day arise a powerful man who believes and acts on the basis of the kingly power of the truth?"[6] The question of the correct use of earthly power in the service of the papal office: this is what Reinhold Schneider calls the most burning of all history's questions, for it is here that we find the entire problematic of existence that we can encounter in this

---

[4] 18:8.

[5] 70:95.

[6] 70:96, 97.

sinful and redeemed world coming together to form a terrible knot: Babylon and Jerusalem gather at the same place for the final decisive struggle. The powers of the temptation that comes from below have nothing else to offer than the open or masked enticements of Caesar's omnipotence in every form; the powers of grace appear on the scene to repel this temptation (which is always the same) through the might of the Cross. The temptation is unavoidable. The victory of Christ is unavoidable. Is the succumbing also inevitable? Or is it possible to untie the knot? Can earthly power be administered without guilt in the service of the heavenly power and powerlessness? When Reinhold Schneider poses this question, he bypasses the Protestant Antichrist polemic, which deals with the competence of the ecclesial office only in an abstract manner, and a Catholic history of the popes that would smoothe over all the problems, since this does not touch the ultimate theological question and at most applies ethical criteria to the personalities of the popes. He poses this question as he is accustomed to ask, on the basis of his own presuppositions: he asks about the supratemporal validity and justification of a historical life and activity before the throne of Christ. One must thank him simply for putting the question, since this is the only question that not merely understands and includes but in principle supersedes all the accusations against individual popes and against the institution of the papacy, including Luther's invectives.

So much for the question as such. The solution will be burdened, in a way that goes beyond all the previous forms of tragedy, with the particular problematic of his Augustinian understanding of Being and value, which looks on all that happens and has value as a *relation-ship* to the ultimate pole. In this view, Christ is the source of every power in heaven and on earth, and the one who is given authority by him on earth is given the first authorization—not independently of his faith and his life!—to share in Christ's omnipotence. It is clear that this points us to the old problematic of the two swords, according to which the state's power, too, comes from the omnipotence of Christ (not only from that of the creator God) and *therefore* must be bestowed in some form by the one who administers this omnipotence on earth, the pope. It is not because of a historical interest far removed from the real world or from a legitimism that looks to the past that Reinhold Schneider once again visits the field of tension between emperor and pope, but because, in his view, it is here that one finds access to the theologically exact position of the question. The power of the state, too, has reference to Christ's omnipotence—this is the language of a concrete historical thinking, which does not wish to stop at an abstract natural ethics—but there is no relationship to Christ except through his visible Church. The old order stands as the expression of a consistent christocentrism. Its practical weakness is of course obvious: the temptation for the Church to make use of the secular sword that she has handed over to the state—for secular or spiritual ends. This contains the deeper temptation to understand herself as the ultimate, transcendental form of the state and now to equate the heavenly kingdom with the earthly, the Christian kingdom with Caesar's kingdom, indeed, with the anti-Christian kingdom. But where, in order to overcome this temptation, secular and ecclesiastical authority are clearly distinguished from one another, as the modern period has done, it is obvious that the opposite danger exists, namely, for all secular power to be left to the secularized state and for the Church to restrict herself to a power of grace that, seen in secular terms, now appears to be only the powerlessness of the grace of the Cross. Depriving herself of all secular power, she carries out the "great renunciation" (*Große Verzicht*) and is caught in the opposite trap, that of betraying her commission in the world. When the dilemma is posed by Reinhold Schneider in this way, it becomes triply lethal. Now it seems as if his initial situation (in *Camoes*), that of a hopeless pantragicism, comes into its own in a definitive manner in the conflict of the pope's existence. The contradiction—which might perhaps be withdrawn if it were understood as an affirmation about the normal Christian existence—becomes once again the fundamental formula, where what is involved is the representative Christian existence. Where the kingdom of God, which is not of this world, is to acquire a breadth in the world in the official sphere, the success of this project means that man can only fail and perish, struck by the swords that inevitably clash. Guilt, from which there is no escape, lies in wait on all sides around him. The temptation of power is by far the strongest: direct power, when the spiritual power is used in a worldly way; indirect power, when the worldly power is given a spiritual blessing and employed as the "secular arm". If a man wants to escape the snare of this temptation, he will fall into the temptation of renunciation, trusting to a pure condition that lies above the world and thus trying to be like God, like Christ. But if he seeks to find, beyond the use of power and its renunciation, a form in which he serves the pure representation of Christ, it will be hard for him to avoid committing both errors simultaneously. All that is questionable is ultimately based on the questionable nature of the basic starting point, that is, the concept of the representation of Christ or, indeed, of ecclesiastical office at all: where a man identifies himself with a commission that comes from the only One in whom commission and life are inseparable. Was Reinhold Schneider correct to portray life in the commission as lethal to the person of the one who receives it (in his *Philipp* and his *Hohenzollern*)?

"And Lead Us Not into Temptation":[7] this is the title of an essay in which Reinhold Schneider describes the depths of this enticement to power in humanity's representatives: power for the sake of the good, for the sake of suprapersonal values, in order to spare people suffering (as Dostoyevsky's "Great Inquisitor" has shown, quite correctly), and only then does the path lead to power for its own sake or for the sake of earthly goods, which become important only where man no longer lives for the sake of the service of God. But who can show the boundary between Peter's well-meaning attempt to prevent the Lord from suffering (since he wants to spare him this suffering) and the misuse of the secular sword that he draws against Malchus? Already the first was a disobedience that the Lord stigmatizes as satanic (Mt 16:23); already there, the apparent compassion concealed the decisive refusal to share in the Lord's suffering. Wherever the Church rejects the powerlessness of the Cross, which is offered her and imposed upon her, she reaches out to take hold of power, and the face of Satan glimmers in her.

One must of course ask whether the opposite is also true: namely, that wherever the Church seeks power, she rejects the powerlessness of the Cross, is disobedient and promotes the work of Satan. His view of power will incline Reinhold Schneider to accept this inversion of his principle. For him, there is no possibility of reconciliation between the worldly sword and the gospel that proclaims nonviolence and, if necessary, the giving of testimony through suffering. This is why he sees the disaster that began with "the arch-plotter Constantine" and continues in Charlemagne, whom he vigorously attacks,[8] the entan-

---

[7] 18:275–82.
[8] 148:98; 116:118; 164:724 (August 10, 1933).

glement of the Church in the nets of the secular power: "all the donations, foundations, documents, wills, treaties", the "boundless fabric" in which "many worn-out colors run together", a continual fresh
weaving of the terrible curtain "that hung in front of the sanctuary
in the temple of the Jews and was rent apart in the night our Lord
died. It twines round itself, holding and supporting itself, impenetra-
ble, impossible to disentangle. And it is no longer possible to hear
the words of him who came to set us free."[9] When the Church has
once become "the religion of the state", all that remains for her is
to bless the weapons of the kings, if the kings need her support for
what they undertake, and to accept the weapons of the kings, when
they are offered her for use in what she herself undertakes. For Reinhold Schneider, this is the real falling away from the nonviolence of
Christ and his power, which is exclusively a power of grace and love
—and this is repeated again and again, with unforeseeable, terrible
consequences.

Here, in face of the Church, we must confront one final time the
problem of weapons, to which we had to apply some nuances in the
case of the state. Do these nuances retain their validity here too? An
aspect of Reinhold Schneider's mission in our age is to pose this question repeatedly, to the point of satiety, in a one-sidedness that makes
the entire destiny of the Church in history dependent on the answer
given. Every mission has one single meaning and purpose; the word
of the prophet likewise bored the people. But this did not give the
people any right to extricate themselves from obedience by means of
a reference to the exceptional quality of the "prophetic existence".[10]
As we have said, it is not a question here of the desire to shake the
reality of the state's authority with its sword as something instituted
by God; both princes of the apostles acknowledge this, after Christ, as
something that is justified in existing. On this level, it is not proper to
cast doubt on the permissibility of personal or collective defense by
means of the force of weapons against an unjust attacker; indeed, in
certain circumstances, this appears to be a simple duty. Nevertheless,
the idea of a weapon in the hands of Jesus Christ is absurd. He takes
evasive action, hides himself; he never strikes back. He also directs
those who follow him not to strike back. Naturally, it is only when

---

[9] 116:118, 119.
[10] 112:51.

he is certain that the hour has come that he offers himself to his suffering. The hour of suffering is not always present, and the same applies to the Church: there is also the hour of evasive action, and this
may perhaps last longer. In this longer hour, the Church lives among
the fellowships of this world, and Christians, at least externally, are
"aliens" who are numbered among the residents of the earthly state
and are subject to its laws. Their behavior has no "universal ethics"
that would provide orientation for their situation: they are something
unique, the exception, something unforeseen in the world, those who
must attempt to follow the will of God, the law of their native land, in
a foreign territory. Thus they must carry out the (legitimate) earthly
law, where this cannot be avoided, but in the spirit of a higher law.
It is here that we have the basis of the ethos of all earthly just wars
that had to be fought by Christians or in which they had to share
—indeed, in keeping with the conscience of the times, here lies the
basis of the ethos of the wars of religion and crusades, the ethos of
the knightly Orders and the Inquisition, wherever the secular sword
(although it derived from an ordering marked by original sin) was
taken up for the spiritual kingdom. But the spiritual dimension must
always necessarily suffer when the secular sword is used; even in the
most just war of defense, the one who puts up resistance, the one
who kills may indeed obey the precept of an earthly solution to the
situation of emergency, and he may do this without harm to his Christian disposition; indeed, he may even preach a crusade out of a supposedly Christian disposition, as saints have done. But he will not be
doing what Christ did. The contradiction can eat away for centuries
at the marrow of the Church, until it breaks out openly one day like a
full-blown ulcer. In this way, the contradiction between Christianity
and slavery became full-blown in the time of Las Casas, and in the
same way, the problem between Christianity and war seems to have
become full-blown today. It was not the Church as institution that
abolished slavery; rather, a humanity that had sought for long enough
to bear the contradiction between slavery and the human dignity bestowed and demonstrated by Christ finally understood the inherent
incompatibility. Nor is it the Church that can abolish war; rather,
if this happens, it will be a humanity that discovers the possibilities
of peaceful mutual understanding under the law of respect for one's
neighbor, something that comes only from Christ. Thus one cannot
say that the form of mutual understanding between the peoples that

is emerging only today, due in significant part to the unification of a world that has become finite and visible at a glance and to the technology of the means of achieving understanding and of transport is something indifferent as far as Christians are concerned, even if the peoples have little or no awareness of the Christian impulse involved here. Perhaps it belongs to the mystery of the Church's powerlessness that she, as the light of the world, mediates her truth ever more intimately to the peoples, although she herself—the source from which the light is shed—scarcely appears any longer to possess truth. Even a secular peace could never be merely a humanitarian affair; it would remain, even for the secularized and perhaps anti-Christian peoples, in a mysterious rapport with the Church, indeed, with the holiness that refuses to strike back; and perhaps this is why this wise peace, if it succeeds in establishing itself one day, will have to be paid for at the price of a suffering of the Church in folly, in keeping with the apostle's words: "We are fools for Christ's sake, while you are wise *in Christ*; we are weak, you are strong; you are honored, we are despised" (1 Cor 4:10).

Thus, the Church does not stand between earthly war and peace in a simple relationship as between sin and obedience, but in such a way that, in her union with the secular sword, she is made to feel most painfully the contradiction between the ordering of original sin and the ordering of Christ; driven by this thorn in the flesh, she must unceasingly bring pressure to bear for the realization of the full ordering of Christ: the ordering of love and holiness within the Church (and this love is perfected in cross and martyrdom) and the ordering of the humanity that arrives at mutual understanding in the state and outside the Church (and this ordering will be a reflection of the holiness that exists within the Church). Naturally, this does not make obsolete the mystery of the relationship between the individual and humanity as a whole: humanity can take a step of "progress" that has its origin in Christ's commission, and yet the individual will always begin anew at the same point of original sin and then purify himself through guilt and repentance as he makes toward love. Since this is the case, humanity will never escape from the ordering of original sin, and the sword will justifiably remain in the hands of the state power until the end of the world. Only its use in war could be limited, perhaps abolished. But even an individual can make this kind of "progress" in keeping with Christ, by making atonement in the

name of all for the law of the sword and exposing himself naked to
the sword: naturally, this can only be the law of the individual, never
that of the totality of men.

The Church must take the full measure of this arc that goes from
the conditional validity of the secular sword (which stands and falls
with the ordering of original sin) to the unconditional ordering of the
law of Christ. But acknowledgment of the validity of the sword in its
sphere does not in the least mean that one accepts its employment for
the spiritual sphere. On the other hand, the Church herself deals with
sinners, and she receives a spiritual sword for these from Christ: the
authority not only to bind Christ but also to loose from the fellowship of the saints. Paul used this authority to excommunicate when he
"handed over" the one guilty of incest "in the authority of our Lord
Jesus Christ to Satan for the destruction of the flesh, so that his soul
may be saved on the day of the Lord Jesus" (1 Cor 5:4f.). But since
this authority is administered in the name of Christ, it is a function
of love and of redemption; it comes from the judicial authority of
the exalted Christ, who judges the world and enacts the separation
as Redeemer; this belongs so much to the judicial function that it
would not be possible for the Church to absolve legitimately from
sin without it. Like all power, this can be misused and has without
doubt often been misused for political purposes; but misuse does not
annul the legitimacy of an authority that is quite simply indispensable
for the Church if she is to rescue and educate those who put up resistance.

One must give careful consideration to all this when one wishes
to determine the correctness and the limits of Schneider's picture of
the ecclesial office. Drawing the boundaries is above all a problem of
getting the *emphasis* right; the boundary seems to us to lie at the point
where Schneider laments the ordering of justice in state and Church,
the ordering of the secular and the spiritual swords, in a gesture that
displays neither God the Creator vis-à-vis his creation nor God the
Son in his redemption. The unveiled look into the horror (which is
typical of Schneider) is not seldom the counterpart of a compassion
with all suffering creatures that we do not find in this form in the
gospel and that thus comes close to reproaching God. Nature is constructed on the basis of transience, of begetting and death, indeed, of
mutual killing; man, the individual, the guilty one, is not responsible for this. Not even the arrival of eternal peace (or even a vegetar-

ian diet) would solve the problem of suffering, still less the religious problem of suffering. If a part of the truth is to be found in Schopenhauer, the same is true of his adversary Nietzsche and his doctrine of the glorious power of weapons and the atoning force of wars; for it was precisely the blending of Schopenhauer and Christianity that so thoroughly put Nietzsche off Christianity. Schneider never managed (like Hans André in his interpretation of nature) to see the harsh law of killing in subhuman nature as the "offertory procession of nature" toward the perfect Cross. And his Christian eye remains fixed on death, behind which the light of the Resurrection shines only dimly.

But the correctness lies at the point where Schneider exhorts the Church never to confuse the kingdom of Christ with the representation of the glorified Christ by his official vicar, the objective holiness of the office with the subjective holiness of souls, the heavenly Jerusalem with the gleam of heavenly splendor that flashes around the visible Church. Rome remains the Babylon of exile, from which the yearning songs rise up to Sion. The Church never has the Cross behind her, so that she can go directly toward glory; she stands with the apostles on the path of Palm Sunday, when Jesus returns in the evening from Jerusalem's "Hosanna" to Bethany: "we must preserve the image of glory and of the genuine ordering and hold this out against the disappointment and the death that arise from the darkness of the vesperal earth",[11] the darkness toward which the Church is ever anew making her way together with her Lord. It is only if she refuses in principle to build the heavenly kingdom on earth that the Church can seek to win something like power among the peoples. The abyss yawns only a hair's breadth to the side of this—a distinction so fine that a human eye is scarcely able to discern the spirits here—the abyss of securing one's own existence (which is secure only in God!) through the means of earthly power, the secret fear of the cross, disguised in the thousand demands made by flourishing existence on earth, and finally disguised in the demands made by the office of representation. The "blessing of weapons" begins in the innermost heart. For Schneider, this is the ultimate of all horrors, the calculation of advantages the Church can gain behind the protecting wall of worldly powers, from the silent agreement among diplomats

---

[11] 57:8.

to the public approval of wars. Wherever this happens, the proclamation of the pure word of Christ becomes impotent and lacks all
credibility (since only the testimony of the life of Christians can give
it credibility), and the contradiction that arises leads not seldom to a
public break, to schism and heresy.

The scandal is already set up on a large scale in *Camoes* when the
Portuguese pirates set sail with a spiritual blessing for an independent
kingdom "where every crime is paid threefold: with gold, glory and
a heavenly reward".[12] In *Inselreich*, the Roman support for the Bastard
and the declaration that Earl Harold has stolen the English throne is
portrayed as decisive for William's victory;[13] despite the opposition
of some cardinals, who defended what was just, Alexander II (coun-
seled by the subsequent Gregory VII) wanted to preserve his own
advantageous position. It is the Church that crowns the Conqueror[14]
and thereby blesses the injustice that perpetuates itself and that will
turn against the Church only in Henry VIII's action. There is an even
cruder description in the *Traum des Eroberers* of the negotiation between naked power and the Roman diplomacy, and the internal decision of Gregory VII in favor of the "Church of power" is ruthlessly
exposed. The powerlessness of the Church bears the guilt for the
confusion of the present-day world, "and therefore I say boldly: Pope
Gregory I would bless William's ships today. . . . Brethren! The only
way we will impose order on this world is through fear and trembling. Are princes saints? Or peoples good? What is more necessary to
us than the sword? And do you think we are keeping Duke William
back? He is already setting sail. That is certain. Ought we not to travel
with him, so that we can demand and gain today what we will be
obliged to concede tomorrow? You speak of justice. Where is justice?
In England? In Normandy? In Germany? Justice is indivisible: it is
in the kingdom of God and proceed from there." And Hildebrand
utters the sentence of excommunication against Bishop Stigand and
King Harold.[15] Sixtus IV's blessing of cannons is discussed in the *Tod
des Mächtigen*.[16] Even Saint Leo IX blesses the warriors who are going into battle against the Normans in "Der Fünfte Kelch",[17] only to
repent this in bitter tears immediately afterward among the ruins and

---

[12] 2:123.

[13] 9:115f.

[14] 9:144f.

[15] 110:53−55.

[16] 67:23.

[17] 34:21.

corpses of the battlefield, after the terrible defeat that he would have been able to ward off. In "Das getilgte Antlitz", the victorious general and criminal Masaniello appears in Naples "on the church tower, with Cardinal Filomarino beside him; the lord of the city stretches out his sword, and the cardinal blessed him and his weapon, while the people knelt down."[18] In *Philipp II* it becomes clear that the decline of Spain in the Netherlands is due to its weapons and that the public proclamation of a price on the head of the Prince of Orange justified his struggle against the Church.[19] Reinhold Schneider agrees with Platen in seeing "in the disaster that struck Rome in the sixteenth century the vengeance over the popes' former presumption in asserting their sovereignty over the emperors, that is, that Rome had aimed at a power that was inappropriate to it".[20] In *Kaiser Lothars Krone*, the danger is named specifically: "Behind the throne of the pope" (Innocent II) "lowered the shade of Caesar: but Caesar's shade followed the emperors, too, and whispered words of indignation in their ears. For it was the Christian task of both in world history to struggle with this shade until the end of the ages and to take up the cross again and again, from day to day, through the entire succession of the generations upon their thrones, and to repel the shades with its help."[21] The same book contains a description of the dreadful, disgraceful struggle between Innocent II and Pierleoni's Pope Anacletus II,[22] and then there is a struggle in ever-new attempts—from the early *Innozenz* from the period of *Hohenzollern* via the relevant sections in *Inselreich* and the essay *Papst Innozenz III und das Abendland* until the concluding five-act drama *Innozenz und Franziskus*—about the figure of this pope in which swords come into conflict between Caesar and Christ in an unparalleled manner. We shall have to discuss him in a section of our own, like Boniface VIII, with whom the scales of power sink down, so that the devil appears on the throne of Peter. The counterpart of Philip II is the "passionate man of hatred", Caraffa, who takes the name Paul IV as pope, formerly an ascetic but now consumed by the fever of power.[23] One could mention many others who succumbed to the tempter; but because of the sublimity

---

[18] 34:133.

[19] 107:334f.

[20] 18:42.

[21] 11:143.

[22] 11:92f.

[23] 107:157f., 166; 71:61f.

of their commission, an unutterably heavy responsibility continued to burden them.

And yet the Lord did not send his disciples in his omnipotence to all the peoples so that they might suffer and perish there but so that the peoples might see their light and come to conversion. Suffering and death are to be at the service of their testimony, not vice versa. Her commission means that the Church is to be active and conquering, just as she must be ready, on the basis of her service, to set the seal of passion on her action. But to be active means coming into contact with power, being familiar with its working, possessing not only the simplicity of the dove but also the cunning of the serpent. This is how the Lord's word wants things to be. His word would not have set the servant on the path of ecclesiastical office if this must necessarily lead to guilt. If one who has been given a commission truly serves his Lord and fastens his gaze unwaveringly upon him, looking to the prototype of all service, then he will not stumble even in the tangle of power. Peter's path is possible because Christ has willed it and guaranteed it. It is not rendered invalid by the errors of history, even when perhaps whole countries have been broken off from the Church through the guilt of her officebearers. Peter denied Jesus, just as Judas betrayed him: the bitterest guilt affects those who are most intimate with the Lord. But the office was bestowed on Peter in the face of his threefold guilt. And the promise that the Church will be hated and persecuted for the sake of Christ is not rendered invalid by any guilt. This is perhaps the ultimate consolation for the Church: behind every persecution of the Church, be it never so justified, stand the words: "They hate me without a cause" (Jn 15:25).

The Renunciation

The cross on which the pope is placed was described by Reinhold Schneider in two mighty historical canvases; they take opposite solutions, but both permit us to see the ultimate tragic dimension. The first, *Der große Verzicht*, concerns the destiny of Celestine V, who renounces the papal throne and thereby opens the door to Boniface VIII. The second is *Innozenz III*. He holds out in Celestine's situation and attempts to carry out Boniface's work in Celestine's inner disposition. These two dramas form in their unity a kind of *summa* of Reinhold Schneider's view of the world.

Peter of Morrone, a hermit who lives in pure contemplation, is elected as pope by a college of cardinals that is fragmented into parties. He is fetched down from his mountain solitude and enthroned as Celestine V. The man of prayer, without realizing what his assent involved, has offered himself as a sacrificial victim for the Church. When he descends from the height of contemplation into the valleys of action, he resolves to allow no other inner disposition to govern him than that of Jesus Christ, the loving, suffering, humiliated Lord. The first thing Charles of Anjou, the representative of the royal power, asks him is to bless his weapons for the Sicilian campaign, and this is logical; it is equally logical for Celestine to refuse this request and to be at once brought as Charles' prisoner to the fortress prison in Naples: a prelude to the "Babylonian captivity" of the Church in Avignon that will soon take place. It is here that the horizons open up now: first the depth. A lordly prisoner from the time of Conradin, Henry of Castile, suffers with those who share his fate in the dungeons of the castle. He is an image of the guilt that lives on, the basis upon which all the power of this world extends itself, kept an unadmitted prisoner in the dark keeps of the conscience, unconfessed, not cleared up, covered over. Charles' son Louis, later a saint and bishop of Toulouse, who will finally abdicate kingly power in order to "break through the ring of destiny", discovers the prisoner, who directs him to Conradin's grave. The dimension of the past opens up: in a dream, the tragedy of the emperor's young son rises up before Louis' mind: one who is pure is defeated because he is the representative and at the same time the one who atones for the age-old sin of his ancestors and his people, but the expiation is accomplished through a new guilt in relation to the victim and enters the foundations of the future in this form. The encounter between the earthly dialectic of power (in the kingship) and supraterrestrial grace in the unruffled holiness of Celestine would be something pure and redemptive! This unfolds gloriously in the scene between the pope and Charles,[1] in which the pope renounces all earthly power and precisely in this moment is able to develop all his spiritual authority ("Before the throne of the apostle, I command you: throw off the burden that presses down upon your

---

[1] 108:112f.

conscience!"), inexorably rebuking the king, rejecting every offer of
hidden compromise and negotiation. Thus he hardens the king's heart
for the time being, indeed, he summons forth the entire anti-Christian
harshness of power. But at the end, he triumphs through his suffering, when Charles finally yields and condescends to go down into the
dungeon to meet the buried guilt without any intervening veils. But
this dialectic remains harmless, compared with the dialectic that only
now unfolds in the heart of the Church. The storm clouds mass in
the scene between Celestine and Mattheo Rosso: the pope becomes
acquainted not only with sin and moral failure but with the struggle
for power and the intrigues within the Church and the hierarchy;
but his assistants lament that he, the contemplative who has no experience of business, does not really grasp what is going on. In his
heart, he has not left his hermitage. So there matures in the spirit of
Benedetto Gaetani, his true counterpart and seduced successor, later
Boniface VIII, the plan to test the pope through a temptation that
is inhumanly heavy, indeed, diabolic, to discover his mission and his
suitability. In a stormy night he stands adjacent to the pope's bed-
room with Jacopone, who is devoted to him, and through a hatch
he whispers—with Jacopone's mouth—words into the pope's prayer
that Celestine understands in the storm to be a voice from heaven:
"Peter, are you chosen? You do not want to bless any weapons. You
refuse to utter the sentence of excommunication. You have proposed
to do something that no pope has ever yet dared to do: Do you in-
tend to challenge the world face to face? . . . This is not truly you,
Peter! It was the tempter who offered you the crown, and your rule,
Papa Angelicus, is in reality a feast of hell, Satan's triumph over the
Church, the form of an angel in the power of the devil! . . . What, are
you now fleeing after all? But from whom are you fleeing? From your
own self, perhaps? (*quietly:*) Peter Celestine, take from your head the
crown that is destroying your soul. . . . You will be able to pray again,
you can expiate and do penance!" Gaetani is aware that: "This is the
ultimate: the temptation by means of peace, sacrifice, renunciation.
If he submits, he is chosen. My God, may he be strong enough!"[2]
But Peter collapses, and the "great renunciation" takes place in the
next act. The pope abdicates in the presence of the cardinals, confess-
ing his "great guilt" in having offered himself to God for an office

---

[2] 108:120–29.

for which he had not been chosen. "I presumed to have faith that I could remain pure in this world in all my weakness and could carry out the highest office without incurring guilt." The people resist this abdication sullenly, contradicting (without being able to know why they do so) Celestine's assertion that he has voluntarily laid aside the crown. Gaetani snatches power for himself, and in no pontificate has the papacy been so naked a claim to power. Peter flees with Louis' help and is from now on the embodiment of the hidden saint in the Church: incomprehensible, feared by those in power, loved by the poor and the sick—Peter's traits combine with those of St. Francis —until he is once again captured by Gaetani's police and brought under his control in prison. For this is what Boniface wants. Celestine, too, wants this, of course, since he surrenders himself freely into the hands of his papal foe and calls on everyone to do the same. "This is a catch of fish—Peter in the net! . . . Do you accept your capture?" Peter replies: "Yes."[3] Meanwhile, world history rolls onward, the mesh of guilt is braided closer and faster: King Adolf falls at Göllheim, Albrecht I (whose wife is Conradin's sister) sends Adolf's gold breastplate to Philip the Fair, the pope's raging claims to power meet only scorn in Paris, his Bull is burned, and he himself is cursed by Nogaret and sent to hell, where Dante will find him; Albrecht is murdered at the Reuß, and Elizabeth takes a terrible revenge on his murderers; but after his experiences with Gaetani, Jacopone has turned to hatred of God and is the leader of all rebellion against the Church. He leads the treachery of the Colonna (whose fortress at Palestrina has been burned down by the pope, allegedly for the sake of a crusade) and also of France against the pope. Terror conquers in Anagni: "Gaetani falls down the steps, his head (from which the crown has fallen) facing downward; the keys fall from his hand."[4] The pope does not long survive this disgrace; from now on, he is a Shakespearean figure surrounded by horrors, a guilty Lear, a Pythia stricken by gloomy madness, in whom the flames from above and from below meet. Peter falls at Jacopone's hand, and Boniface does not survive the news: "The holy Peter is dead, and I am his murderer!"[5] But Anjou encounters the face of the concealed guilt; the prisoner, too, is already dead, and Charles exchanges his crown with

---

[3] 108:216.

[4] 108:228.

[5] 108:271.

him; the patient man in the night receives his golden crown, and he puts on the crown of straw that the prisoner had woven for himself.

If we ask what the author intends and thinks about the action and suffering of his holy hero, the two mottoes he prefixes to the drama could guide us: "If the foundations are destroyed, what can the righteous do?" (Ps 10:3). "Nunc tuae patens est malum discessionis (Now the evil of your renunciation is obvious)" (from the Antichrist play).

The first is easy to understand and is supported and illuminated by many passages of the drama, as when Conradin says: "When the people no longer want the highest crown, then not even the strongest man can wear it. My fathers and their enemies consumed my invisible inheritance before I was born. How could I ever win back the visible inheritance? All is guilt." [6] And Gaetani says about Celestine: "I have the feeling of sinking into a bottomless pit. If he is not what he is, what then does the election mean? And where can I then still recognize the mystery of the Church? But what is the right thing to do in a world that no longer knows this mystery, that spoils it and has lost it?" [7] Finally, Celestine himself: "I was given the office of pasturing the peoples. But you have tried me beyond my strength. And that was the devil in you. It is true that I have sunk in the waves, because my faith was weak. The Lord did not come to meet me. The Lord— that would have been your love." [8] At the end, Hugo Sotin says: "I often think, venerable brethren, that we ought not to have left him so alone." [9] Seen from this vantage point, the tragedy of the saint in the Church is the tragedy of the one who finds no help, no appropriate response, no love. Holiness would have been able to embody itself in the office, contemplation to embody itself in action, only where an answering holiness had come to embrace it from the office and from the sphere of action. It is not the fault of the saint that the Church of the office and the Church of the saints diverge so terribly—so far that pure holiness must flee from the realm of the office in order to remain holy but thereby abandons the office to the demonic power. This is the fault of the dark power that a priori refused to accept the light but at best *looked on* to see how the saint made use of power, but did not feel the obligation to be holy itself, in order to salvage

---

[6] 108:88.
[7] 108:102.

[8] 108:251.
[9] 108:272.

what was holy in the Church. "We yearned for the saint, but for the kind of saint who has power", says Rosso.[10] And he is right in a certain sense, for there does exist a power in the office. And he and the others incur guilt because they wanted the power of the saint without being holy themselves. And so they are in agreement with those who have power, with Charles and Philip, who decide in favor of the saint (and against Boniface) because he is powerless and is a plaything of their power.

But now the darker second motto begins to shine out: "Now the evil of your renunciation is obvious." Not that this is an evil belonging to the saint, who does indeed confess his supposed guilt (that he loved the Church and offered himself for the papal tiara so that he might obtain the cross); it is the Church's guilt, and all join in bearing it, those who wanted this evil and those who did not want it, a guilt that becomes plain in all, those who wanted the evil and those who did not want it, by means of the curse adhering to power. Celestine bears this curse by shattering his earthly mission and enduring it only as expiation (something it was not initially intended to be). But this act of bearing and expiating cannot prevent the guilt from sitting on the papal throne in the heart of the Church and blessing weapons.

This interpretation is supported by the earlier drama *Der Kronprinz*, where the center was already occupied by one who performed an act of renunciation, namely, the crown prince himself, who exchanged the secular crown for the spiritual crown of the priesthood, thereby taking the path of penitence but also (like Celestine) opening the door to the free passage of naked power. This is the tragedy of the nobility today: kingship and aristocracy have outlived their roles, since they no longer find any noble echo in the soul of the masses, so that, if they nevertheless want to rule, they are obliged to ally themselves with the lower instincts in the people but also draw the shorter straw here and prepare the paths for monarchy's ape, tyranny. In this historical situation, it is simply too late for the idea of the genuine crown; the presuppositions for the acknowledgment of its sacral character are lacking; this is why the exchange of the secular for the spiritual crown is not only defensible but is in fact the only path that is left.[11] There is no longer any solution for the crowd but only for the individual. His

---

[10] 108:111.   [11] 101:85–87.

path is that of vicarious penitence, indeed, vicarious bearing of the night of this age. Crown Prince Rudolf ends in this night, in which he is spared neither torment nor doubt, not even the doubt whether his choice was in reality merely a flight, a flight into the sacral realm, out of action into contemplation, a withdrawal of the Church onto the heights,[12] with the result that the lower ground is left to its own devices. Rudolf feels the "contradiction of his existence" as something insoluble within himself; he looks to Christ, who is simultaneously priest and king, but it is no longer possible to combine both in the earthly office. He knows that having been born a king, he "would have had to believe in the law of the crown",[13] but "he believed in his own age and sacrificed" what he "ought to have administered". But the Queen Mother recognizes in this despair the "beginning of martyrdom". "God has handed him over to the tempter because he wants to purify him, so that he will become a saint. That, too, is a kingly work: a saint would be the highest gift of the royal house to the country." "We have been given the grace of being obliged to sacrifice ourselves in the night."[14]

This situation, too, points farther back, into Reinhold Schneider's beginnings, into the tragic dialectic between the pure height and the turbid depth, between the suprahistorical purity of the soul and its historical entanglement, the necessity of its descent into this realm of guilt, in order to purify itself here through self-denial so that it can return into the pure sphere. One must keep in view the myth of the "Libussa"[15] and of Brunhild in *Tarnkappe*, and the tragedy of St. Joan of Arc, on the other hand, in order to see the extreme point— the intimate entwining of a mythical and a Christian idea. Out of the mythical material of the peoples comes the idea of the descent of the pure soul into the realm of history, whether it is guilt that compels the soul to descend or whether the soul becomes entangled in guilt only by its descent into the confusion. Already the Church Fathers were tempted to equate this scheme with the Christian scheme of con- templation and action, and they largely succumbed to the temptation. Seen along this trajectory, the "great renunciation" would become all too unambiguous: the saint cannot live in the world of power but

---

[12] 101:67.

[13] 101:70.

[14] 101:70f., 87.

[15] 55:47f.

flees from it in order to live holiness on the heights of renunciation, doing penance for the devastation he has left behind him through his flight. Thus the holy renouncer is "guilty" of the corruption of the Church, just as the corrupt Church bears the guilt for the fact that the saint cannot live in her. This line would be all too unambiguous; in order to be wholly ecclesial, the remnant of mythology would have to disappear from it. For it is not true that the soul is pure before it enters the body and history: for it is born in original sin. Nor is it true that contemplation is pure and clear while action is turbid, for Christ is just as pure in his action as in his contemplation. But it is true that the soul came forth from the pure hands of the Creator and Redeemer and must return thither and that all pure action must derive from pure contemplation if it is to stand the test. Schneider is completely aware of how exposed his line of argument is: "Let us not forget that the antecedent history of the camps and prisons [of the Nazis] goes very far back, . . . that Christians' renunciation of responsibility for the world is a great theme of this history. Is the result of this renunciation really the emergence of torturers who have become brute animals, of a hatred struck by madness, something that casts shame on the people and on all humanity? Has this renunciation not been definitively overcome by those who breathed out their soul deprived of all power, in fetters, hidden under a table, in the uniform of prisoners, at the foot of the most wretched of all altars, making expiation for all?"[16] And we have already heard that those "who are resolved not to sacrifice their souls to power must accept that wicked men rule on earth; those who make the renunciation are no longer justified in expressing their indignation about the spread of the destruction—their words are basically meaningless." "Man, who is born to be the regent of the earth, is not permitted to make this renunciation."[17] As a counterargument, one can point to the great idea that all prayer, and suffering too, has an effect on history and that it can be meaningful to leave the realm of action in order to influence it all the more effectively from above.[18] Nor will one be able to dismiss the thesis of *Kronprinz* that a period of renunciation in the sense of sacrifice can present itself as the only remaining solution. But despite all this, *Große Verzicht* does not yeat appear to be fully

---

[16] 89:10f.

[17] 91:12, 20.

[18] 70:106f.

justified. The aim of this drama, beyond all the explanatory reasons, is to uncover the enormous tragedy of the existence of the one who bears office and to make visible the deep ecclesial guilt that consists in the mutual exclusion of action and contemplation. It does indeed always remain true that the offices in the Church are distributed, so that the one who is called to pure contemplation is to be answerable to God for the world, and the one who is called to action ought not to peer furtively up in the direction of pure contemplation. But God remains free to call every servant to cross from the one sphere to the other. Since the offices depend on his call, they are not opposed to one another in an exclusive manner, nor is one superior to the other: what God ordains is the best. But woe if the flight onto the mountain and into "holiness" be caused by the internal treachery of the Church: by the vile deceit of Gaetani, who heaps an excessive burden on Celestine as he painstakingly acts, instead of helping him. This is what *Innozenz und Franziskus* calls the primal conspiracy of power: instigated by the kings, but supported by those in the Church who lust for power, who make those who ought to have been saints in the center of the Church into saints on the periphery of the visible Church; it is these who light the flame of Rouen, it is these who make the Jerusalem that languishes in Babylon to become herself the Babylon that kills the saints who languish in her as Jerusalem and becomes drunk on their blood. The flame that leaps up out of this gulf is a flame from above and from below, and the one burned therein truly becomes an expiator for the one who burns him. This is the fire of the Lord's judgment on his Church: "You have abandoned your first love. Reflect on the height from which you have fallen!" (Rev 2:4–5). Reinhold Schneider here joins another warning voice of our age, Erich Przywara, and those patristic texts that recognize the judgment on the great harlot Jerusalem (Ezek 16) in these words of judgment but also with those pronounced upon the great harlot Babylon. Only here can Luther's slanders against Babel in Rome, against the Antichrist on Christ's throne, be completely overcome. Luther's anger, which cast off the burden of the Church, costs too little; it is only the one who is willing to bear the burden to the very end who is also entitled to hold the clear mirror of truth and holiness up to the face of the Church.

"The angel was there; he could appear in no other way. If the Church were to be great enough to canonize Peter of Morrone, it would be something unheard of, but perhaps it would be reconciliation."[1] The Church did so, whereas Dante buried the man of renunciation in the same hell as his opponent Gaetani. Is the gulf that yawns between these two judgments something definitive, or may it one day close, as a sign that existence in the Church is something possible, not only tragically impossible? Reinhold Schneider captured the greatest papal figure of the Middle Ages, in all his secular power, in a second drama: the pope with Celestine's heart and Boniface's deeds, *Innozenz*, who began in his youth with a very profound turning away from the world (*De contemptu mundi*) and then climbed in this abiding disposition to the highest peak of papal power, to rule over all the kings of Christendom, installing them and deposing them, demanding their obedience and excommunicating them, one who was virtually almighty and yet was more and more deeply humiliated by the godless whirlwind of power. In his old age, he sees himself again as the young man he once was: "Lothair of Segni, if I, Pope Innocent, were now to come into your cold room, I would fall on your neck and sob. The shadows around your eyes are the proclamations of terrible sufferings!"[2] The fact that he had to enter the realm of contradictions is not testimony against him: perhaps he did his best along the Via Dolorosa on which he was placed—he was the pope of St. Francis and St. Elizabeth of Hungary. But not poverty but "triumph was his mission, the triumph of the risen King of the world"; and it could be a law of the Church's being that he had those saints for him and against him: "Every mission is chained to its denial."[3] After long reflection, out of the internal power of his own renunciation, he acknowledged the mission of St. Francis and gave him his place in the Church; ultimately, as one eaten up by the tragedy of power, he was permitted to die physically in the arms of the seraphic saint and to be clothed with the religious habit of poverty.[4] But he burns feverishly to see the realization of the earthly glory of the Church: "I will summon the Church; she

---

[1] 108:274.
[2] 116:207.
[3] 116:215.
[4] 116:281.

is to appear in a form never seen before, casting her radiance over centuries to come; the peoples are to hear the Church and see her in heavenly ornaments, in the bridal garments of her offices and ordinations. I summon the great Council to the Lateran."[5] His aim here is to crown his work, as the mad Boniface wanted: "Hurry! Summon the cardinals! I am summoning the great Council that will call the kings of the earth before its judgment seat. I am holding the Last Day. Here, this is the throne of the judge of the world! . . ."[6] No one would contradict the excommunicated emperor Otto IV when he calls the pope "the lamb with the jaws of a lion", "the bloodthirsty lamb in Rome",[7] even seeing in him the woman in purple and gold who is drunk with the blood of the kings.[8] At the very beginning, the pope is introduced as the one who considers the choice among three candidates for the imperial throne and assesses them in terms of the three questions: "What is permitted? What is admissible? What is useful?" These questions prove each time to be ambivalent, just like everything—even all "justice"—that fills the sphere of earthly power; and thus the final consideration is the choice of Otto of Brunswick, not Philip of Swabia or the boy Frederick in Sicily, for it serves the Church "to crown the one who conducts armed warfare on her behalf".[9] These weapons and this earthly power become meaningful only when they are made dependent on the highest power, that of Christ: and since what is involved is earthly and visible power, this can happen only through the mediation of Christ's official vicar. It is not for nothing that the pope has an eagle on his seal, casting lightning flashes, with the inscription: "Give me a sign, so that things may go well for me."[10] When Otto makes enquiries about what kind of man he is, he is given the answer: "He is at one and the same time sober and stormy, a born ruler, one who watches over the world without loving it. He is the office."[11] This answer does not satisfy Otto; he enquires about the soul "in which peoples can meet", and when he sees the Pope in Rome later and encounters only the office, not the soul, a final discussion remains impossible: "I understand very well that you live your office, not your own self. You will understand me,

---

[5] 116:177.
[6] 108:258.
[7] 116:249, 252.
[8] 116:252f.

[9] 116:23.
[10] 116:28.
[11] 116:34.

too, if I transform myself into the office."[12] But the office makes the
pope "more than a human being";[13] in his own view, he cannot be
the "soul" that a Francis is permitted to live. When he speaks with
Cencio Savelli, referring to the "donations", about the conspiracy
that has caught the Church in the spider's web of secular power, the
utopian future vision arises of a Peter who has finally regained his
freedom: "It will happen one day. Peter will wander on the shore,
looking for a ship; the only thing he will have with him will be the
ring on his finger. He looks back to Rome, and it glows as in the
time of Nero, and this overwhelming structure of justice and injustice
will turn to dust. For the promise is contained in his ring. It is *not*
in all these writings and works. And it is said that the one whose
work is burned up will be blessed. Thus the Church, too, will be
blessed on the day of the fire." And yet Savelli must turn the page
after this dream by observing: "The office is directed to the world
and has the form of the world."[14] For Innocent, too, the dream has
vanished next morning, and the former view has reestablished itself:
"All authority is collected in me; it becomes the flash of lightning that
hurls the rebel out of his saddle; it remains grace if he obeys. How did
it come about that I doubted?"[15] When Otto is driven out of Italy
and returns home, he meets Francis en route and complains about
the injustice of the excommunication; the saint confirms the secular quality of the office by pointing at the same time to its heavenly
dimension: "The offices are visible and exist for visibility. God can
lead through that which is invisible."[16] On the one hand, the office
is "more than a human being" because it makes present the power of
Christ; on the other hand, it is "less than God", who remains free
to lead through invisibility; indeed, the office is not even "soul", yet
this is demanded of every man. This is the terrible situation of this
powerful man. The old question arises anew: How can one who rules
in the name of the glorified Christ at the same time follow the poor,
humiliated Christ—something that he is obliged to do? How can the
one who is installed in office "to build and to plant, to uproot and to
destroy", as Innocent says of himself (in the words of the prophet), at
the same time be the one who does not break the bruised reed? Are

---

[12] 116:132.
[13] 116:86.
[14] 116:121.

[15] 116:129.
[16] 116:182.

not contradictory demands made of a man here? Innocent is held fast in a threefold constellation of power that is skillfully interwoven in the drama: he must struggle with the three emperors. He encounters a terribly radical heresy that poses harder problems than the external power, since it responds to what is most hidden in him: namely, the Cathars, whom he will extirpate with fire and sword. Finally, he is the counterpart of the great saints, and they will bear him at the last moment over the abyss opened up before him by the theology of the heretics.

The first field of conflict is characterized by the tragic twilight that does not allow any earthly justice to appear as something absolute but fetters each justice tightly to its counterpart, the possibility of casting doubt on it and abolishing it. Otto wants what is good; he prays, but not in such a way that his will to power is wholly submitted to the good. And the oath he swears to the pope's legate against his own conscience, in order to attain power through submission, alienates the princes from him only because it has already involved him internally in a conflict with his own true self. Nevertheless, he has the consecration and the office through this, and he is not disobedient to this consecration when he tramples down the political barrier imposed on him by Innocent, viz. to refrain from attacking Sicily, which belongs to Frederick, the pope's ward. He is excommunicated by the pope and abandoned by the princes, consuming himself in the lethal contradiction between the law of his consecration and the excommunication that closes the doors of grace in his face: "(*sighing:*) Where shall I go? I cannot leave the crown, nor can I lose my soul!"[17] His end is intensely dramatic: the pope refuses to listen to the messenger who is sent to him: "Otto will be released from the excommunication only when he abdicates his claim to the crown";[18] Otto dies on the Harzburg in sight of the peak of the mountain, the "place where the damned dance", with a hellish mist swirling about it; he has monks scourge him in penance, he makes confession in tears, admitting that he has rebelled against the pope's exhortations, but since he cannot renounce the crown, he is refused Communion. At the last moment there appears the abbot of Walkenried, who had spoken on his behalf to Innocent; he assumes the responsibility for releasing the dying

---

[17] Ibid.   [18] 116:216.

man *in articulo mortis* from the excommunication, in the name of the pope, who had refused him this. Francis had been able to tell him that God has paths in the invisible dimension, lying beyond the visible offices of the Church, and now Otto in his distress knows "an utterly profound word: God is in hell too. He is in hell in wrath and fury, the form of which is the satanic disciplinarian" (he means the pope).[19] He entrusts to his brother the imperial treasures: "Here is emperor Lothair's cross. Where the beams meet, there shines out the face of the emperor Augustus. Does he not look like Christ? That would have been the solution. Something impossible ought to have happened. Now take the crown. I am glad that I did not have any son. No one is to be what I was."[20] Beside him is his uncle, Philip of Swabia, the mild man who once wanted to become a priest but who, like Otto, only has half a right to the crown and is also personally touched by the shadow of guilt, when he accepts the pope's urging and promises his daughter (whom he had promised to Otto of Wittelsbach) to his nephew and is killed by Wittelsbach for this.[21] Finally, we have the third man, whose rights were maintained by Innocent and to whom he finally gives the crown yet who will be the first openly anti-Christian figure among Western rulers: Frederick II with the pagan soul, alienated from the Christian faith and therefore intrinsically inaccessible to the excommunication Rome hurls at him; excommunication seems to him a normal fate for all emperors.[22] "He is like the hero of the saga, whom no weapon can scratch."[23] "The one who will now wear the crown slips through the meshes in the Fisher's net."[24] After the coronation in Nuremberg, he ascends his throne in solitude and discloses in a soliloquy what lies within him:

> Is it comprehensible that mighty rulers, century after century, from father to son, want to do something that is crazy: to administer a kingdom in the world in the name of the one who explicitly withdrew his kingdom from the world? This is the lance that makes them bleed to death, along with the peoples. They all bear in their heart a thorn from the heavenly crown of suffering, and the priests know superlatively well how to apply

[19] 116:252.
[20] 116:259.
[21] 116:66, 72–75.

[22] 116:165f.
[23] 116:176.
[24] 116:260.

pressure to this spot. No! The one who wants to be lord over the earth must be totally free.[25]

So Frederick enters the state of excommunication with a "cool" head. Bishop Egbert saw him sitting there: "Grace withdraws from him. When I entered, it was as if the Antichrist were sitting on the throne."[26]

But it is not the fate of the three kings that fascinates Reinhold Schneider but its dark relationship to the pope. We can understand the drama only when it becomes clear how the fates of all three fall on the shoulders of the ruler of the world in Rome as an unforeseeable guilt. It is he who saw what he was doing when he declared Otto's half right to be full; it was he who laid down the barrier of Sicily for him and who imposed on him the spiritual excommunication for his political disobedience, robbing him of the earthly crown and casting him down into the infernal contradiction. But it is also he who bears the guilt for Philip's murder, because he does not shrink from ignoring Otto of Wittelsbach's rights and demanding Beatrix for his own nephew Paolo: when Guido of Praeneste reminds the pope that the Count Palatinate is a man given to furious outbursts, Innocent replies: "You have been in Germany too long. The marriage of the families of the pope and the emperor is worth the anger of a petty prince."[27] But ultimately the guilt of Frederick's profound apostasy lies on him too: the sentence of excommunication can no longer affect Frederick, because the pope's power has lost its sharp edge in being misused in the political sphere. And Frederick is not the only one involved here but is the representative of all that is to come: "Contradiction: that is what is coming."[28]

The second struggle is between Innocent and the Cathars. The drama begins with a scene in which the sleeping pope sees in a vision Francis, who is holding up the Lateran, and immediately afterward summons to his presence a heretic from Viterbo; it ends with the pope's death scene. This time, he sees the heretic in a vision and struggles with him until Francis enters in person and chases the image away. The whole progress of the drama lies in this exchange of image and reality. At the beginning, the heretic stands between the

---

[25] 116:268.

[26] 116:270.

[27] 116:70.

[28] 116:215.

pope and Francis; at the end Francis stands between the pope and the heretic. There is a subterranean relatedness between the man who wrote the book *On Contempt for the World* and those who want to be pure, those who allow the validity only of the spirit and see the entire fleshly existence of man and Church as deriving from a dark opposing power. Reinhold Schneider is bold enough here to put his own gospel of the nonviolence of grace and of the kingdom of God on the lips of the heretics; for him, they are indeed in error as far as doctrine is concerned, but they are moved by a deep and unquenchable yearning for the greater truth, a truth that is covered over by the Church's earthly lordship in power and appears thereby as something all the more urgently required. Innocent senses this: "The terrible thing is that he is right—not in the doctrine, for that is nonsense—but I understand his yearning. One who thinks like that has experienced something. He has suffered. Melancholy! Melancholy! What a humiliation it was for God to take on this body. But we are of God, and so we too are humiliated."[29] But he summons Peter of Castelnau to his presence in order to send him to Toulouse; the start of the terrible Albigensian wars, in which Peter dies as a martyr, but thousands perish under the horrors of the religious war. And the more the crusaders rage and ravage, the more do the heretics appear to be proved right; the pope is the idol, the beast that arises out of the earth with hell's crown on its head.[30] Count Raymond of Toulouse defends them, although he is not one of them: "Those whom you call heretics live more strictly than many whom you have canonized as saints. They do not venture to eat either meat or fish; they do not bear any swords; they do not shed one drop of blood."[31] And after the conquest of Lavaur, where all the women and children of the city were gathered in the church and were burned alive, while the crusaders poured pitch on the prisoners and led them off to be burned alive, the Cathars rejoice that their prison is collapsing around them and kiss each other in the love of the Spirit, until a young priest who sees all this breaks down and cries out: "I cannot bear this. Who will believe us if we burn saints alive?"[32] The Cathar triumphs: "Thus Scripture says: The harlot in Babylon gets drunk on blood."

---

[29] 116:13f., 110f., 113.

[30] 116:52.

[31] 116:44; cf. 109.

[32] 116:143.

And when he appears to the dying pope and reproaches him for the falsity of his doctrine: "Do you think that the flames would have contradicted it? Think of Lavaur and Béziers . . . , you have literally demonstrated that the Church is hell."[33] The crusaders reel off their usual words: "The Church sheds no blood. *Ecclesia abhorret a sanguine.* She condemns, and the judgment belongs to the secular power. It is not the Church who wishes that blood be shed, but God. Lead them away!"[34] But the Count of Foix gives the decisive reply to the leader of the crusaders: "The Church sheds no blood. No, she gets others to shed it for her."[35] Innocent himself, in his great opening speech at the Council, senses that the sword cannot achieve anything in matters of the faith, since the demonstration of the truth lies quite elsewhere. "What does the Church do? Does she relieve the Lord of his suffering? Does she offer a sacrifice that is to fly ahead of the crusaders? We will be told that we have lacked faith, since we have not set out for Jerusalem; because we have not left Babylon. (*With great emotion*) I have been praised because I am powerful. But I do not have the power to call forth this sign of departure."[36] In theory, Innocent had declared himself with all his soul in favor of the "two swords";[37] but early on the morning of the day the Council met, the young Raymond of Toulouse had shown him what the praxis was by bringing him a charred and melted cross from the burned church of Lavaur, excavated from the ashes of twenty thousand corpses. From then onward, the pope bears this cross hidden on his breast; it is there when he makes his speech to the Council. But what does this mean? Does not his office include the necessity of punishment, excommunication and curse? Does he not have the obligation to purify the Church from heresy?[38] And must not this obligation lead to a "crusade without mercy"[39] in which ultimately "every robber who fears the gallows takes the cross and wreaks havoc under the pope's blessing"?[40] But does not the responsibility for this contradiction then rebound upon the office as such, indeed, on the One who is the origin of the office? It is not enough to be zealous for the kingdom (the zeal that wears out the pope); the question is whether the instruments that he can take

---

[33] 116:275.
[34] 116:142.
[35] 116:45.
[36] 116:217-19.

[37] 116:112f.
[38] 116:62f.
[39] 116:136-40.
[40] 116:144f.

up, as the man who holds the office, are not more inclined to remove the kingdom to the farthest distance possible? "Fire and sword" or "fasting and prayer":[41] that was the alternative at the beginning of the war. At the end of the Council speech, an old abbot says: "This is marvelous. But the question remains: What is the kingdom of God? Is it lordship? Is it only testimony?"[42] When the pope, worn out on his deathbed, yearns passionately for the great crusade that he himself wants to lead to Jerusalem (since Frederick will not go)—while the song of children is heard outside the window, "the naked feet that feel their way in flight on the streets of all the countries, seeking their own destruction":[43] the children's crusade—his plan is indeed a moving gesture, but it does not provide any help, nor does it drive away the apparition of the heretic, the "word consumed by fire", at his bedside. Burdened down with the guilt of the three kings, the man of office must now take on the additional burden of guilt for the heresy. "Very quietly, turning aside", he had asked forgiveness of the young Raymond when he brought him the cross: "Your country must forgive what has been done to it. I ask this of your country."[44] The only solution now lies with the saints.

And now there is the third front. In the pope's dream, Francis holds up the Church. Through his great renunciation and his poverty, he is the one who is wholly pure. But he is not wholly pure like the heretics, in an arrogance that takes its stand against the office, but in total, humble submission to the Church.[45] Innocent objects: "Those who want to be the least of all are in great danger of believing that they are the first of all", but Francis replies: "That is the affliction we bear patiently. That is why we praise obedience." Just as the Cathars quote John, so the path of St. Francis is placed under the word about adoration in spirit and truth. His path, which seems impossible, becomes possible by the fact that he takes it.[46] It is not a flight from the world but a living of poverty in the midst of the world. Not flight from the world's resistance, but nonresistance to the world.[47] It leads finally, when Brother Elias is already beginning to calculate, where

---

[41] 116:48.
[42] 116:220.
[43] 116:276.
[44] 116:211.

[45] 116:87ff.
[46] 116:89.
[47] 116:185.

Francis had wanted only to give everything away, to the sacrifice even of his own work on Alverna:

> Lord! What is happening now is not the commission you gave me. The brothers think we must have a house; the bread they receive at the doors of houses is too scanty for them. And yet you have always arranged things so that we were able to live. . . . Ought I to leave the brothers? Ought I to become completely free again? Speak, dear Lord, do not leave me this night. (*After a pause:*) No, Lord, my prayer is not right. I wanted to be all alone with your word. You do not want that. You want something else: sacrifice. You want—yes, dear Lord, now I recognize your will— you do not want my work. You want me to see how it suffers, how people get it wrong. Perhaps you want me to see how it perishes. (*A light appears.*) How can I keep on talking about sacrifice? Look into my heart: all I want is you, holy and crucified Lord! (*The light takes on the form of crossed swords; Francis spreads out his arms and cries:*) All I want is you, light that brings death![48]

It is this sacrificed man who finally spreads out the cloak of poverty over the dying pope and at the same instant makes the apparition of the heretic disappear.

Elizabeth of Hungary received his message of poverty; what she does is done in imitation of the poor man of Assisi.[49] Heinrich Raspe has driven her out of her castle, the Wartburg, and his later fate is transposed by the author back into the time of Innocent, in order to provide the counterpart to Elizabeth, who makes atonement where power is raging.[50] She pits her expiation against the excommunication of Otto and thereby against the ravages caused by the pope's edict of excommunication. She rejects Frederick II as suitor, not so that she can exonerate herself of responsibility for his soul, but because it is only through her expiation that she can bear the immense burden of his hubris.[51] But she must suffer the ultimate pain when she is compelled by Conrad of Marburg to choose between the children of her own body and the poor of God; the office of father confessor takes on this scarcely endurable harshness here, going beyond the harshness of physical punishment (which we see on the stage inflicted on Raymond of Toulouse and Otto of Brunswick). Conrad knows exactly

---

[48] 116:271–73.
[49] 116:183f.

[50] 116:199.
[51] 116:293ff., 244.

what he is doing. We have the following dialogue between Bishop
Egbert of Bamberg and Conrad:

EGBERT: You are terrible. You want to destroy her.

CONRAD: She must be destroyed if she is to attain what is determined
by God for her.

EGBERT: I once looked on while a master artist used a glowing graver to
work the image of a saint out of the bronze. That is how you are.

CONRAD: Commission.

EGBERT: And would you think it right, even if the graver were heated in
the fire of hell?

CONRAD: Bishop Egbert, do you know how the figures that stand on our
altars came into being? (*To Elizabeth:*) You stand at the half-way point.
The one who does not abandon everything cannot be the disciple of
the Lord.[52]

Here, too, the final point is poverty, where all that remains is the fact
of hanging on. Like Jane Frances de Chantal later, Elizabeth walks
over her children to get to the Lord. What the strict Conrad does
here, the mild Francis de Sales will allow to happen there. But unlike
the saint of Assisi, Conrad rises up beside the saint in all the strictness
of office. He does what is right, but in his action, love has wrapped
itself in the office in such a way that it is virtually unrecognizable:
as unrecognizable as was the Father's love on the Cross. And perhaps
the solution lies here, going farther than Reinhold Schneider actu-
ally intended. It does not lie in Elizabeth alone, but in Elizabeth and
Conrad as a pair: where God's love in the Church suffers harsh pain
and imposes harsh pain—provided that this is the harshness of love.
This harshness belongs to the mystery of redemption. Not only the
suffering of the Cross is entrusted to the Church's administration but
also the preparation of the Cross, since it is a mystery between the
Father and the Son even before being a mystery between the Son and
sinners. And we are not told that this preparation in the Church must
always be the work of the sinners who unconsciously and reluctantly
carry out God's will for his saints. There can also exist in the Church
the official representation of the Father on Golgotha. If one wishes
to call what happens between Father and Son here a "contradiction"

[52] 116:237f.

—that love is abandoned, that light is darkness, that life is death—then one will be able to seek and to find the reflection of this contradiction in the Church even without sin. It is here that everything is decided: if one admits that the sacred contradiction of the Cross is deeper and earlier in the thoughts of God than the contradiction between holiness and unholiness in the world and in the Church, that the outlines of the first contradiction can be discerned as they gleam through the second contradiction, then one may join Reinhold Schneider in unearthing the contradiction everywhere and not resting until one has found it under all the wrappings that conceal it, seeing the ultimate dimension in it. Then one may join him in reducing the real kingdom to one single point that flashes here and there, without ever being able to spread itself out extensively in time. For all that spreads out is only a metaphor and must first pass through the fire if it is to be able to enter the kingdom definitively.

> CONRAD: No goal is higher than the perfection of the saints.
>
> EGBERT: But where would the kingdom be then?
>
> CONRAD: Do you not see it? It has begun here.
>
> EGBERT: In the hospital at Marburg? Then everything would be hidden.
>
> CONRAD: We know exactly the place where the kingdom enters the state of hiddenness. And we ought to stand at this place.
>
> EGBERT: Then there would scarcely be any need for pope and emperor over the peoples. We will never agree, Brother Conrad.
>
> CONRAD: Never, Bishop Egbert.[53]

The contradiction that yawns wide open in Innocent ("first the No full of sadness; then the lordly, terrible Yes. The apostle looked on the world as refuse. But the Lord was in the world and sanctified it. That is the contradiction"),[54] the contradiction between poverty and triumph in the Church,[55] the contradiction that Christ is in his Church and yet cannot be in his Church ("He is the vicar appointed by Jesus Christ. But who dares to say that Christ is in his vicar? The authority is not the Lord"; "How am I to bear the contradiction that Christ would not be where his Church is?"),[56] the contradiction that

---

[53] 116:244f.
[54] 116:207.

[55] 116:215.
[56] 116:149.

a secular justice can be mediated only through the Church and that this idea repeatedly dissolves ("Otto: It is impossible for the law of Christ and the highest offices on earth to be in conflict with one another. Innocent: No, it is impossible for someone to be right in the eyes of Christ but not in my eyes. Otto: I will not be able to keep the oath I have sworn"),[57] the contradiction between guilt in the eyes of God and innocence in the eyes of the world, a contradiction that cuts clean through all those who receive a divine commission ("We have not forgotten the legend that says that the first knights were angels sent to the earth: guilty in God's eyes, but chosen for a ministry sober in its holiness"):[58] this endlessly varied contradiction has its final form on Alverna, where the light takes the form of the intersecting swords in order to pierce Francis through and through. Here, in the innermost sanctuary of the light, where sin does not occur, in the unity of the suffering of the Father and the Son that is simultaneously love and separation, here where man is drawn into the divine contradiction of the redemption: here there is solution and absolution—even for every tragic, sinful form of contradiction. Because he acknowledges Francis and gives him space in the Church, Innocent receives absolution. The kingdom comes to him with its glowing tip. " 'Now I see the nails in your hands and the blood on your breast. You are the kingdom. You alone.' Francis puts his finger to his lips."[59]

"The kingdom never existed and will never exist",[60] sings the melancholy poet at the Wartburg castle in the presence of his shocked drinking companions. The kingdom is "a handsbreadth of earth. For nothing more than this was necessary in order to ram the Cross firmly into place." The kingdom has the form of "the intersecting beams".[61] The kingdom had to be grasped in a purely dynamic way, yet it can never lack here below the static quality that contradicts this.[62] When Innocent dreams his utopia of a Church that would be only poor and free and then recognizes the worldly form of the office, he seeks to summarize the contradiction in the image of the lightning flash that corresponds to his seal: "The victory" (of the poverty of Peter) "would strike a blow to the heart of the world; it would be a testi-

---

[57] 116:133, 134.
[58] 116:234.
[59] 116:281.

[60] 116:194.
[61] 116:159, 85, 259.
[62] 116:244.

mony, the *lightning flash of power*. For the power that is truly involved
here can only be the flash of lightning, from the rising of the sun
to its setting, for one moment—and only this power brings Satan
down."[63] Everything that lacks penetrating force and thus falls short
of this lightning flash would perhaps be evidence that the heretics
were right. Innocent, captivated by the straight line taken by their
thoughts, feels the earth shaking under him: "I wonder if you know
this, Cencio Savelli: at the most dangerous point of all, the countries
slip out of our hands, as if a magician had snatched them up into the
air . . .", and he conjures up the "demonic heretic Marcion", who
"taught more than a thousand years ago that there had been a conspiracy in the Church at work against the truth of Christ".[64] And
there can be no doubt that the earth shakes under the feet of the author when he goes so far now as to put the gnostic logion of Christ
onto the lips of the pope in his broodings: " 'I have come in order
to destroy the works of the female.' Remarkable! Not the woman,
but the works of the female. What are these? Birth, the maintenance
of the world? No. This word is not true. It was uttered by a yearning that addressed itself to Christ but that he did not answer—just
as he left so many questions unanswered."[65] At this point we reach
the boundary of this literary work: just one more step, and it would
be transformed from a theology of the Cross back into a Schopen-
haueresque pan-tragicism, so that the exalted mystery would be subjected to a gnostic distortion. It is as if the author has preferred to
place too high a tension on the string, rather than too low, out of fear
that the terrible tension of the ecclesial situation might be reduced
again to something "safe". In any case, this tension always relaxes
of its own accord. "It is also a hidden martyrdom to be consumed
by an unquenchable yearning, the soul's heavenly impatience to fly
up to the peak for which it was born and yet to which it is refused
access."[66] And he says to Hugh of Ostia: "Something different ought
to happen, something completely different. For in the circle in which
I work, that which already took place must continue always to take
place: something insufficient, something intolerable."[67] Savelli is right
to say: "The fever is consuming the pope completely. Time's flight

---

[63] 116:121.
[64] 116:117f.
[65] 116:207.

[66] 116:17.
[67] 116:176.

tortures him. He would like to establish a tower for eternity on the slender span on his life."[68] So he becomes, with all the good and the bad that are in him, an image of the bride who yearns with all that she is, with the Spirit of God and with her sin, for the Bridegroom: "Come soon!"

Is the question of *Der Große Verzicht* clarified and carried farther in *Innozenz*? In the former play, the discontinuity between action and contemplation remained open: the saint had to flee from action, but the demonized action ultimately canonized the man of renunciation. Here, the one who made the act of renunciation in his heart was to master action in the world. He was assuredly unable to do this, and he became guilty (as the author sees it) to a much greater extent than he himself was aware: only, the atoning saints and men of renunciation expiated him and justified him. This means that the promising mid-point has not yet been discovered. The third point that would now need to be made visible would be the mastering of action through one who was totally a saint. If Schneider succeeds in drawing such a figure, then the suspicion of gnosticism would disappear once and for all, and the divine founder of the Church's office would have proved himself to be the almighty One in whom there is no contradiction, through providing the possibility for men to become saints in this office (as far as this is possible for sinful men).

In his *Papst Gregor der Große*,[69] Reinhold Schneider has sketched at least the outlines of such an existence in office. The background of this pope, who was first city prefect and led the entire civil administration and then became a monk of St. Benedict, meant that action and contemplation were united in him. Like Celestine, he was chosen against his will and resisted the election, "making the irrevocable sacrifice of the contemplative life for which his heart longed"; and, as with Innocent, the basis of his work is the *contemptus mundi*, perhaps the deepest "contempt" any pope ever had: he lives a truly eschatological existence in the storms and collapses of the age of the Goths, ever prepared to see the Lord coming for the judgment of the Last Day in a Rome that was sunk in ruins and daily sank even farther. In a sermon, he uses the image of the cooking pot, which once had portrayed the fate of Jerusalem, to describe the condition

---

[68] 116:27.   [69] 51:119–33; cf. 9:39ff.; 18:32f.

of Rome: "Where is the senate? Where are the people? The bones
have been cooked away to nothing, the meat has been consumed, all
the splendor has been extinguished. Empty Rome is burning." But he
has a powerful effect on his age: he protects his city from hunger; he
installs governors over Italy and exhorts them to practice justice; he
sends Abbot Augustine to England to proclaim the Cross there. "A
new form of power and the administration of power can now be seen,
with clear contours marking it off from the old world, although it
makes use of the form of this older world and thereby salvages it: this
is a power whose innermost life is love." Gregory works on the basis
of his office, "he stands at a fixed point. He was not consumed by history like others, who succeeded indeed in unleashing their voice but
knew nothing of the word with which the Lord of all the ages calmed
the storms." And thus this pope, who stands so close to Schneider, is
a kind of reconciling evening light after the storms of the great dramas. Here it appears natural that the man with the keys should stand
at the point where eternity and history intersect, "his eyes fixed on
the raging stream of earth's history as it crashes terribly onward, his
head bathed in light of the gravity of his office, of the grace of Christ's
peace." The working of such popes "takes charge of all the events
of history; but their steadfastness, that of the holy place where they
stand, is not subjected to historical variation".[70] And the mystery of
this Rome, its formative power, summoned all the peoples around it,
one by one, to a higher, a Christian destiny. This destiny is never
achieved complete purity, but it can be perceived in outline thanks
to the open and the hidden relationships to Rome.

---

[70] 51:128, 129, 132, 120.

MARIENBURG—KNIGHTHOOD

The Fortress

After humid days, a storm had brewed up over the broad plain, and this broke out with terrible power in the night; in the flashes of lightning, the fortress appeared closer than it was in reality, with all its towers and battlements, lit up by flames in harsh colors; the image of Mary, which faced east, shone out, and was extinguished, and shone out again, until finally the darkness filled the mighty space of the sky that had been convulsed earlier by the fire. The fortress, with all its fantastic splendor, with the image of the heavenly protectress who had given it its name, had disappeared.[1]

The author's experience is full of symbolism; it is not by chance that he stood there before the fortress that rises steeply over river and plain, where the inviolate severity of form dominates, from the earthy heaviness of the towers in the battlements, via the choir of the chapel of our Lady as it juts out boldly, up to the tip of the Gothic arch. "The gravity of service and struggle determined the entire form, seeing no consolation but that which came from this service and struggle itself."[2]

But the constraint and severity of the external dimension and at the same time of the life that was led here in the regular rhythm of service, always following the stroke of the same hours on the clock, nevertheless preserved a great freedom and breadth of the internal sphere; at the place where the Master gave the command in summer, the groins of the vaults emerge from the granite column like jets of water that separate, are broken and then unite again between the broad windows, then, as it were, run down the walls, to be sent out anew and create a vault of light through which the reflected lights of the river, thrown

---

[1] 60:17.
[2] 8:109f.

upward, glide along; and the three granite supporting columns in the
great refectory cast one to another the weights that radiate out, slide
down and are gathered together again, like fountains that consume one
another without beginning or end. And this unquenchable fullness of
inner being, won from the stone, a fullness that needs only the granite
column of the law, runs through all the vaults and chambers: from the
dark dormitory of the knights, where they lay fully clothed and with
the light on, as the Rule required, via the narrow stairs and corridors,
which were as if cut into the stone; it is gathered in the chapel, where the
heavy choir stalls still stand in the twilight of the many-colored old light
of faith, and even outside in the sober courtyard; and finally, it reaches
the most important room, from the windows of which the Master, in
the privilege of solitude, looked out over river and land; this is a heavy
vault, and those who lived here needed still another space in order to
fulfill the commission laid upon them, namely, the adjacent chapel, in
which, while the brethren assembled in the high castle when the bell
rang for the Hours of the Office, they prayed alone in order to subject
the house and the conquered land laying around it to the One who was
its true Lord.[3]

The knights had set this form in the midst of the endless plain that
ran eastward, in order to bring it to a formless world along with the
Cross: and what they brought was their own life: "human form that
found its expression in stone, and grew and lasted in perpetual service". If the peoples flowed together as if into a river that stormed
against the rock, murdering the new inhabitants with unutterable cruelty, "this was hatred of the form and its superiority."

But the form lives from renunciation, and it remains alive only if the
renunciation is renewed from day to day: weapons and worldly pride,
every kind of happiness and possessions, even the ties that bound them to
their own blood relations, must be left behind by the knight who entered
the fortress; indeed, even the dignities that the brethren bestowed on
him were something he lost again, when his year of office was over. . . .
The knights' destiny was man's own true destiny, namely, to be sent
out into a foreign land, in which the only one who can survive is the
one who gives himself a law. Under this law, the knights gave form
to the land that hitherto had been given over to the oppressive power
of the elements; they acquired, defended and cultivated something that
nevertheless did not belong to them; they were powerful and yet poor;

---

[3] 8:110f.

their orders were issued along the northern coast as far as Latvia, and across the sea to Gotland, and as far as Pomerania in the west, and yet they did not have the right to a key to their own chests or a horse of their own.[4]

The Order perished when the knights rose up in rebellion against the Grand Master Heinrich Plauen, in the struggle to have property and power of their own: "The fortress had to fall into the hands of the peoples of the plain, after the knights themselves had rebelled against the law of form." But "the symbol of the form removed above the plain, at the border"; no matter how many foreigners came here, they had above themselves an image that imprinted itself not only on the eye but on all the limbs, just like that other fortress in the west, built once out into the waters and now towering above the illimitable sands, *Mont-Saint-Michel*, which holds out the image of the eternal form to that which is eternally unformable.

Eastward went the repelling of formlessness (that is the rebellion of the masses), the gradual subjection of the earth to the law of the Cross and of culture; westward went the sending out of the same unity of Cross and culture across the seas, with the border fortress as a warning not to succumb to the enticements of infinity. In both cases, this was an appeal to the discipline of the West in its purest origins and its highest realizations, in order to bear the patrimony of the West beyond her own boundaries and to present it as an idea to the world as a whole. For the West was born of the spirit of chivalry: the Cross is salvation; man submits unconditionally to its law, which sets its mark upon the life of the one who serves and gives him the power to set his mark on the world. "I live, yet no longer I; Christ lives in me": this is the origin of the knightly set of values, according to which the servant assesses everything: through his serving, he gives the true Ruler expression in himself, mediating his will and his majesty. The basis of secular knighthood is a spiritual knighthood, which presents itself in pure form in the knightly Orders and breathes the Christian soul into the secular feudal system. Since it is the pope—representing Another, who himself ruled as one who served—who gives the form, it is not possible for the idea of the sacred kingdom, which is at once spiritual and secular, to perish. The foundations for this are laid by men who choose as the law of their life the form of representation

---

[4] 8:111, 112f.

as the form of Christ, in order to give the world the form of Christ on the basis of this lived form. The mediaeval kingdom has crumbled away, the knightly Orders and the sociological forms of the feudal system have disappeared. But no bourgeoisie can suffocate the Christian knighthood: the man who follows Christ to the full, who denies himself and dies to himself and to the world in poverty and chastity and obedience, in order to clothe himself in the mind of Christ and to take up the weapons of the Spirit, can never, ever be a "bourgeois". He is not himself (as the bourgeois is): he is the image of Another. He does not strive on his own behalf (like the bourgeois), but on behalf of the will and for the glorification of Another. He defends the form but never the boundary (like the bourgeois), for his innermost reality is the fact that he is sent by his Lord out beyond all boundaries. This is why the body of knights was the supportive structure of the West, as long as it existed, even when the external face had become a bourgeois face; and it will remain the supportive structure, even if this takes on the rougher traits of a proletarian face. Francis was a knight of Christ,[5] as was Ignatius in turn,[6] while Newman's refinement resists every temptation to take things easy. Knighthood changes its form, depending on whether Christians and the world are willing or unwilling to receive the imprint of its spirit; but it does not change its soul. Were this soul to die, then the salt of the earth would also have perished, and the Church in turn must die. But since she is immortal as long as the world lasts, the glorification of the body of knights is no backward-looking romanticism, no *ancien régime* that turns its face aside from the march of time, no secret front against the birth of tomorrow's humanity, but the only effective equipment with which the Christian can meet the present day. No effectiveness can ultimately come from everything that is moved by a hidden resentment against Christian knighthood to speak on behalf of the culture and development of the "religious personality" and its "free responsibility for its own self": *that* is a romanticism that has already been left behind by the harshness of today's world, as it gets on with its own agenda. Care is taken of the personality only where the ultimate dimension, that of perfect service, is guaranteed. "He who gains his life will lose it; but he who loses his life for my sake will gain it."

---

[5] 26:23.

[6] 28:10.

One who begins by seeking synthesis with the world will gain neither Christ nor the world, but the one who lets go of the world for the sake of Christ will receive it back in the mission he receives from Christ. Schneider upheld this law immovably and calmly. While even religious lose their heads today and are often willing to sacrifice the alleged old-fashionedness of their form on the altar of a modernity that has just been snatched down from the pegs of the world's cloak-room, he looks steadfastly at the skies.

What is involved in the defense of the West is not a historical-geographical principle (as when a bourgeois ideology defends the West) but a Christian idea, as we see when it is a question of mission or the crossing of boundaries. The idea of the West that has become traditional is closed: territory, home, the absolutized tradition are defended. The knightly idea is open: Christian existence lives on the basis of mission and loses its *raison d'être* if it loses its mission. "It is not the 'West' as a cultural area that is the ground that will bear us; but Western Christianity will bear us. Christianity is opened up to the world, for it must bear responsibility for the world."[7] This Western mission has been demanded twice with all sharpness and clarity. The first time was when the mist dissolved before the dazzled eyes of the Europeans, disclosing the far realms of America, Africa, India and Oceania, and the Christian mission par excellence was laid in the hands of the West: the extension of the previous kingdom to become a kingdom embracing the whole world. We stand in the midst of the second demand, which begins with the French Revolution and lasts, via the Russian Revolution, into the future: in the collapse of the old forms of societal consciousness, in the fact that the new forms have not yet appeared, in the emptiness and intermediary status of today lies the demand to imprint form on the new element in the mission and on the basis of the mission. Both situations are unheard-of demands that go beyond the natural powers of the West, a violent widening of its horizons—geographical the first time, intellectual the second time—and the only way to master both is from an equally unheard-of massing of Christian, supernatural powers.

How does the man of service survive the discovery of the world; how does he survive the revolution? This is the fundamental question of great Christian authors today. Claudel posed it in *Soulier de Saint*

---

[7] 52:151.

and *L'Otage*, Bloy in his *Columbus*, Gertrud von Le Fort in *Letzte am Schafott* and *Kranz der Engel*, Bernanos in his political writings and in *Dialogues des Carmélites*. The new situation is transparent for all these authors to the second situation: the external totality of the globe becomes the presupposition for the internal consciousness of the world, for the opening of the spirit to the totality. In this sense, the continents are loaded in Claudel with the same intellectual symbolism as the European countries in Reinhold Schneider, and the hymns to the world that has finally become one take a broad course in their onward flow and embrace both space and spirit. In a similar manner, Claudel, too, chooses his starting point in the Spain of chivalry, the world of Charles V and Don Pelayos, which dares to take the step out into the boundlessness of its mission; this step is taken by Rodrigo, once a Jesuit novice but now given back to the world, under the accompanying prayer of his brother, a martyr of the same Order—naturally, in the questionable dimension that attaches to this act of leaving the Order: the yearning for God coupled with the yearning for a woman, the severity of the infinite commission mingled with the melancholy of an infinite eros, the border fortress with the image of the Mother of God demonized to become the desert city of Mogador, where the chivalry of Doña Proëza must be confronted directly with the devil of unbelief and of Islam, until finally the world of representation, the Escorial, closes the tragedy (but in a pale, dying light) and grace takes the decision that sends heavenward the human failure with all its significance for world history. This is the same horizon that stretches behind the works of Reinhold Schneider, the same question, the same solution. "The conscience called to rule can take its measure only against the totality of the world and the responsibility for all . . . : it must bear the stamp of Jesus Christ's conscience vis-à-vis the world. Such a Christian conscience vis-à-vis the world comes to rule, however, only when it pulses in a man as the life of his life, the alertness of his spirit, the heart of his heart."[8] In the sonnet "Die Menschheit", we are shown the necessity of the choice to let consciousness and conscience become universal, renouncing the specific "conflictual muddle",[9] in order to keep the totality in view and take up the mission of the earth. And in the sonnet "Das Abendland", the validity of the

---

[8] 91:34, 35.
[9] 98:85.

West is made dependent on whether it refers its values back to the Cross, which essentially rules the whole earth and demands that the West enter the service of the totality.[10] Only the absolute kernel of the West will understand this call, viz. the body of knights that has always prevailed in the most sublime motifs and forms of its literature, in Dante, in Camões, in Calderon and Corneille, in the best of Shakespeare and in the few peaks of German literature that attain to this sphere. "It is here that the great motifs of Western literature shine out. All of them are basically an inheritance from the crusaders: chivalry and a mighty yearning for the great breadths, for the totality of the world, for eternal life and eternal honor."[11] Reinhold Schneider unfolded the sphere of *Soulier de Satin* in his *Camoes* and *Philipp*, in the former in an infinite tragic dynamic, in the latter in a form that lives out of death. In *Las Casas* we find the problem of the unity of the two (of Camões' ideal unity of the world and the real unity to which Philip gives form), the same unity that fascinates Rodrigo; like Claudel, Schneider sees the same image of the island kingdom and its cold, seductive queen as the opposing power. But the knight Rodrigo—even though he is guilty and fails disgracefully—wins the unity of the world and the victory for himself at the point where, for Reinhold Schneider, the epic of the Western discoveries must end with a judgment on Europe. The immense drama, which begins in Claudel, too, in the improvisation of the stage and runs its course in poetic disorder—while nevertheless allowing the highest order to shine through—remains in Schneider something that is lacerated and subject to an annihilating verdict:

> While the West grew darker and that which hitherto had been solid began to quake again, and the armies entered the field to fight about the faith, the mists slowly cleared from the sea; at the very instant when the innermost dimension was at stake and perhaps peoples and individuals would have had to be alone by themselves, space opened up. The cue was given, the curtain rose, but the actors were not yet ready; they ran about among themselves, undecided which gesture they should choose; indeed, it seemed as if they were not familiar with the drama that the invisible Lord of the stage demanded them to present. First Portuguese and Spaniards, still wearing their old armor, came onto the apron stage,

---

[10] 35:65.

[11] 52:135.

but the others did not join in their play; each one began by himself, and even the bold knights at the front of the stage soon enough showed their confusion and fell into roles that were ill-suited to their venerable clothing and banners. The peoples were given a tremendous task, but they were unable to carry it out precisely in this vital hour. The West was asked what it had done and acquired in the one and a half millennia since the Word had been spoken to it. . . . Now, at the end of this period, the world demanded the service of the West: it was to bear out the Cross, under the protection of which it had lived up to now; but it was precisely about the Cross that the battle was joined.[12]

The mission is borne out, doubly lacerated: with the rending in doctrine, for which Luther bears the blame, and with the split between doctrine and life that was made by each of the conquerors in their thirst for booty, resulting in a terror—forever indelible—on the part of the peoples with whom they came into contact, many of whom refused baptism, since they were so afraid of ending up in the same heaven as their tormentors. The ousting of the Europeans from the lands they once conquered, which we witness today, is a paltry atonement for the guilt they incurred.

The second situation, to which Claudel gives form in *L'Otage*, is the continued existence of the old chivalry when the new commonness arrives. The solution is Sygne de Coufontaine's sacrifice of the secular order of feudality, in the spirit of feudality, in order to save the spiritual feudality—the pope and the Church's order of service. Whereas her brother Georges is unable to make the distinction between the spirit and the external form, and consequently becomes the representative of the *ancient régime* and of the later Action Française, Sygne goes back to the spiritual root of the secular form and abandons the latter in order to cling exclusively to the former. She is torn to pieces as a human being and personality in this rending of her existence, surviving in her extinction only as a sign, a glint of grace falling on the world of commonness. This is the deepest and basically the only tragedy of today's Catholicism; a tragedy that cannot be understood by any non-Catholic or, unfortunately, even by many Catholics: that the world takes on a form and demands of its citizens a form that no longer seems compatible with the form of service and the spirit of representation, thus dissolving the Catholic human being

---

[12] 9:336f.; cf. 18:184–93.

into the representative of a tradition that has vanished forever, of a historical form that is not alive, on the one hand, and the witness of a living spirit, who however has no more space in which to live and becomes with ever greater necessity *martyrs* in the strict sense of the word, the one who gives the testimony of his blood. Rudolf in the *Kronprinz* stands spiritually at the same place as Sygne, the same place too, as Gertrud von Le Fort's and Bernanos' Blanche: they cannot avoid taking the step that brings the person rooted in the old over the threshold of the new age, but this step brings them death. This is a step taken by pure ecclesial faith in its night: what it sees to be black counts as white to it, because this is what obedience—obedience to the tragic situation—demands of it. No grass grows on the side of the traditionalists; they have been put in the wrong by history; but does grass grow on the side of the "spiritualists" who sacrifice themselves blindly and renounce all order? Neither Claudel nor Reinhold Schneider dares to accept this question in a visible, empirical sense. The ultimate point that they can display is the death of the chivalrous human being in his testimony, with the light from above that transfigures him.

One must, however, ask both authors whether they fully preserve and defend the Catholic dimension here. Claudel's knight is not the knight of Marienburg, the real religious knight in an ecclesial form, but one derived from this, secularized in an aesthetic manner, who does indeed keep the "spirit" of chivalry but does not keep any of its vows in a real sense. Instead of simple chastity, we find the tragic eros that cannot find fulfillment; instead of simple poverty, the superabundance of the world that deprives one of power; instead of simple obedience, the command of a higher ego that resounds higher than all one's own will. The air of a spiritual Catholicity blows everywhere in *Soulier de Satin*, but one does not meet the form of the Catholic existence, so that this air is always at risk of changing into the spectral existence of the Faustian dimension of the noble creatureliness that is never satisfied. The same is true to an even higher degree of another man who praises the idea of Catholic religious life, Ludwig Derleth in his *Proklamationen*, in which the responsibility for the world exercised by the man of renunciation oscillates into the Dionysian and Caesarean realms, and the border fortress, a modern Monsalvatsch, comes suspiciously close to the fortress of Hitler's ordering. Both have rightly observed the shift today in the boundary between re-

ligious life and the world, as this penetrates more deeply into the
world and responsibility for the world, in keeping with Marienburg.
But they pull down the dividing wall that the sober reality of the
Church demands and arrive at a unity of ecclesial and secular spirit,
Catholic and pagan spirit, a unity that is really only a confusion, a
unity in which the decision has already been taken secretly in favor
of the world, because the barriers that Christ and the Church give
the true man of renunciation have been overrun. Ecclesial seriousness becomes here a utopia impossible of realization—in fact, mere
literature. It would be unjust to say something similar of Reinhold
Schneider. He portrays the true monk at the beginning of Western
history, and he portrays the genuine priest in *Kronprinz*. It is only in
the middle of the history that the unity threatens to become "spiritualistic" in Schneider: Camões and Philip die to this world in order to create the form, but their death is a "metaphysical" death, not
one in keeping with religious life—as we see from their attitude to
women—with the result that the form they succeed in creating is
directly or indirectly an aesthetic form. But the more this creation of
form is rendered impossible by the brutal laws of the revolutionized
world, the more does the "spiritualistic" solution—"a noble disposition"—seem the only one that really remains. Reinhold Schneider
knows well that the spirit is not enough, that it very quickly expires
if it no longer has any historical embodiment. Ultimately, therefore,
all that helps is to look to that form that stood at the origin of the
Christian West, the form in which the great renunciation is carried
out really and ecclesially and in which the power of the renunciation
is transmitted into the mission to the real world. There is no other
point in the modern world at which it is still possible to hope for and
to educate the knightly spirit that transforms the world. Nothing can
be said against Rudolf's priesthood, but it does not help those who
rule. It would be necessary to think anew the idea of Philip—not a
priest, but a man of renunciation—on the basis of the Church and
to attempt it afresh on this basis. Sygne's sacrifice is tremendous, but
it cannot be repeated once the family of the Coufontaines has died
out. It can be looked for at a later date only from the ecclesial form
that sets its mark on the nobility. The crossing of the boundary in
Kranz der Engel and in the existence of a Péguy, a Simone Weil on the
threshold, becomes the public renunciation of the form of the visible
Church. The redeeming element can come only from the innermost

kernel of the ecclesial existence; it can be sure of the great promise of Christ, which ensures it both the spiritual blessing and the secular basis.

No doubt, the new knight of Christ will no longer bind on the secular sword, and he will scarcely get himself a visible expression that could stand comparison to Marienburg. Compared with the struggle of the knights of old, his will be a hidden, a spiritualized struggle in the world. Nevertheless, he will distinguish himself from the world not only through the spirit but also through the form, since the Catholic Church is a visible Church as are the forms of her states of life: the religious state cannot be invisible, any more than marriage or the priesthood. Only in this way will the cross between Church and world be constructed in all its harshness for the new knight—precisely that cross that Reinhold Schneider glimpsed, the cross before which the man of little faith cries out: "Impossibility!"

The Spirit

In order to understand chivalry, we are told in a lecture about Eichendorff, as this author conceived of it, one must perhaps go as far back as *Parzival*.

> The chivalry that the author affirmed as an inheritance entrusted to him, as an inalienable part of his own self, through the whole of his life against the tendencies of his century, is a simple inability to be anything else than what one is, a form printed on the soul and a way of life that imposed a particular attitude and obligations. The knight, as Wolfram von Eschenbach saw him, is sent into the world in order to resist injustice and to preserve justice; but he can do this only by serving that which is holy, the hidden Grail and the order that radiates out from this. Such a chivalry means responsibility, which was of course exercised under specific conditions of property by those who found their orientation here in the world and in history; but even if this kind of property no longer exists, the *mission* of the knight still remains: there must always be men who serve that which is holy in this world without reservation and without salary, caring for the weak, the persecuted and the insulted, renewing the authority of law and fighting against injustice. The knight exists for the sake of everyone: that is his proper position in the world.[1]

---

[1] 113:150, 151 (24, 25).

"Marienburg perishes because chivalry is no longer lived. But chivalry itself cannot die: it is a mystery of the one who is chosen and equipped for it by the King of the world."[2]

> The body of knights: that is the fellowship under obligation to the King of kings: those who extend the sway of justice, who cannot make compromises with injustice, the consecrated protective lordship, going across all boundaries, extending the guardianship of the valorous over the persecuted, those deprived of their rights, those insulted and distressed, those who take care of the creation as it groans, and of the bruised reed, because it is God's will that it not be broken. If the world is torn by divisions, if the peoples are thrown into the confusion of mutual hostility, how is the world to be healed, how are the peoples to be reconciled, if not through such a new body of knights, which is nothing other than the carrying out of the will of Jesus Christ, here and now, in this time?[3]

And the sovereign Lady of Marienburg "is with us at the border and awaits a wholly new service. The boundary is no longer allowed to be fluid; here, at the point to which we have been pressed, the fortress must be constructed, a building with a boldness and a strength that cannot be visible to earthly eyes."[4] These are invisible because the collapse of the old form has reduced chivalry to that spirit from which all form and culture are continually generated anew.

As long as the form of life remains alive, at least as an inheritance, everything is easy, and it is also possible to grasp the possibility of the transposition from the tradition to the spirit. The work of the authors of knightly family—Chamisso and Eichendorff, both of whom lost their castles, Novalis and Arnim, Anastasius Grün and Droste—is inspired by the aim of salvaging the inheritance and giving it a home in the spirit. Droste, for example,

> certainly lived within her ancestral rank and station in life. Since she lived according to her rank, she understood the people, the boy on the moorland, the forester and shepherd, of her homeland, as well as the pious peasant woman of the Pyrenees. We must make a sharp distinction between such an existence and the existence in a social class. One's station has living links to all the articulations in which it exists, whereas the social class is something exclusive, which provokes opposition. To live within a station means, under particular conditions and presuppositions,

---

[2] 113:152 (26).   [4] 60:22.
[3] 113:157 (31).

to exist for the totality; the station can congeal into a social class and degenerate into this and will then be a contributory factor to revolution or decadence: this development need not automatically take place, as long as the station remains conscious of what it is and what its obligations are in its mutual relationship to its own age and as long as the people retain the image of living articulation. It is not property that decides this, or the law that has declined and been humiliated into a question of property; but it is from the law of the task that it is accomplished, a task posed by history and modified by history.[5]

The ordering of society in ranks was as such spirit that had become form; and those authors, who had survived the decaying of the form, could transpose it back into spirit; "One of her great achievements is the spiritualization of chivalry."[6] But once again, how is this spiritualization to succeed when the forms of society no longer offer any points of departure, when man no longer possesses the framework that indicates to him that he is one who serves, that his life is a "life for all"? In *Philip II*, everyone saw how much the king's existence justifies and makes possible the existence of all the social ranks and of all the persons they contain. But what if there is no king, no social rank? This truly raises the question: "Is nobility still possible?"[7] The only answer Reinhold Schneider has to this is that of a "spiritual rank": an attitude that joins those who have it to a rank that cannot be perceived in sociological categories. The hope for the world lies in the

decision of a rank to refrain from doing anything ignoble and to form itself in such a way and to choose its members in such a way that each one will feel the ignoble to be something impossible. The effect of this would be immeasurable; in a profound sense, it would be a spiritual effect, since it would share in determining the form of the people's life. Such a decision could be taken and kept alive only out of a great historical consciousness, in the veneration of the fathers. The more men are brought low by distress, by the monotony of work and the ordinariness of their thought and the impoverishment of their forms of life, the more are we directed to the example of the one who cannot bring himself down without dying. . . . Now the work of the uttermost abnegation,

---

[5] 99:9f.

[6] 99:11.

[7] 52:36.

the work of building in the heart the castles that have been removed, must succeed.[8]

But how is this "rank" to be formed? Reinhold Schneider's words to the young generation appeal to its chivalry[9]—but does this exist? He must express as a wish what *ought* to be the case: his wish is that it may indeed exist. "We wish with all our heart that this chivalry may not have died in our people, that it may find the form in which it can meet this age, just as chivalry as an inalienable human value penetrated past ages and made itself their companion in order to direct actions and attitudes. The strongest are without any doubt those who do not live for themselves."[10] For it is indeed true that everything depends on the form that is required here. Neither the spirit as such suffices nor the doctrine that is proclaimed (and that will be infallible until the end of time), but only the lived life that makes visible the spirit and the doctrine. And so, in our view, it is necessary to go back to the chivalry that lies established in the *Church's indestructible order of forms*: where Christ's act of election and the total renunciation that answers him establish not only a spirit but a form of life in the visible ecclesial sphere, a rank that is spiritual but nevertheless possesses form. This rank must not be confused with the Church's office, which is indeed a service and a dignity and demands a form of life for both these; but the office itself does not bestow these. The articulation and gradation that establish the form of life in ranks is not the distinction between the hierarchy and the laity but that between a vow made exclusively to God and a vow made to a human being (in marriage): the former is the rank of service *tout court* in the Church ("*instrumentaliter*", says Thomas Aquinas), which must raise up for those who live in the ordering of the world the image of total abnegation and the readiness for every mission. Reinhold Schneider's words are completely true: "*Only* the body of knights summoned into being by Christ is imperishable; it has given life to all the genuine bodies of knights that have had their hour and their service on earth and have assuredly never carried these out without making mistakes. But the world remains dependent on Christ's body of knights."[11] Only, one must bear in mind that this chivalry has a visible form in the Church, established

---

[8] 52:39, 40.
[9] 78:6f.

[10] 76:24f.
[11] 60:19f.

by the promise at Matthew 19:29 and developed in all the forms of the vowed life. Monasticism is only one of these possible forms; historically speaking, it was often too much turned away from the world and placed too much emphasis on the individual for it to be able to do justice to all the demands of the task in the world that Schneider assigns to chivalry. The spirit that must inspire monasticism at the present hour must bear in itself the entire span that goes between renunciation and making use (on the basis of one's mission), and it must also have the span between Spain and Russia, between Ignatius with his form and John with his all-embracing love, and this tension must be lived in the ecclesial form that, as Marienburg shows, offers a place to the most exposed positions of the Christian in the world.

The Cross

In Christ's sacrifice, the internal gift of himself is antecedent to the external Passion that the world inflicts on him; and in the Passion itself, the execution of the sacrifice by the Father who hides himself is antecedent to the execution by the gathering darkness of the world. The *occasion* for the sacrifice of Christ's gift of himself and for its execution as an action between Father and Son is the sin of the world: so the first aspect of the Cross is its position between the purity of the kingdom of God and the lost state of the kingdom of the world. But the occasion of the redemption is surpassed by the true *reason* for the redemption, namely, God's love, so that the first aspect becomes the Cross that love imposes on itself. Without the internal Cross, the external Cross would be meaningless: only love justifies the suffering, only love's suffering justifies the terrible distress of the world.

The Church inherits both Crosses: the external state of being crucified between God and the world and through the world; but also the internal state of being crucified by God for the world. Both Crosses have been visibly imprinted on the structure of the Church. Although every Christian life shares in both, the Cross between the soul and the world has its particular place in life in the world, while the Cross between God and the soul has its particular place in the life of the evangelical counsels. One who lives by the counsels carries out for the whole Church in an existential manner what the office of the priesthood carries out liturgically for all, the sacrifice of the body of the Church as a participation in the sacrifice of the Body of Christ. The hierarchical ordering of the Church emphasizes the priority of the internal Cross to the external Cross, which is based in the former and receives its own fruitfulness thence; this means that life in the counsels has priority over the state of life in the world. Although the life of the counsels renounces the good things of the state of life in the world, it is not opposed to this like one part to another part of the totality, for Christ, who renounced property, marriage and freedom, does not stand opposed to the world as one part of the totality to another. It is the mystery of the internal Cross, which establishes the state of life in the counsels, that it universalizes this state of life vis-à-vis the world, and also vis-à-vis Christian life in the world. It is based on a choice out of the world and a life that is not of the world and empowers for a mission out into the whole world and to a spiritual fatherhood and motherhood vis-à-vis the whole world. One cannot say that this mission to all the world is limited or even reduced by the fact that one does not make use of the world, a renunciation exemplified by Christ and imposed on the one who takes religious vows. But this nonlimitation cannot be grasped in sociological or psychological categories: it belongs to the wonderful paradoxes of the suffering and Resurrection of Christ. This is why it was right for the great founders to place their disciples at a point deep in the world; before the internal Cross, the barriers blocking access to the world collapse in principle. Teresa of Avila rolled along in her wagon drawn by mules, in a "traveling convent" on the bad roads of Castile from town to town.[1] Francis wants his sons "to live in the midst of the world as hermits. For", he says, "wherever we go, wherever we stop, we bring our cell with us. Brother Body is our cell, and the soul sits therein like a hermit, thinking of God and praying to him."[2] Ignatius says to those who listen to him in Azpeitia: "We are no religious; for us, there is to be no house, no homeland, but only the ministry; and we want to try to belong inseparably to the Lord and yet to be familiar with the things of the world, so that we can serve him at every single place."[3] Francis de Sales unfolds his "great plan" to Madame de Chantal: he "did not want to found a new Order that would be milder than the others and therefore less than them; it was to stand between the world and

---

[1] 16:50.
[2] 26:41f.
[3] 28:82.

the monasteries, reconciling and helping."[4] The second aspect of the
"great renunciation" becomes ever clearer in the course of Church
history: existence for the world, being sent outward, responsibility for
the totality. The societal element of responsibility for the world sets
its mark even in the most utterly hidden contemplation of Carmel.
It is the weakness of our nature under original sin, not the inherent
logic of the matter, that obliges boundaries to be set up between the
one who takes religious vows and the world: boundaries that give
protection, boundaries urged by the Church's caution, the care for
the greater number of persons. The more a chosen one accomplishes
in his life the sanctity of his Cross, the more will his only cloister
be the power of the Lord, and the more deeply can he penetrate as
the light of the world into the darkness, like the main characters in
Sebastian vom Wedding or Bernanos' *Diary of a Country Priest*. For the
light, the darkness is only a receding boundary. And there is no reason
in principle why this mission should be reserved exclusively to those
humbled and afflicted: May it not also apply to the complete sanctification of the work of administration? Marienburg was no dream, and
the Escorial still stands to bear witness to the reality of its founder.
And all those who seek today to live the perfection of Christ in pro-
fessions in the world have in their turn pushed the borders farther
back.

But the internal Cross would not be what it is if it were assured of
more than the fact of its mission, that is, if it were certain of victory
in the sphere of the world. In this march into the world, the internal
Cross goes to meet the external Cross that awaits it. "Another will
bind you and lead you where you do not wish to go." But the resistance does not begin only with the wickedness of those who per-
secute the Spirit of Christ in the disciples; it begins in the structures
themselves, which, as we have said above, share in the fallenness of
nature. The external Cross is the tension, to the point of contradiction, between the world that moves in these structures and the laws
of the kingdom of Christ. But men of the Church are chosen to take
up their position primarily in this external Cross, whether they rule
as kings and bear the authority of the sword or lead a modest life
with their wife and their money. These people cannot die the death
of the one who is called to live the life of the counsels, so that he may

---

[4] 27:30.

continue to live for the world out of Christ's life alone. As Paul says, they are divided. And since this division cuts clean through them, the only choice left to them is to impart to the external Cross the spirit of the internal Cross: to use possessions and marriage as if they were not using them, to exercise their freedom as if they were people bound by service. There is only *one* Christian love, and its law is the gift of what is one's own, renunciation, a vow that binds itself eternally to the beloved. The Christian who lives in the world will inexorably be placed in spirit under the law of the life of the counsels because of the unity of the crucified love: "Genuine love impels one to take a vow; it cannot let itself be divided; it lays claim to the whole person to make the total gift of self, forever."[5] And what does love have to give if not possessions and body and spirit? Schneider's whole ethos can be interpreted as the spirit of the vows in the accomplishment of one's mission in the world. "The only one who can carry out the task of administration is the one who has no desire to possess but stands in the service of One who is higher, in the great total context."[6] And this comes from the essence of secular power itself: "Power cannot be possessed, only administered."[7] We have seen that this proposition is valid only under certain qualifications: there is not only a transcendent power but also a power immanent to the world. But what we must now say is not affected by this qualification. This is shown clearly enough by the Gospel text about the steward. The truth is that man is only a representative. The radicality of the Franciscan poverty "was in a certain sense the basis of the truth itself".[8] This is why Schneider also sees that virginity, understood in Christian terms, is no renunciation, so that the renunciation imposed by Christian marriage is no restriction but a widening:

> For a purity of this kind, which preserves the body out of love for Him, renunciation would not be the correct name; the traits of the Lord's countenance are not marked by renunciation. He went in total freedom through the things of earth; he did not deny them; he did not take those who were his out of the world: but evil had no share in him. Renunciation always means the gift of self to a *part*. But the Christian life is concerned with the *totality*, not with the life of individuals, but with the

---

[5] 78:12.

[6] 76:27.

[7] 91:17.

[8] 26:40.

life of the world, and it is only in this context that the existence of the person comes to fulfillment, out of a responsibility for the totality that is assumed in full awareness.[9]

And obedience is engraved as the final rune on this existence. Man has not chosen his life; "along with life, he was given a certainty, namely, that he is to live: he did not wish this, but this is what is laid down for him. And now he obeys this determination."[10] He does not obey himself but Another, his Creator, and this is why he must also perform the Creator's will in his own will. And he does this precisely by assuming responsibility for his life. He knows "that obedience never releases him from responsibility".[11] In obedience, as the spirit's sacrifice of love, every vow is included: "There is no genuine poverty without obedience, nor any purity."[12] Thus the appeal can be addressed to the dignity of the Christian: "Oh, if only you were proud enough to bind yourself!"[13] But the one who is obedient does not choose himself: he lets himself be chosen. He does not even choose his state of life: by choosing it, he obeys God's choice. This act of being chosen is unique, a deed beyond both activity and passivity, and everything that the man is must simply be flung into this deed. "The heart must at least have been obedient to the angel and his severity, which brings our earthly planning over into God's plan and glory with the grace of a terrible pain."[14] "For we are free at one point. There is an hour that determines our life, and this hour belongs to us."[15] Destiny and life depend on the sublimity of this choice and decision, far beyond the boundary of the person himself. The one who is chosen is to take the path of holiness in the visible vow. The one who is not chosen for this will stand in the external Cross and will not be dispensed from holiness, which is the crown that must hover above the decisions he makes; in the conflict between the kingdom of the world and the kingdom of God, he must be on the watch for holiness, in order to make the right decision. Holiness is demanded of life in the world too.[16] And the more this life, too, allows the internal Cross to become the form of the external Cross, making the great renunciation the source of the great responsibility,

[9] 78:25, 26.
[10] 91:98.
[11] 7:219f., 225.
[12] 71:38.

[13] 98:68.
[14] 62:40.
[15] 3:56.
[16] 78:29f.

the more will the one holiness of the Bride of Christ shine out purely from both lives.

To seek to remove the boundaries between the external forms of the states of life would mean spiritualizing the visible Church. The encounter between the king and the saint, between the saint and the pope, between the king and the pope, remains here below an ultimate figure that cannot be superseded. Reinhold Schneider knows this better than anyone else; he does not turn this mutual relatedness into an identity. But the mutual relatedness demands the highest compenetration: the king *ought* to be a saint, that is, he "ought to have had the experience of the monk and to rule with this experience".[17] But the saint must not imagine that the form of holiness dispenses him from the *substance* of holiness: to hang with Christ on the Cross, blessing and redeeming the world. Benedict Labre says to the young man in Rome: "Go right into the midst of it! You will not save anything. For it is the Lord who saves, not men. But you must know what you are accepting responsibility for."[18] The renunciation does not dispense from responsibility but rather imposes a greater and more profound responsibility. There can be no doubt that the new body of knights that is demanded by the present hour of the world's history is called to this intimate encounter between the monk who bears responsibility for the world and the man of the world who administers state and culture out of the spirit of renunciation. With his *oeuvre* as a whole, Schneider has powerfully prepared the paths for this encounter.

> But it remains a mystery between man and God which form of the body of knights is appropriate to a particular age; Dominic responded to the gravest danger of his age when he gathered his disciples around him, and Ignatius of Loyola responded to a different kind of danger in a quite different way. Perhaps the hour has come again for such a response; perhaps the grace of a great danger has brought with it such an hour. But it is for grace to speak; it alone will shape the form of the new body of knights and will do so only if we pray for this work and make ourselves ready to seek it everywhere and to hear it in the midst of the storm of our age but with a recollected soul. No human consideration creates the form; the light from above, the heavenly fire that outlasts all

---

[17] 37:82.   [18] 34:250.

the lightning flashes, must fall into the soul and consume a man. The one who burns in this way will become a sign.[19]

But it belongs to the mysteries of grace not only to grant the fulfillments but also to grant every promise. To plead, to struggle, to grope—all this is grace, just as much as finding and possessing. Elijah's courage is grace, when he arranges the pyre in its layers and pours water over it to challenge his enemy; his weariness unto death is grace, when he is the only one left, no better than his fathers; his strengthening through a mysterious food is also grace—this is a food that the world does not know, but a food that empowers him to go on his pilgrimage to the holy mountain and to experience God in the still, small voice of the breeze. The testimony given to Schneider is also grace, a testimony that he must give in the same spirit as Elijah when he spoke in the presence of Ahab and his priests and also before the holy people. In this transient world, it may seem that the wind has blown it away, but all testimony is eternal in God, and when God takes up Schneider's testimony in the chariot of fire to that place where it has its home, then may its clothing, the mantle, fall down upon us, for this mantle makes the waters divide.

---

[19] 60:20.

CURTAIN

The Departure

"You are there in order to see how a whole age is cleared away, so to speak. . . . How rotten everything is."[1] The situation in which Reinhold Schneider looks on while his family house is pulled down in Baden-Baden in the winter of 1956–1957 is a central symbol of his last years, which were marked by autobiographical writings. For the slender volume *Der Balkon* had as its first title: *Der Abbruch, Notizen eines Zuschauers* (The demolition. Notes of an onlooker). The author's life had become harder than ever after 1945, and especially in the years 1950–1951. ("It was a delight to live under Hitler, compared with what I have to endure now.")[2] Expressions of hostility, calumnies of all kinds, the boycott of all Catholic newspapers and periodicals, which caused him to have his statement against rearmament printed in East Berlin, with the consequence of general indignation —and then honor upon honor (Pour le mérite, the Peace Prize of the German publishers' union) and many other decorations, numberless lecture tours, invitations to take part in the rehearsals of his dramas. Mountains of printers' proofs exhausted him to such an extent that he prefixed Paracelsus' word to the *Balkon*: "The works show that the work is over."

Why is *Der Balkon* so important? The house in which he was born was the once famous Hôtel Messmer, in which the entire upper crust of Europe had gathered at the end of the last century, King Wilhelm with Prime Minister von Bismarck, Napoleon III, Austrian and Russian princes. But what among this noble company corresponded even to the slightest degree to what the concept of "crown" had portrayed for Schneider? He was aware that the crown had long since lost its valid meaning and that (as has been shown) this meaning could survive, if at all, only in a Christian transformation. But this "demolition of the house every day"[3] hammers the known truth mercilessly into his consciousness: "Rubble, no form any more. Should I take a souvenir away with me, the fragment of a window? No. A labyrinth that was built by a time now past, a labyrinth in which we were held captive, has been cleared away. A blessing once lay upon it. But the

---

[1] 132:61.
[2] 168:117.
[3] 132:175.

blessing was not taken good care of. The entire splendor of those years was based on sins."[4]

This passing away brings the author into an unfamiliar external relationship to a security that embraces the whole of secular and Christian history, a security in which he had always moved. He reads works about astronomy and shares Pascal's feeling of terror at the endless emptiness of space; he studies paleontology and trembles at the immeasurability of prehistoric times. "We shudder utterly at the sublime meaninglessness, lifeless fires going round in circles, cast out arbitrarily and thrown together in clumps, under the superior power of nature despite all their own power—and wandering between these, at an insignificant place, this magic isle of our life and spirit, of guilt and death . . . who can understand the God whom man meets within himself . . . as the God of *this* universe! It is perhaps here that there comes the deepest discontinuity in our religious existence." Nicholas of Cusa (as Schneider now says more frequently)

> in his mysterious knowledge had perhaps accomplished this virtually impossible task: the unsurpassable superior might of grandiose meaninglessness must coincide with revelation and the certainty of salvation. But who will condemn the one who is overwhelmed by the question of the universe? . . . Who can truly find calm by means of theological expositions of modern knowledge, of the cosmic problem, of the problem of the will and of history? Who can escape the feeling of being conquered and of perishing in the ocean of sparkling night? It is hubris to seek to find the meaning in oneself, in personal intellectuality, as Pascal and Fichte wished. It is annihilation, if one does not do so.[5]

In keeping with his conversion experience, Schneider holds together in the uniqueness of Christ things that he sees threatening to fly apart:

> We do not displace the word that everything is created in Christ and that he is the head of the universe, in whom everything—matter itself —is renewed. In the abysses of the universe we must recognize the countenance of Jesus Christ instead of our own confused face. It is not a question of science's having the possibility or the obligation of abolishing faith. . . . If we do not succeed as Christians in being at home in endless space, then we are failing in our duty to the age in which we live. . . .

---

[4] 132:181.   [5] 132:168–69.

Do we perhaps believe that there are aspects of the world for which Christianity has no answer? That is the one thing that must not happen. And it is better to die with a burning question pressing on one's heart than to die with a faith that is no longer wholly honest: better to die in agony than under anesthetic. The hope remains that humanity will one day see Christ walking through space, as Peter once saw him walking on the sea.

But Schneider does not allow any soothing end: "Is it a 'ghost', a reflection of the earth? Is it the Lord? Almost as great as this hope is the danger that we send our cry upward while we sink down in endless space."[6] But this danger in turn is overtaken by the liberating thought that Christianity cannot be understood without the element of tragedy. "The modern image of the world does not in the least refute the faith. But it does demand a quite different armory of spiritual power than the Middle Ages, for example, or the apostolic age. . . . God does not contradict himself because the contradictions coincide in him. Christianity has given a metaphysical answer to tragedy, but it has not abolished tragedy." The best introduction to Christianity remains Greek tragedy:

> The simultaneity of failure and accomplishment, geniality and crime, illumination and blinding; here is the beginning of the deification of suffering, which is brought to its completion in Christianity . . . the unfathomable entry suffering makes into the Godhead. Perhaps we might understand in this mystery this earth that is broken open and lacerated, where the One appeared and suffered and sacrificed himself, submitting himself to his own creatures. In the presence of this cosmos that almost annihilates us, we must see him and the act of redemption. For it is in him, as its head, that the cosmos is recapitulated and in him that it will be saved.[7]

But once again the pendulum swings back. Schneider knows Christ only as the Crucified, who bears the contradiction in himself: "Christ is not the one who brings order to the world. He is our lethal freedom. But we must realize clearly that this freedom passed over into a world that has been substantially changed by the intelligible deed carried out in our lifetime—by something that concerns us all. The

---

[6] 136:241, 242.   [7] 126:75-76.

creation of Mozart, of Stifter, of Mell will not change, but the ques-
tioning experiment has conquered the whole earth."[8]

The experiment has totally desacralized knowledge, and this brings
us to the neuralgic point in Schneider's worldview. He still speaks in
Winter in Wien of the "sacral crown", "the anointed ruler is a worker
of miracles, a saving power; in England and France, one particular
illness could be healed by his touch, scrofula was called *mal du roi*, or
the king's evil. . . . He is a magus, a prophet."[9] Can this "sacrality"
be linked seriously to the Christian coronation of the emperor? This
may have been the case in the mediaeval faith that drew on the images of Constantine and Charlemagne, and the crown that descended
through the air upon Lothair in Bari could be seen as a confirmation of this—not only by his contemporaries, but by Schneider too.
But did Christianity lose much when increasing secularization meant
the disappearance of this faith? At the very latest, the Hitler regime
must have made it clear that "The crown of sovereignty has changed
into the crown of mockery; from now on, nobility attests its presence by the fact of its humiliation."[10] The shift becomes clear in the
way he judges the theater: the Christian truth "demands the illusory
world of the theater, which is not sacred *after* the classical period,
and cannot be; it was indeed possible to go onto the stage in the
presence of the classical gods and summon them onto the stage; one
cannot do this in the presence of Christ, nor can he appear on the
stage."[11] The transformation of the old lordly crown into something
new, something that was now truly Christian, was already portrayed
in *Kronprinz*, and Schneider had noted as early as 1933: "The relationship to the crown is the relationship to the law, to the strictest
ordering, which is not determined by that which is of this earth. . . .
The crown remains what it is: the greatest symbol of all the laws that
have validity among men, the symbol that determines destinies. It is
an expression of the responsibility that an individual must assume."[12]
In the sonnet "Bezeugen will ich es zum letzten Male" (I will attest
one last time that a crown sheds its glory on every brow), this crown
becomes the gift to man "from the freedom of the kingly blood"
of Christ: "only the conscience, which with boldest courage takes its

[8] 135:18.
[9] 135:78.
[10] 146:26.

[11] 126:70.
[12] 164:699–700.

position and deliberates before the eternal throne" and thereby "exercises its administration like justice itself".[13] The cases of Droste and of Marienburg have made it clear that the phenomenon of secularization, which Schneider certainly regretted, was also something he knew to be the occasion for the necessary transposition of the sacral out of its pagan origins into Christian authenticity. Thus the description in the early *Innozenz III* of the provenance of the Christian world from the catacombs into an existence above the earth as a phenomenon of the striving for Caesar's power was a grave distortion. For all the pain it caused the onlookers, the demolition of the Hôtel Messmer had its function as a corrective.

Nada

In a state of total exhaustion and utter weariness, Schneider wrote his *Winter in Wien* (1957–1958), and it is above all these last words that have enkindled curiosity: Can one read out of these pages, drenched in melancholy, something like a sensational apostasy from the whole of his earlier work since his conversion at the time of the book he wrote about England? For this reason, new editions rapidly followed. Appeal was made to Schneider's return to his first "teacher", Schopenhauer; he had written an introduction to a selection from his works. A deeper unease may have been caused by the fact that he had exchanged letters since 1951 with Erich Przywara, whose supradialectical theology of the Cross and transcendence seemed to Schneider intellectually related to an ideology of Carmel; but one should note how much it is Przywara who takes the initiative in the letters.[1]

It is indeed true that until the very end—but also from the very beginning—the Cross of the Son of God, and thereby "the most terrible suffering: the suffering of God", "the consent of the Father to the horrible sacrifice of the Son",[2] was the door through which Schneider found his entrance to the Christian faith. And let us hasten to add that the *idée fixe* that we have already mentioned, and which pursued him all his life, the idea of the happiness of being permitted to sleep forever, lent a rather weaker note to the Resurrection. There

---

[13] 124:216.

[1] 145.

[2] 126:93, 94.

was nothing at all new when he wrote about the Church in *Winter in Wien*: "Firmly convinced of her divine foundation and of her duration until the end of history, nevertheless I prefer to withdraw into the crypt; I hear the song far off. I know that he is risen; but my vital force has sunk so far that it is unable to reach out beyond the grave, in a yearning and a fear that go beyond death. I cannot imagine a God who would be so lacking in mercy that he would awaken a dead-tired sleeper under his feet, a sick man who had finally managed to fall asleep."[3]

But it is worthwhile to compare this nihilism, seemingly akin to Buddhism, with Schneider's whole attitude to this great Asian religion. The confrontation begins already in his early diary: "nihilism" here means initially that transcendence beyond what belongs to the world, although this "is the surest support of the earthly". "For even Schopenhauer's denial is only the contradiction of everything that is known and experienced, but not the affirmation of absolute nothing."[4] But is this not true of the Buddha too? "It would seem to me to be necessary to look at Europe from the soil of India. . . . It goes without saying that I would merely be a guest there. But the Indian experience is the only additional experience that I truly felt to be desirable, indeed necessary, whereas what others understand as pleasure, happiness, enjoyment, reconciliation is inaccessible to me."[5] But one year later (1932): "One can indeed make distress the starting point for thought that shapes the world, but not suffering. The fact that he does the latter separates me from Buddhism."[6] The seductive closeness becomes a definitive distance: "The traditions of India and China could have been a powerful temptation for me had not the ever more rapid descent of European history driven me toward Christ."[7] "Christ deified suffering. He bore up into the mystery of the Godhead the wounds inflicted by hatred and disgrace as victorious signs of love. . . . My deepest nature was oriented to the veneration of deified suffering."[8] Naturally, according to Schneider, the confrontation between Buddha's religion and Christ's must be carried out with a quite different kind of passion: "The dialogue of Christians with

---

[3] 135:79.
[4] 164:161f.
[5] 164:489f.
[6] 164:551.
[7] 123:77.
[8] 123:130.

Asia has still scarcely begun."[9] "Why cannot one learn from India as a Christian? I find the opinion of Indian Christians that the Westerners completely failed to understand Christ convincing. It is a terrible thing that Christianity is scarcely mentioned in India."[10] There must be a dialogue between the refusal to suffer and Christ's will to bring salvation through suffering.[11] "The enlightened One knew nothing of the Physician of the world and sought to be the world's physician by taking his full leave of it, without love and without hatred. . . . Could he take any other path, since God had not revealed himself to him?"[12] We have already observed how little Schneider truly returns to Schopenhauer in his late introduction to this thinker; he draws a portrait from a superior height of Schopenhauer with all his contradictions; even in the diary, the transition to the central value of "life" is irreversible, no matter how deep the contradiction may sit in this: life is a "relationship to infinity",[13] even if this also means that it is the "tragic necessity of the impossible"[14]—but does this in fact bring us to the Augustinian-Thomistic paradox that human nature cannot be perfected in itself without the free condescension of grace, which must take on the form of the Cross in the sinful world?

It is here, of course, that Schneider's most extreme words are uttered, words that appear to take him beyond the boundary drawn by the Christian faith. The lawyer's question, "Master, what must I do to attain eternal life?", "describes the spiritual situation on which the gospel is based. . . . But is this situation something essential to man? No. Neither the Presocratics nor the Stoics posed it. . . . The question answered by the coming of Christ, the question that preceded him, has a precise historical location and is thus the voice of a variable constellation that is very specific. This is the reason why preaching and mission fail at one particular place."[15] Formulated with even greater seriousness: "For me, the revelation of love is a personal word to the one who believes, who is able to believe, not a word addressed to the (animal) creature, to space, the stars, or to history, no matter how paradoxical this may appear. One single star shines weakly out of a boundless cosmic dark cloud; this must suffice for us;

---

[9] 127:39.
[10] 148:105.
[11] 146:249.
[12] 146:248.
[13] 164:708, cf. 556, 680–82, 696:98.
[14] 164:682.
[15] 135:98, 99.

nothing more is revealed. Naturally, no theologian can accept this."[16] But why not? The Christian revelation is de facto a word addressed to each individual; it does not include any information about the millions of years of evolution or about the innumerable light years of the cosmos. Is it impossible to give these quantities a home in a unique, absolute quality? If so, why then does Schneider speak of the "entry into Jesus Christ's cosmic and historical abandonment", seeing in his own suffering "perhaps indeed a participation in" this abandonment?[17] And why does the author, despite everything, go into the church to pray every morning, "praying beyond faith, against faith, against one's own self, every single day the clandestine path taken to the church by the bad conscience. . . . As long as this need is felt, grace is there. . . . And this need could even be a promise: *numen adest*."[18] "One must pray, even when one cannot do so. . . . I have a deep need for prayer, that is what sustains me, what calls me into the church in the morning; I cannot pray for myself; and the Father's countenance has become wholly obscured in darkness."[19] It is quite in order, quite understandable, that Schneider can no longer pray for himself in the face of the world catastrophe whose herald he feels himself to be. But it suffices to hold one's shattered existence before the veiled image of God. Schneider will not cease to pray, in all his darkness; he will collapse and die on the street on Holy Saturday 1958 on his way back from church. When this man, "tired of wandering, tired of the world and of faith",[20] asks for a sleep that will release him from all the clashing swords of this existence, this is closely related to the Church's most common prayer for the dead: "Eternal rest grant unto them." What Schneider cannot conceive beyond death is a "resurrection" that would repeal love's pouring out of itself into the lowest depths, an installation of the Son in the power of his victory that would abolish the powerlessness of his descent. For Schneider, this victorious power would consist in the inalterable attitude of Christ's having handed himself over once and for all to the world, as the world realistically exists, so that the Eucharist is the uttermost gift of Christ. When Schneider allows himself to sink down wearily, this is a pious (though hidden) following of the crucified Christ, who

---

[16] 135:241.
[17] 135:261.
[18] Ibid.

[19] 135:119.
[20] 135:121.

no longer sees or understands, into the hands (which can no longer be felt) of the Father who created this terrible world and bears the responsibility for it: "power and grace": power of the creation that has been given its freedom (through the Father's power) and grace that is shattered in its contact with this power and yet discerns the benevolence of the One who has given this freedom, behind the power that is indispensable and yet is utterly misused.

Finally, a word about Schneider's criticism of the Church, which lies wholly within the framework of what a consistent Christian thinker can state about avoidable, and sometimes unavoidable, compromises by theologians and those who hold office. Many theological solutions are too cheaply bought in his eyes; but above all, he cannot bear the defense of the war (of resistance) that is still common today. "All that has been achieved hitherto in history and in culture is unthinkable without the justification of violence and the exercise of violence; every individual is free to defend his family and his own person. But as for the defensive war, it is a fire that cannot escape blazing out into the dimension of the indefensible."[21] Schneider is aware that he is making a demand here that is "higher than the dominant doctrine of moral theology, which contradicts it. Something that has never yet happened must happen, if the world we know and love is to be saved."[22] "Our casuistry does not protect us. Its dams will be swept away by the waters of the living conscience."[23] Thus he "can no longer accept the existing forms of Christian preaching; the problem of war has made me more aware of the tragic contradiction between the gospel and our life but also of a certain doctrine of the state and a theology. . . . The summit of my loneliness consists in the fact that I profess my allegiance to the Catholic Church; I would not be so alone in the Evangelical Church."[24] The Roman politics of concordats gets on his nerves, too,[25] and he finds the solidarity with Israel too weak: "On the day when the synagogues were stormed, the Church ought to have appeared beside the synagogue as her sister. It is a decisive fact that this did not happen."[26] But which sincere Christian could

---

[21] 135:158.
[22] 146:91.
[23] 126:72.

[24] 148:91, 125.
[25] 123:152.
[26] 123:155.

be without concern about the Church?[27] If one considers this sufficiently, it is a sign of fidelity to her.

Reinhold Schneider wrote in detail about the "dark night" of St.
John of the Cross, and the attempt has been made to explain the darkness portrayed in his last autobiographical writings as a participation
in the "mystical night". But the melancholy that accompanied him all
his life, and now breaks out anew and overwhelms him, and his total
physical exhaustion point in a different direction. The "dark night"
is a supernatural withdrawal of deep and blessed experience of God,
and there is no path leading there from the condition of melancholy.
Schneider's consciousness of having Kierkegaard, Strindberg and Unamuno as forefathers who were akin to his spirit points away from the
experience of the "dark night". This is not to deny that melancholics
(like depressives) can be exposed to great trials. But in Schneider's
case, it is above all intellectual insights that lead to the obscuring of
his relationship to God: the unfathomable suffering of creatures, the
meaningless guilt of historical existence, which has never been dis-
charged, the inconceivability of the cosmic dimensions, the world as
a "rotating hell",[28] as a process of devouring and being devoured.[29]
All of this obscures the face of the loving Father for him, but what lies
before him is not (as in the "dark night") the Father of Jesus Christ
who turned away or disappeared but "the dreadful mask of the One
who hurls to the ground and shatters, the treader of the winepress".
This is not to disparage the sufferings of the author, only to assign
them their correct theological position.

One last misunderstanding must be cleared up here. Reinhold Schneider is often decried superficially as a pacifist. But no one knew better than he that power is indispensable in the construction of a state
worthy of man, although this power is always ambiguous and, therefore, dangerous.[30] He expressed himself most clearly about this in *Wesen und Verwaltung der Macht* (The essence and the administration of
power).[31] But he never stopped struggling to define the boundaries
of what was permissible. When Bernt von Heiseler drove him into

---

[27] 135:211.
[28] 135:171.
[29] 135:184.

[30] 160:217; 164:701f.
[31] 160:79-108.

a corner ("The desire to 'disembark' from the contradiction, so to speak, to flee from the river of violence to the shore of purity, seems to me—something Indian, a heresy"),[32] when the necessity of a police force is pointed out ("An entire people cannot be medical orderlies"),[33] Schneider has no more answers, although he himself had understood *Große Verzicht* as opening the path to violence. "I see that I am compelled once again to think through the problem of peace, one of the most tragic problems of history."[34] Schneider was selective and guarded about accepting the label "pacifist". As early as 1930, he can say: "It is possible to conceive of a pacifism that is aware of destiny but keeps silent about this for the sake of its goal; one must have a great respect for such a pacifism."[35] But he looks more and more from the historical necessity of the aggressive war (*Die Hohenzollern*) and the war of defense (*Prinz Eugen*) to the inhuman machinery of the modern war of annihilation; in the face of this war, he is not able to see any use in a cheap pacifism ("I do not know how to deal with this world at all";[36] pacifism is "a No to life").[37] "But alongside this exists a strong, manly pacifism based on knowledge and familiar with history",[38] the No at all costs to the piling up of the atomic weapons that mean that "the catastrophe" is in reality already "present".[39] But Christianity has always demanded of the believer something that is historically impossible, since "Christianity is freedom" from every inner-worldly coercion. "Here we stand and fall, at the point where the kingdom of Christ encounters the secularized kingdom of God. This is our continuity"; "it is Christianity, not the law of causality, that must become the cosmic religion."[40] This demand of a courage superior to the world, in what seems to be the most extreme hour of the world's history, brings us to Reinhold Schneider's bequest to our age.

Bequest

The decisive word that must be uttered here is *tradition*, but not at all in the superficial sense of the return into a supposedly ideal past.

---

[32] 148:103.
[33] 148:112.
[34] 148:182.
[35] 164:189.
[36] 164:431.

[37] 164:445.
[38] 146:77.
[39] 123:199.
[40] 127:49, 50, 51.

One should note statements like the following: "I no longer believe that something like a Christian ordering of the world existed in the Middle Ages; only, both the individual and the family could live as Christians in the Middle Ages. This has become almost an impossibility today."[1] And in greater detail:

> If Charlemagne had received the commission—and how do we know this?—then he sinned against this commission in the most terrible way, by seeking to spread the kingdom of Jesus Christ with the sword, with persecutions and oppression, thereby giving a clearly insuperable impetus to the unholy tragedy that is the history of power and the history of the Church. It is not possible to bring crusades in Jerusalem and against the Slavs, the history of emperors and popes, into any kind of bearable relationship to the gospel, which yet is supposed to be the only basis of the claim made by both parties. Nevertheless, it is possible that the commission did exist and that it was inherited subsequently—although, as I have said, I do not venture to make a sure statement about this. If something of it still exists today, this could only be the commission to the Germans to give an *answer* to the finished history of the empire, that is, now genuinely, in a radical sense, to seek the empire and its promise through a life and testimony in keeping with the gospel. The power of such a testimony to bind all things together has not yet become the reality in history that it could become. The old empire produced truly great men, works and deeds, but the contradiction between preaching, deeds and thinking is so dreadful that I must at least hold the form itself to be definitively exhausted. . . . But this ought not to make us lose courage; one must get fed up at some point with the constellation of problems that get worse and worse, a constellation that is effective on the stage but is not essentially dramatic.[2]

"It is obvious that research cannot abolish faith."[3] Thus, tradition based on Christ means something quite different from traditionalism —indeed, means its exact opposite. In *Erbe und Freiheit* (1955, the last work Schneider composed in his sovereign manner) he plays variations on this theme in six chapters. The motto for this book is in *Der christliche Protest* (1954): "If we are not what we ought to be, then our existence is meaningless. It is clear that what is commanded in history is something impossible, but it must be done; faith has the hope that grace makes the impossible possible. Out of this relationship to the

---

[1] 149:97.
[2] 148:98–99.
[3] 127:50.

world, the knightly spirit forms itself for a resistance that will demand more than everything."[4] There are five aspects. (1) European community is based only in Christ; where political power is no longer subordinate to him (as in Charlemagne and his followers), the "Body built up by Christ through his sacrifice must tear itself to pieces". Men want the historical figure of the kingdom, whether as a Church or through revolutions or through reformations that have turned the living tradition of Christ into a book. Thus, "after two thousand years of venerable tradition, it is as if Christianity had scarcely begun." We are reminded of Paul's shipwreck. It would be better if the conquistadors' ships, loaded down with gold, had also been shipwrecked. Christ is the criterion of our tradition, "but we must seek him in the unsparing encounter with this world of ours, with the cosmos of the fourth dimension . . . of the forces that explode it through the crimes of the human spirit: yet it *is* the cosmos meant by the singer of the Portiuncula; sanctified world."[5] (2) Despite everything, the presence of Greece is evoked again, the great warning against the political power that led to the city-states' devouring of their own selves; in Socrates, man has become "question-able", and we could save ourselves "if we exposed ourselves to the great questioners and questions of the beginning".[6] (3) Drama as historical power: drama speaks from the very outset—against all of philosophy's explanations—about the incurable conflict of the existence that looks for justice and attains this only in the death of the hero; but alas for the age that would like to have left tragedy behind. "History itself is a stage" that convinces us of the wrongness of every attempt to leave behind us the tragedy of the Cross.[7] (4) The example of Schiller—against the author's passion for freedom—is even more deeply a "prophetic" portrayal of the inevitability of tragedy: "Freedom is established only through violence." But it is "not the Redeemer God but the judge" who "shines above the plays that are acted out in the Christian sphere".[8] (5) In *Karl V, Erbe und Verzicht*, Schneider grasps the moment when the old empire, at the apogee of its fullness, internally collapses: politically, but also religiously when Luther appears. We have the "definitive dismissal of a great form of life, the form of the empire", but the "pietàs"

---

[4] 126:110–12.

[5] 127:13–54, 55.

[6] 127:76.

[7] 127:83–106.

[8] 127:109–50.

with which the emperor abdicated "saved the continuity": "Charles collapsed and brought thereby a burden of unheard-of value over the bridge: the image of unity, of the Christian coherence with the present day of the various periods of time, peoples, traditions and the Roman inheritance; he did not save the imperial office, but he saved its image, which continues to shine."[9] (6) Finally, *Das Kreuz im Osten*: from the beginning, despite Byzantium, an essentially nonviolent Christianity, continually called into question by the West, by Sweden, by its own rulers, while ever new witnesses suffer for the nonviolence of Christ: Metropolitan Philip against Ivan the Terrible, later Avvakum against the reform of Nikon. "The rejection of violence is not an invention of Tolstoy: it is already expressed in the Middle Ages." Dostoyevsky's prophetic look into the future sees not only the coming unbelief, but also that "Christ will be victorious in a hundred years." "No one can prove that the Cross has truly fallen in the East."[10]

Thus tradition is for Reinhold Schneider the handing on of the gospel and of the fundamental attitude of Christ and of those who are called to follow him vis-à-vis the earthly power that overwhelms them.

One can interpret the deepest meaning of tradition, as Schneider understands it and bequeathes it, in yet another way. For him, subject to so many stimuli, the Christian tradition became the catalyzing unification that provided an evaluation and discrimination. He did not deny the numerous and contradictory elements in his own provenance, "but they are ordered as around a magnet". One need only listen to the following confession, which contains only the principal names (to them he could have added Jean Paul, Gerhard Hauptmann and Walt Whitman):

> My first great teacher was Hebbel, and after Nietzsche had appeared only like a lightning flash, there followed Schopenhauer, then Dostoyevsky, who found at the very end the Yes to life that was decisive for me; in Unamuno, I found the teacher who led me to tragedy; in Nietzsche I found the one who brought tragedy to its perfection. Goethe always affected me but never led to a decision—the same is true of Shakespeare. It would be a great and important task to reveal Schiller's educa-

---

[9] 127:153–86.   [10] 127:189–234, 220, 229.

tive power once again to a new generation; but this is a very difficult task. The two greatest hindrances are Rousseau and ethics—Hölderlin, Novalis and Kleist are no educators; they are beacons that flare above the abysses in which the new element rests.[11]

How could this autodidact succeed by a process of divination in forming out of this chaotic fullness—which later took on immeasurable dimensions through the endless reading of historical works—the strict hierarchy that characterizes his mature work, without (as he himself observes several times) dropping some essential stage: everything was taken up and used in his own construction? Seen from a purely formal perspective, the "form" (*Gestalt*) matures ever more clearly and solidly from one work to the next (this is what he calls the *Form*), first dreamlike, then historical, linked to the concept of the religious transcendence of existence, without defining this more specifically: "When I portrayed Christianity hitherto, I did not do so as a Christian. . . . Christianity (is) only one of many languages to express this experience (of that which lies above this world)."[12] A twofold decision became necessary. On the one hand, the tragic was the deepest essence of existence for Schneider, but Christ with his Cross "has taken tragedy on himself and thus withdrawn it from the world: he wanted to live tragedy on behalf of all."[13] "As soon as Christ appears, the whole tragic world perishes: the terrible confusion is no longer possible. As soon as the tragedian meets Christ, he loses his ability to write tragedy."[14] This is why the young Schneider formulates the existential alternative that confronted him as "either Christ or Shakespeare". But a second dilemma joined the first: "Our greatest task is our own life. The most important question is whether we give it a true form and make it a pure impression and expression of our being. Individual deeds or works can never justify us, but only the totality of our life."[15] The confluence of the problem of work and the problem of existence brought the decisive insight to maturity: Christ existentially supersedes all tragedy of the stage and of life, but by bringing it to perfection, and existence lives in the truth when it resolves to enter into the highest form, which gives shelter to everything. In his conversion, Schneider resolved both the question of his work and the

---

[11] 164:437.
[12] 164:764.
[13] 164:610.

[14] 164:670.
[15] 164:696.

question of his life. He discerns the solution in a contemplation of history: "The world lives from the course of such lives, which bear in themselves the demand for imitation, although they can never be repeated; in this perspective, Christ's life appears as the most gigantic of all."[16] Thus "There are only two possibilities: to lead a tragic life or to lead a Christian life." But "tragedy is indignant revolt: Christianity means the total penetration of the world in the spirit of unwearying love. Christ handed himself over publicly to the world in order to transform it . . . he himself lives this task unconditionally; but much has already happened, if others feel even as much as one spark from the great fire." In the face of the "continuous contradiction between indignation and reverence", Schneider chose the second alternative: reverence in following Christ.[17] This made the internal form of his life the origin of the external power to give form to the enormous masses of historical material. Everything in these masses can be referred back to his existential decision as criterion. This is already seen formally in *Philipp*, and the book about England shows it explicitly and materially.

Here lies the nobility—let us not use the word "chivalry" once again—that shines out from the whole of Reinhold Schneider's work and life, and that is one of the reasons why he no longer finds many readers today. Schneider could also sing a high praise of the bourgeoisie, but it concludes with the words: "There is no republic without an aristocracy."[18] This is not meant absolutely as a social caste but certainly as a spirit. He could only concern himself with noble souls; common souls revealed themselves automatically by a comparison with these. "It is not possible for the masses to become a people." "It is typical of the modern period that it does nothing for the nobility. Its concept of the people remains revolutionary-proletarian: a mass of equal persons who allow themselves to be ruled. In reality, a people is an articulated organism with a natural summit. Where the instinct for the nobility has been extinguished, we no longer find the instinct for order and for the great laws of life."[19]

There remain three words that ring out most seriously and urgently in Schneider's late writings, words that presuppose the nobility of

[16] 164:350.
[17] 164:670, 671.

[18] 164:750.
[19] 164:747, 737.

the heart if they are to be heard: freedom, conscience, responsibility. These are words spoken in the face of the "impossible possibility" that the world, as it has become, should continue to exist; words that only a pure Christian heart can perceive and understand, taking charge of them through the gift of one's own life and thus making them an effective reality.

BIBLIOGRAPHY

This list contains only the works that were published by themselves in book or pamphlet form. Articles in newspapers and periodicals, as well as some small pamphlets, are not listed here; the same applies to descriptions of landscapes that can be found collected in the volume *Schicksal und Landschaft* (Herder, 1960). Normally, only the first edition is noted. Very many individual publications were printed again in collections, some edited by Reinhold Schneider himself, others after his death. Only the most important of these volumes, and of the collections of letters, are listed here. Bruno Scherer has prepared a complete bibliography (88 pages) in: *Reinhold Schneider, Leben und Werk in Dokumenten* (Karlsruhe: Badenia-Verlag, 1973).

Hans Urs von Balthasar himself revised and extended before his death the bibliography of this *new edition* of his work *Reinhold Schneider: Sein Weg und sein Werk*, which was first published in 1953, which was based mostly on the first editions of Schneider's publications. As far as possible, references to the *Ausgewählten* und *Gesammelten Werke* have been added.

References in the footnotes of this book are to the number of the work in this Bibliography, followed by the page number(s).

1 Grimm. *Baden-Baden in 100 Zeichnungen*. With an introduction and sonnets by Reinhold Schneider. Baden-Baden: Kunstkreis, 1928. 135 p.

2 *Das Leiden des Camoes oder Untergang und Vollendung der portugiesischen Macht*. Hellerau: J. Hegner, 1930. 242 p. Cf. 107 and 153.

3 *Portugal. Ein Reisetagebuch*. Munich: A. Langen/G. Müller, 1931. 175 p. Rev. ed., Insel, 1947. 149 p.

4 *Philipp II oder Religion und Macht*. Leipzig: Hegner, 1931. 343 p. Cf. 107 and 153.

5 *Das Erdbeben: Drei Erzählungen*. Leipzig: Hegner, 1932. 151 p. Cf. 117 and 156.

6 *Fichte. Der Weg der Nation*. Munich: A. Langen/G. Müller, 1932. 250 p.

7 *Die Hohenzollern. Tragik und Königtum*. Leipzig: Hegner, 1933. 311 p.

8 *Auf Wegen deutscher Geshichte. Eine Fahrt ins Reich*. Leipzig: Insel, 1934. 131 p.

9 *Der Inselreich. Gesetz und Größe der britischen Macht.* Leipzig: Insel, 1936. 574 p. Cf. 154.

10 *Gestalt und Seele. Das Werk des Malers Leo von König.* Preface by Reinhold Schneider. Leipzig: Insel, 1936. 30 p. 64 illus.

11 *Kaiser Lothars Krone. Leben und Herrschaft Lothars von Supplinburg.* Leipzig: Insel, 1937. 211 p.

12 *Las Casas vor Karl V. Szenen aus der Konquistadorenzeit.* Leipzig: Insel, 1938. 203 p. Cf. 155.

13 *Corneilles Ethos in der Ära Ludwigs XIV. Eine Studie.* Leipzig: Insel, 1939. 100 p. Cf. 119 and 158.

14 *Sonette.* Leipzig: Insel, 1939. 63 p. Cf. 157.

15 *Elisabeth Tarakanow: Erzählung.* Leipzig: Insel, 1939. 79 p. Cf. 118 and 156.

16 *Theresia von Spanien.* Munich: Schnell und Steiner, 1939. 77 p.

17 *Der Jüngling.* Freiburg: Herder, 1940. 8 p., 25 illus.

18 *Macht und Gnade. Gestalten, Bilder und Werte in der Geschichte.* Wiesbaden: Insel, 1940. 330 p. Cf. 158.

19 *An den Engel in der Wüste. Die Wende Clemens Brentanos.* Würzburg: Werkbund, 1940. 31 p.

20 *Der Katarakt. Das Schicksal Nikolaus Lenaus.* Würzburg: Werkbund, 1940. 36 p. Cf. 119.

21 *Der Pilger. Eichendorffs Weltgefühl.* Würzburg: Werkbund, 1940. 28 p. Cf. 90.

22 *Zur Zeit der Scheide zwischen Tag und Nacht. Der Lebenskampf der Droste.* Würzburg: Werkbund, 1940. 40 p. Cf. 90.

23 *Das Vaterunser.* Colmar: Alsatia, 1941. 55 p.

24 *Nach dem großen Kriege: Die letzte Reise des Kurfürsten Maximilian. Der fromme Herzog. Zwei Erzählungen.* 1941. 84 p.

25 *Das Antlitz des Mächtigen.* Freiburg: Herder, 1941. 12 p., 25 illus.

26 *Die Stunde des heiligen Franz von Assisi.* Colmar: Alsatia, c. 1941. 101 p.

27 *Der Abschied der Frau von Chantal.* Colmar: Alsatia, 1941. 36 p. Cf. 118 and 156.

28 *Der Überwinder: Zwei Erzählungen* ("Der Abgrund", "Der Gast"). Colmar: Alsatia, 1941. 70 p. Cf. 118 and 156.

29 *Der Kreuzweg.* Colmar: Alsatia, 1942. 63 p.

30 *Sankt Odilien.* Colmar: Alsatia, 1942. 16 p.

31 *Ehrwürdiges Alter.* Colmar: Alsatia, 1943. 14 p., 25 illus.

32 *Das Weltgericht.* Colmar: Alsatia, 1943. 14 p., 25 illus.

33 *Laß uns zur Stimme deiner Liebe werden. Worte an einen Gefallenen.* Colmar: Alsatia, 1943. 11 p.

34 *Die dunkle Nacht: Sieben Erzählungen.* Colmar: Alsatia, 1943. 239 p. Cf. 117 and 156.

35 *Jetzt ist des Heiligen Zeit: Sonette.* Colmar: Alsatia, 1943. 76 p. Cf. 157.

36 *Der Dichter vor der Geschichte Hölderlin, Novalis.* Colmar: Alsatia, 1944. 72 p.

37 *Stimme des Abendlandes.* Colmar: Alsatia, 1944. 151 p.

38 *Das Gebet in der Zeit. Ein Volk der Beter und Büßer.* Freiburg: Herder, 1945. 14 p. Cf. 51.

39 *Gott der Vater und Herr.* Freiburg: Herder, 1945. 14 p. Cf. 51.

40 *Papst Gregor der Große.* Freiburg: Herder, 1945. 21 p. Cf. 120 and 161.

41 *Jesus Christus gestern und heute.* Freiburg: Herder, 1945. 14 p.

42 *Die Kirche in der Geschichte.* Freiburg: Herder, 1945. 14 p. Cf. 51.

43 *Die Macht der Friedfertigen.* Freiburg: Herder, 1945. 16 p. Cf. 51 and 160.

44 *Das Unzerstörbare.* Freiburg: Herder, 1945. 14 p. Cf. 51 and 161.

45 *Versöhnung der Gläubigen. Daß alle eins werden.* Freiburg: Herder, 1945.

46 *Die Verwaltung der Macht.* Freiburg: Herder, 1945. 16 p. Cf. 51 and 160.

47 *Weihnacht der Gefangenen.* 1945. 13 p. Cf. 51.

48 *Von der Würde des Menschen.* Freiburg: Herder, 1945. 22 p. Cf. 51 and 161.

49 *Auffindung des Kreuzes.* 1945. 15 p. Cf. 51.

50 *Legt das Große in das Leben. Aus Schillers Briefen.* Postscript by Reinhold Schneider. Munich: Alber, 1945. 106 p.

51 *Gedanken des Friedens: Gesammelte Kleinschriften.* Freiburg: Herder, 1946. 152 p. Enlarged ed., 1956. Cf. 120 and 160.

52 *Erbe im Feuer. Betrachtungen und Rufe.* Freiburg: Herder, 1946. 174 p. Cf. 160.

53　*Der Glaube.* Görres-Lesebogen 38. Nuremberg: Glock und Lutz, 1946.

54　*Die Heimkehr des deutschen Geistes. Über das Bild Christi in der deutschen Philosophie des 19. Jahrhunderts.* Baden-Baden: H. Bühler/Heidelberg: Kerle, 1946. 83 p.

55　*Im Anfang leigt das Ende. Grillparzers Epilog auf die Geschichte.* Baden-Baden: H. Bühler, 1946. 64 p. Cf. 119.

56　*Macht des Geistes.* Bonn: Borromäusverein, 1946. 21 p.

57　*Sein Reich.* Bonn: Borromäusverein, 1946. 16 p.

58　*Apokalypse: Sonette.* Baden-Baden: H. Bühler, 1946. 39 p. Cf. 157.

59　*Neue deutsche Gedichte.* Dokumente des andern Deutschland, vol. 3. New York, F. Krause. Cf. 157.

60　*Die neue Ehre.* Bonn: Borromäusverein, 1946. 24 p.

61　*Der Mensch vor dem Gericht der Geschichte.* Baden-Baden: H. Bühler/Augsburg: J. W. Naumann, 1946. 47 p. Cf. 160.

62　*Der Priester im Kirchenjahr der Zeit.* Freiburg: Caritas, 1946.

63　*Fausts Rettung.* Baden-Baden: H. Bühler/Berlin: Suhrkamp, 1946. 45 p. Cf. 119 and 158.

64　*Von der Streitmacht des Gebetes.* Munich: Schnell und Steiner, 1946. 11 p.

65　*Taganrog: Erzählung.* Freiburg: Herder, 1946. 98 p. Cf. 118 and 156.

66　*Die letzten Tage: Sonette.* Baden-Baden: H. Bühler, 1945/Recklinghausen: Paulus, 1946. 47 p. Cf. 157.

67　*Der Tod des Mächtigen: Erzählungen.* Freiburg: Herder, 1946. 79 p. Cf. 118 and 155.

68　*Newmans Entscheidung.* 1946. 31 p. Cf. 71 and 161.

69　*Die neuen Türme: Ausgewählte Sonette.* Wiesbaden: Insel, 1946. 54 p. Cf. 157.

70　*Und Petrus stieg aus dem Schiffe.* Baden-Baden: H. Bühler, 1946. 143 p. Cf. 161.

71　*Weltreich und Gottesreich: Drei Vorträge* (Innozenz, Philipp, Newman). Munich: Schnell und Steiner, 1946. 139 p.

72　*Erscheinung des Herrn.* Waibstedt: Kemper, 1946. 36 p.

73　*Kleists Ende.* Munich: Alber, 1946. 31 p. Cf. 90 and 158.

74 *Allerseelen 1946. Einem verschwundenen Freunde.* Mannheim: Wohlgemuth, 1946. 24 p.

75 *Der Sinn aller Opfer. Brief in ein Kriegsgefangenenlager.* Munich: Schnell und Steiner, 1947. 13 p. Cf. 161.

76 *Gedenkwort zum 20. Juli.* Freiburg: Herder/Calw: Hatje, 1947. 27 p.

77 *Macht und Gewissen in Shakespeares Tragödie.* Berlin: Suhrkamp, 1947. 46 p.

78 *Stolz und Verantwortung. Von der Sendung der Jugend.* Berlin: Morus, 1947. 31 p.

79 *Über den Selbstmord.* Baden-Baden: H. Bühler, 1947. 39 p. Cf. 161.

80 *An Alle. Ein Aufruf.* Freiburg: Caritas, 1947. 16 p. Cf. 161.

81 *Das Heilige in der Geschichte* (selection). Heidelberg: Kerle, 1947. 95 p.

82 *Herz am Erdensaume: Gedichte.* Heidelberg: Kerle, 1947. 59 p. Cf. 157.

83 *Duldet mutig, Millionen!* Mannheim: Wohlgemuth, 1945. 105 p. 2d ed., 1947.

84 *Die Verborgenen.* Paderborn: Schöningh, 1947. 13 p.

85 *Das Antlitz der Not.* Bonn: Borromäusverein, 1947. 36 p.

86 *Der Mensch und das Leid in der griechischen Tragödie.* Munich: Schnell und Steiner, 1947. 31 p. Cf. 158.

87 *Der Dichter vor der heraufziehenden Zeit.* Freiburg: Herder, 1947. 31 p. Cf. 160.

88 *Das Kreuz in der Zeit* (a) "Das Vaterunser"; (b) "Der Kreuzweg"; (c) "Die sieben Worte am Kreuz". 1947. 149 p., also published in individual vols.

89 *Sieger in Fesseln. Christuszeugnisse aus Lagern und Gefängnissen. Das christliche Deutschland 1933–1945.* Edited together with Paul Hofmann. Freiburg: Herder/Tübingen: Furche, 1947. 175 p.

90 *Dämonie und Verklärung: Sammlung literarischer Essays.* Vaduz: Liechtenstein, 1947. 375 p. Cf. 119 and 160.

91 *Die Nacht des Heils: Essays.* Zurich: Scientia, 1947. 160 p.

92 *Im Schatten Mephistos: Drei Essays.* Stuttgart: Deutsche Verlagsanstalt, 1947. 46 p. Cf. 160.

93 *Anthologie. Worte der Besinnung aus dem Werk Reinhold Schneiders.* Munich: Schnell und Steiner, 1948. 155 p.

94 *Die gerettete Krone: Erzählungen.* Munich: Schnell und Steiner, 1948. 178 p.

95 *Vom Tun der Wahrheit* (Bruder Klaus, Ignatius von Loyola, Franz von Sales). Munich: Schnell und Steiner, 1948. 92 p. Cf. 120 and 161.

96 *Schwermut und Zuversicht: Lenau, Eichendorff.* Heidelberg: Kerle, 1948. 81 p.

97 *Aar mit gebrochener Schwinge* (Clemens Brentano, Annette von Droste-Hülshoff). Heidelberg: Kerle, 1948. 88 p.

98 *Stern der Zeit: Sonette.* Krefeld: Scherpe, 1948. 97 p. Cf. 157.

99 *Erworbenes Erbe. Zum Gedächtnis der Droste.* Munich: Alber, 1948. 23 p. Cf. 119 and 158.

100 *Lessings Drama.* Munich: Alber, 1948. 27 p. Cf. 119 and 158.

101 *Der Kronprinz. Politisches Drama.* Munich: Alber, 1948. 88 p.

102 *Abendländische Bücherei.* Edited and introduced by Reinhold Schneider. Freiburg, Herder (13 vols. 1947–1949). German titles: (a) Byron: *Kain.* (b) Corneille: *Polyeucte.* (c) Goethe: *Die Natürliche Tochter.* (d) Milton: *Simson der Kämpfer.* (e) Molière: *Le Misanthrope.* (f) Sophocles: *Ödipus.* (g) Vergil: *Äneis, zweiter Gesang.* (h) Leskow: *Am Ende der Welt.* (i) De Vigny: *Hauptmann Renaud.* (k) Tennyson: *Enoch Arden.* (l) Shakespeare: *Heinrich IV.* (m) Grillparzer: *König Ottokars Glück und Ende.* (n) Pushkin: *Die Hauptmannstochter.*

103 *Der Widerschein: Drei Erzählungen.* Düsseldorf: Christophorus, 1948. 78 p.

104 *Kreuz und Geschichte.* Stuttgart: J. B. Metzler, 1949. 95 p.

105 *Das Spiel vom Menschen. Belsazar: Frei gestaltet nach Calderon.* Graz: A. Pustet, 1949. 143 p.

106 *Dreißig Sonette.* Privately printed. Helle: Burg Giebichenstein, no date. Cf. 157.

107 *Iberisches Erbe* (Camões, Philip II, with a new introduction). Olten: Summa-Verlag, 1949. 376 p. Cf. 2, 3 and 153.

108 *Der große Verzicht.* Wiesbaden: Insel, 1950. 279 p. Cf. 155.

109 *Geschichte und Gewissen: Velhagen und Klasings Schulausgaben.* Selection with a postscript. 1950.

110 *Der Traum des Eroberers. Zar Alexander: Zwei Dramen.* Wiesbaden: Insel, 1951. 183 p. Cf. 120.

111 *Die Tarnkappe: Drama.* Inselbücherei 486. Wiesbaden: Insel, 1951. 68 p.

112 *Rechenschaft. Worte zur Jahrhundertmitte.* Johannes Verlag, 1951. 99 p.

113 *Vom Geschichtsbewußtsein der Romantik: Drei Essays* (Arnim, Eichendorff, Uhland). Mainz: Akademie der Wissenschaften und der Literatur. Abhdl. der Klasse der Literatur, 1951. No. 5. 51 p.

114 *Die Beter.* Freiburg: Herder, 1951. 13 p., 25 illus.

115 *Die Lampe der Toten: Eine Auswahl deutscher Lyrik* (with B. von Heiseler). Das kleine Buch 36. Bertelsmann. 79 p.

116 *Innozenz und Franziskus* (Drama). Wiesbaden: Insel, 1952. 282 p. Cf. 120.

Ausgewählte Werke in 4 vols., Cologne/Olten: Hegner, 1953:

117 Vol. 1: *Das getilgte Antlitz: Novellen und Erzählungen.* 288 p.

118 Vol. 2: *Der fünfte Kelch: Novellen und Erzählungen.* 296 p.

119 Vol. 3: *Über Dichter und Dichtung.* 352 p.

120 Vol. 4: *Herrscher und Heilige.* 300 p.

121 *Wesen und Verwaltung der Macht.* Wiesbaden: Steiner, 1954. 42 p. Cf. 160.

122 *Die ewige Krone.* Oltener Bücherfreunde, 1954. 71 p.

123 *Verhüllter Tag.* Cologne/Olten: Hegner, 1954. 229 p. Cf. 162.

124 *Die Sonette von Leben und Zeit. Vom Glauben und der Geschichte.* Cologne/Olten: Hegner, 1954. 239 p. Cf. 157.

125 *Adel: Zum 75. Geburtstag von Otto Freiherr v. Taube.* Oltener Bücherfreunde, 1954.

126 *Der christliche Protest.* Zurich: Arche, 1954. 148 p.

127 *Erbe und Freiheit.* Cologne/Olten: Hegner, 1955. 234 p.

128 *Die silberne Ampel. Ein Roman.* Cologne/Olten: Hegner, 1956. 344 p.

129 *Der Friede der Welt.* Wiesbaden: Insel, 1956. 115 p. Cf. 160.

130 *Soll die Dichtung das Leben bessern? Gespräch mit Gottfried Benn.* Wiesbaden: Limes, 1956. 34 p.

131 *Die Rose des Königs und andere Erzählungen.* Freiburg: Herder, 1957. 161 p. Cf. 117 and 156.

132 *Der Balkon. Aufzeichnungen eines Müßiggängers in Baden-Baden.* Wiesbaden: Insel, 1957. 182 p.

133 *Europa als Lebensform.* Cologne/Olten: Hegner, 1957. 60 p. Cf. 160.

134 *Die letzten Jahre des Prinzen Eugen. Ein Fragment.* Cologne/Olten: Hegner, 1957. 57 p. Cf. 120.

135 *Winter in Wien. Aus meinen Notizbüchern 1957/1958.* Freiburg: Herder, 1958. 301 p. Cf. 162.

136 *Pfeiler im Strom.* Wiesbaden: Insel, 1958. 418 p.

137 *Der ferne König. Erzählungen.* Freiburg: Herder, 1959. 297 p.

138 *Innozenz der Dritte.* Edited with a postscript by J. Rast. Cologne/Olten, 1960. 231 p.

139 *Schicksal und Landschaft.* Postscript by C. Winterhalter. Freiburg: Herder, 1960. 392 p.

140 *Briefwechsel Reinhold Schneider—Leopold Ziegler.* Freiburg: Herder, 1961. 264 p.

141 *Gelebtes Wort.* Edited by C. Winterhalter. Freiburg: Herder, 1961. 364 p.

142 *Briefe an einen Freund* (Otto Heuschele). Cologne/Olten: Hegner, 190 p.

143 *Allein der Wahrheit Stimme will ich sein.* Edited by C. Winterhalter. Freiburg, Herder. 255 p.

144 *Begegnung und Bekenntnis.* Edited by C. Winterhalter. Freiburg, Herder. 271 p.

145 *Erich Przywara Briefwechsel mit Reinhold Schneider.* Introduction by W. Bergengruen, Theodor Heuß. Zurich: Arche, 1963. 147 p.

146 *Erfüllte Einsamkeit.* Mit zwei Gedenkworten von W. Bergengruen. Freiburg: Herder, 1963. 264 p.

147 *Verpflichtung und Liebe: Literarische Essays.* Edited by C. Winterhalter. Freiburg: Herder, 1964. 256 p.

148 *Briefwechsel Reinhold Schneider—Bernt von Heiseler.* Stuttgart: Steinkopf, 1965. 199 p.

149 *Briefwechsel Reinhold Schneider—Werner Bergengruen.* Freiburg: Herder, 1966. 157 p.

150 *Aus dem Briefwechsel Reinhold Schneider—Paul Mahnert.* In: Leni Mahnert, ed., *Reinhold Schneider in Essen.* Essen, privately published by the editor, 1970. 43–85.

151 *Briefwechsel Reinhold Schneider—Jochen Klepper.* In: *Jochen Klepper, Briefwechsel.* Stuttgart, 1973. 61–157.

152 *Gesammelte Werke* in 10 vols. Edited by E. M. Landau, commissioned by the Reinhold Schneider-Gesellschaft. Frankfurt: Insel, 1977–1978. (Vols. 2, 3, 5, 6, 8, 9 and 10 have also appeared in paperback as Suhrkamp-Taschenbuch.)

153 Vol. 1: *Camoes—Philip II*. 477 p.

154 Vol. 2: *Das Inselreich*. 633 p.

155 Vol. 3: *Der große Verzicht*. 476 p.

156 Vol. 4: *Zeugen im Feuer*. 497 p.

157 Vol. 5: *Lyrik*. 442 p.

158 Vol. 6: *Dem lebendigen Geist*. 627 p.

159 Vol. 7: *Geschichte und Landschaft*. 463 p.

160 Vol. 8: *Schwert und Friede*. 477 p.

161 Vol. 9: *Das Unzerstörbare*. 524 p.

162 Vol. 10: *Verhüllter Tag—Winter in Wien*. 465 p.

163 *Reinhold Schneider, Lektüre für Minuten. Gedanken aus seinen Büchern und Briefen*. Selection with a postscript by Primin Meier. Frankfurt: Insel, 1980. 208 p.

164 *Tagebücher 1930–1935*. Frankfurt: Insel, 1983. 943 p.

Books about Reinhold Schneider

Out of the immense bibliography drawn up by Bruno Scherer (cf. 165, 325–67), we mention only the works that have been drawn on most frequently.

165 Franz Anselm Schmitt and Bruno Scherer. *Reinhold Schneider, Leben und Werk in Dokumenten*. Karlsruhe: Badenia, 1973.

166 Bruno Scherer. *Tragik unter dem Kreuz. Leben und Geisteswelt Reinhold Schneiders*. Freiburg: Herder, 1966.

167 *Widerruf oder Vollendung. Reinhold Schneiders "Winter in Wien" in der Diskussion*. Freiburg: Herder, 1981.

168 Maria van Look: *Jahre der Freundschaft mit Reinhold Schneider. Aus Tagebuchblättern*. Weilheim: O. W. Barth, 1965. 276 p.